LETTERS
TO MY
DAUGHTER

LETTERS
TO MY
DAUGHTER

A Father Writes about
Torah and the Jewish Woman

Walter Orenstein

JASON ARONSON INC.
Northvale, New Jersey
London

This book was set in 11 pt. Berkeley Oldstyle by Alpha Graphics of Pittsfield, N.H.

10 9 8 7 6 5 4 3 2 1

Library of Congress Cataloging-in-Publication Data

Orenstein, Walter,
   Letters to my daughter : a father writes about Torah and
 the Jewish woman / by Walter Orenstein.
    p. cm.
   Includes bibliographical references and index.
   ISBN 1-56821-387-5
   1. Women in Judaism. 2. Judaism—Doctrines. I. Title.
 BM729.W6073 1995
 296'.082—dc20   94-45801

Manufactured in the United States of America. Jason Aronson Inc. offers books and cassettes. For information and catalog write to Jason Aronson Inc., 230 Livingston Street, Northvale, New Jersey 07647.

To my daughters
Leslie Cytryn and Suri Drucker
who were among my first students
to ask challenging questions
in matters of Torah

Contents

Preface		ix
First Letter	Women in the Torah	1
Second Letter	Women and *Mitzvot*	7
Third Letter	Women and Prayer	17
Fourth Letter	Women and Torah Study	53
Fifth Letter	The Written and the Oral Law	63
Sixth Letter	The Codes	83
Seventh Letter	The Ten Commandments—Man and God	99
Eighth Letter	The Ten Commandments—Man and Man	125
Ninth Letter	The Concept of God	139
Tenth Letter	The Prophecy Phenomenon	155
Eleventh Letter	The Meaning of Miracles	167
Twelfth Letter	The Theodicy—The Problem of Evil	177
Thirteenth Letter	The Messianic Era and Resurrection	201
Postscript		229
Notes		235
Index		253

Preface

Of the countless number of wise sayings found in the Talmud and the Midrash, the one that has been most influential in my approach to Jewish education and, therefore, most meaningful to me personally is *talmidim k'ruyim banim v'haRav karuy Av*, "students are called children and a teacher is called father" (*Sifre*, Deuteronomy 6:7). Throughout my career I have tried to live up to this ideal, and if I have had a measure of success in my work, it is primarily because I regard my students as my own children, and I have never limited my time for them to the hours I spent in the classroom. Since most of my teaching and administrative career has been in colleges and seminaries for women, I felt that it was appropriate for this book to be written as a father-daughter dialogue. The letters themselves, of course, are fictitious, but the questions posed are those with which I am confronted almost daily throughout my career in Jewish education.

Some of the books addressed to the Jewish woman focus on the nobility of the traditional role of a Jewish mother, while others focus on women's rights and obligations in Jewish law and ritual. This book is concerned with these important matters as well, but it subsequently goes far beyond the others. It traces women in the Torah and proves through text and commentary that their status is equal to the status of men though their function is usually different. It introduces women to the Oral Law, the exciting realm of Halakhah, and some of the essential principles of Jewish philosophy, a world that is strange to most Jewish women, indeed, a world that many of them today seek desperately to know and comprehend.

Although this work is addressed to a college student, it is meant for all Jewish women regardless of their backgrounds. The observant woman who has a limited background in Jewish studies and seeks an understanding of the principles of Jewish belief and the way that these principles should impact on her life will find that this book will get her started on the road to Jewish scholarship. The *yeshivah* student whose education has taken her far beyond the rudiments of Torah knowledge, but who is concerned with her status and lacks the training to probe the sources on her own, will find this book enlightening. Last, the noncommitted, nonobservant Jewish woman who has lived in the secular world, found that it leaves much to be desired, and after serious deliberation on the matter has come to realize that life without God and without Torah has no real value—indeed, the woman who recognizes the moral bankruptcy of today's secular society and is willing to listen to the comforting message of Torah—will find this book spiritually uplifting.

The selection of topics, the source material, and the general approach of this book is the product of many years of teaching and religious counseling. The topics are not only fundamental to Jewish thought; they are of crucial concern to today's generation. The material has been culled from the Bible, the Talmud, and the Midrash as well as the classical works of Jewish philosophy of both medieval and contemporary times. The approach of the book is in full accord with Jewish tradition.

I would like to express my sincere appreciation to Mr. Avi Goldstein and Ms. Faige Silverman for their editing skills, to Ms. Janet Kirchheimer for allowing me to benefit from her extensive knowledge of computer technology, and to my wife, Nellie, for her creative suggestions and her continuous encouragement in this project.

Women in the Torah

My dearest daughter,

I read your letter with great interest, and it deeply disturbs me. I am not at all surprised that you find that the disciplines to which you are being exposed at the university pose a formidable challenge to the veracity of some of your most cherished notions about our people, its Torah, its philosophy, its ethics, and its history. I am not shocked by the fact that some of your Jewish professors do not merely reject the existence of God and the revelation of the Torah at Sinai but try to dissuade their students from these beliefs whenever the opportunity presents itself. Those of us who have attended secular universities have all experienced these sobering confrontations with reality at one time or another. Of course, to some, the experience is more traumatic than to others, but most of us have managed to emerge from the environment of the secular university unscathed, our pride somewhat bruised perhaps, but essentially as strong in our faith and in our commitment to Torah and *mitzvot* as we ever were.

You say that you feel intellectually deprived when it comes to matters of Jewish law and philosophy, that you have been plunged into a confrontational, hostile world unarmed and frightened. This disturbs me. You claim that because you are a woman, you were never given a proper Jewish education, that the *yeshivah* where

1

you studied for twelve years never prepared you with a sophisticated defense to uphold the doctrines and beliefs of Judaism, a
defense you say you desperately need in order to handle yourself in the secular world. What's worse, you say, the *yeshivah*
lacked even the foresight to equip you with the methods and
techniques you would need to research matters on your own, had
you chosen to do so. And now you begin to question the role of
the traditional Jewish woman. You have been listening to the
arguments of the "feminist movement," whose superficial knowledge of Judaism has led them to assert that our sages were simply male chauvinists who relegated women to second-class citi-
zenship. You have come under their spell, and now you, too, begin
to question the acceptability of the traditional role of the Jewish
woman.

   You tell me that you need answers, and that's encouraging to
me because I know that it means that despite your disappoint-
ment and anxiety, you still maintain an allegiance to our faith and
a commitment to our traditions. So let us communicate. While
you're studying at the university, I can see you only a few times
a year. I would therefore propose that we communicate by letter:
you pose the questions, and I will attempt to answer them. More
importantly, I will offer an approach to the Jewish way of life that
will appeal to both your intelligence and your emotions, your
sense of reason and your spirituality. We will embark on the road
to enlightenment, which I hope and pray will lead to a better
understanding of Torah and a commitment to *emunat hakhamim*,
which might best be explained as a trust in the integrity of our
sages and the acceptance of their words as truth. We will begin
with the role of the Jewish woman because I believe that putting
that role into proper perspective is where the road to enlightenment begins.

   One cannot help but admire and commend the women at the
helm of the "women's liberation movement" for their noble and
sincere efforts to obtain equal status and equal treatment for

women in our society. There is no doubt in my mind that they will go down in history among the most praiseworthy women of this century. It is, therefore, much to my dismay that these women do not have a better understanding of the position of Judaism on these matters. For not only have women always been held in high regard in Judaism, but what is perhaps of even greater importance and relevance to the issue, in terms of status, is that women have always been considered equal to men.

Judaism has come under attack by many women for its alleged unfairness and insensitivity to women in important areas of Jewish practice. While such attacks pose no problem to the rabbinic scholar who knows them to be unfounded, many a woman is intimidated by them, particularly those who, like yourself, are unable to research the issues on their own, in consequence of which they cannot defend the halakhic position.

It is crucially important to recognize that equality of *status* does not have to mean equality of *function*, nor should it. To illustrate: a corporation may have five vice presidents, each with his or her own realm of activity and responsibility; they are equal to one another in title, in salary, and in status, but each serves a different function. Judaism has always posited and preached that men and women have equal status, and at times, for its own reasons, it has given them equal function as well. Abraham, the first patriarch, dedicated much of his adult life to teaching ethical monotheism to the people of his generation; his wife Sarah shared that calling with him. When he left the land of Haran, the Torah records, "And Abraham took his wife Sarah and his nephew Lot . . . and the souls that they had acquired in Haran; and they set out for the land of Canaan" (Genesis 12:5). In explanation of the phrase "the souls that they had acquired in Haran," *Rashi*, the great French commentator of the eleventh century, tells us: "He brought them under the wings of the Divine Presence. Abraham converted the men and Sarah converted the women." Clearly, in this regard, Abraham and Sarah were equal in function. Of course, Sarah's "classroom" was limited to women, but then Abraham's was limited to men. The Torah indicates this separation of the sexes in Abraham's house when it came to socialization as well. Abraham is visited by three guests, and the Torah records: "Then one said: 'I will return to you when life is due, and your wife Sarah shall have a son.' Sarah was listening at the entrance of the tent which was behind him" (Genesis 18:10). Sarah did not socialize with the men; she stayed outside the tent listening.

Sarah's status and her superior judgment in certain situations is also noted in the Torah. When she perceived Ishmael's negative influence on Isaac, she advised Abraham to send him and his mother away. Abraham was hesitant, but the Almighty insisted, "Do not be distressed over the boy or your slave; whatever Sarah tells you, do as she says, for it is through Isaac that offspring shall be continued for you" (Genesis 21:12).

The equal status of the other matriarchs is also alluded to in the Torah. When Isaac prayed for a son, the Torah records: "Isaac pleaded with the Lord on behalf of [lit. opposite] his wife because she was barren; and the Lord responded to his plea, and his wife Rebecca conceived" (Genesis 25:21). Focusing on the literal meaning of the text, the Talmud comments: "He stood in his corner and prayed and she stood in her corner and prayed" (*Yevamot* 64b). When Jacob was instructed by the Almighty to return home to Canaan, one would have expected him to tell his wives to prepare for the journey. Not so! He first consulted with them, and pled his case before them. Only after Rachel and Leah responded, "Do all that God has spoken to you," do we read, "Thereupon Jacob put his children and wives on camels; and he drove off all his livestock and all the wealth that he had amassed, the livestock that he had acquired in Paddan-aram, to go to his father Isaac in the land of Canaan" (Genesis 31:16-18). He would not act without their approval.

The last of such examples in the Torah concerns the daughters of Zelophehad. Their father had died leaving no sons to inherit his land. Displeased with the prospect of the land going to their uncles, they approached Moses with the words: "Our father died in the wilderness. He was not one of the faction, Korah's faction, which bonded together against the Lord, but died for his own sin; and he had left no sons. Let not our father's name be lost to his clan just because he had no son! Give us a holding among our father's kinsmen!" (Numbers 27:3-4).

Moses brought the matter to the Lord, and the Lord responded: "The plea of Zelophehad's daughters is just; you should give them a hereditary holding among their father's kinsmen; transfer their father's share to them" (Numbers 27:7). The fact that they were women did not preclude their inheritance of what rightly belonged to their family.

My dearest daughter, if we were to peruse the pages of Jewish history, we would find Miriam, the sister of Moses, who was a prophetess; Deborah, the wife of Lapidot, who was a judge; and Esther, the cousin of Mordecai, who was summoned to take the reins of leadership and lead the Jewish community of Persia through a terrible crisis. Indeed, it was regarding Esther that the late Rabbi Dr. Joseph Soloveitchik remarked:

> The most important task assigned to man is not to be counted as the tenth person in a minyan, but to make history. As far as history is concerned, Judaism has never discriminated against women. From the days of Sarah, the woman was on a par with the man as a history maker. And perhaps at certain times—times of crisis—the woman contributed more than the man. The phrase in the Pentateuch which we read every Rosh Hashanah, "Whatever Sarah tells you, do as she says," has never been forgotten by the Jewish community. . . . Both men and women were created in the image of God. Both were endowed with dignity and majesty. Both were called upon in Persia when disaster was about to strike.[1]

Now while it is true that in the span of Jewish history merely a handful of Jewish women have attained prophecy and leadership, it must be recognized that there were not many men who attained these heights either. Historically, excellence has always been limited to the few, all the more so leadership. It is not a matter of numbers, but qualifications, and it is clear from Jewish history that both men and women have had the qualifications. Also to be considered is the fact that Judaism recognizes women's other role in life—caring for the children and the home—as being of primary importance. Had women been relegated to inferior status, not a single one of them could have risen to such spiritual heights.

Study all that I have written to you in this letter very carefully. Digest it and ponder it. Confirm my ideas from the sources I have mentioned, or refute them if you believe that I am in error. Then write to me, and let me share your thoughts.

Women and *Mitzvot*

My dearest daughter,

It's good to hear from you again, and I am ready to answer your questions. You concede that in terms of the biblical narrative, both men and women are created in the image of God, and you admit that the patriarchs and matriarchs had equal status. Although you understand that equality of status does not have to mean equality of function, you can't understand why women have so few obligations when it comes to *mitzvot*. "Doesn't the fact that men recite a benediction every morning thanking God for not creating them as women prove conclusively that Judaism does not regard women as highly as it does men?" you ask. The answer to your question is a definitive "No, it doesn't," and I will discuss the significance of that misunderstood and misinterpreted benediction with you in this letter. Let me begin with an introduction to the matter of women and *mitzvot*.

Judaism recognizes the heterogeneity of nature, that the world is composed of a multiplicity of species and forms, all of which were created by the Almighty and each of which conforms to His Will. Indeed, the totality of nature is "good." The point is made quite succinctly in the Torah narrative.

At the close of each day of Creation, we read, "And God saw that it was good," and at the end of the six-day cycle, "And God

saw all that He had made and found it very good" (Genesis 1:3).
Echoing this idea, King David wrote: "How many are the things
You have made, O Lord: You have made them all with wisdom;
the earth is full of Your creations" (Psalms 134:24).[1] Yes, nature
is heterogeneous, but it is unified by the Will of God, manifested
in what is called "the law of nature." This is the meaning of the
appellative *Lord of Hosts*, namely, the Lord who creates and governs the multiplicity of things that exist in nature. But the Torah
goes still further in its discussion of Creation; it circumscribes each
form as the work of God alone and endows it with significance
and permanence. This is the meaning of the phrase "after its kind,"
which is reiterated with the creation of each living creature.

What we have here is *havdalah* ("separation" or "differentiation"), a principle that is of fundamental importance in Judaism.
By specifying the forms in nature and rendering them permanent
through a fixed set of laws, the Torah implies that each living thing
has its own Divinely designated function, its own role in the Divine
plan, the fulfillment of which is "good" in God's eyes. There is no
need to cross the natural barriers, for in all realms there is meaning and fulfillment. *Havdalah* not only affirms the significance of
each creation, it also fosters its dignity, as a whole and in its individual components. To "create" means to make the whole and its
parts, the aggregate and the individual, and Judaism teaches that
in the human species, the individual is of no less importance than
the group.

The principle of *havdalah* begins with the creation of the first
quantum of light, as we read, "And God saw that the light was
good, and God separated the light from the darkness" (Genesis
1:4). As put by Rabbi Samson Raphael Hirsch in his commentary, "God called to the light and appointed it to the tasks of the
day, and God called to the darkness and appointed it to the tasks
of the night."[2] Both light and darkness have their roles in the
universe; they are separate from one another, but each is important in its own right.

How is *havdalah* expressed in Jewish literature? In a rather unique way. The subjects are not defined but rather set in contrast to one another. For example, the *havdalah* recited after *Shabbat* reads: "He [God] separates between the sacred and the profane, between light and darkness, between Israel and the other nations, and between the seventh day and the six days of Creation." One subject is contrasted to the other, and as a result, the uniqueness of each subject, while not defined, is put somewhat in perspective. The sacred is *not* the profane, light is *not* darkness, Israel is *not* like the other nations, and *Shabbat* is not like the weekdays. It should be clearly understood, however, that *havdalah* is a statement of uniqueness, not a value judgment. Considering that the purpose of *havdalah* is not to define but merely to put in perspective, contrast is the best formula.

In *Birkhot haShahar* ("the morning benedictions") there is a series of three benedictions that are interrelated and relevant to our discussion.

> Blessed are You, Lord our God, who has not made me a heathen.

> Blessed are You, Lord our God, who has not made me a [heathen] slave.

> Blessed are You, Lord our God, who has not made me a woman.

Much to our chagrin, these benedictions have been misinterpreted and subjected to unfounded criticism, not only by individuals whose understanding of Judaism is limited at best, but even by those whose knowledge should have inspired them to speak otherwise or be silent. Unbridled zealousness is not only self-defeating, it is dangerous. Our task shall be to examine the sources carefully and ascertain the intended meaning of these benedictions.

As we have indicated, one of the examples of *havdalah* is "separation of the sacred from the profane." It would seem that this was the guiding motif of the three benedictions above, for they focus on the unique character of each group mentioned with regard to its obligation to *mitzvot*, and only in this regard.

The uniqueness of the Jew manifests itself in his responsibility and commitment to observe the *mitzvot*. While this commitment requires attentiveness, time, and effort, the Jew does not regard it as a burden. Quite the contrary. He accepts it upon himself with enthusiasm. For the more the Jew involves himself with *mitzvot*, the closer he feels to God, and drawing near to God is what Judaism is all about. In recognition of this responsibility, which he considers a privilege, *and only in this regard*, the Jew recites the benediction " . . . who has not made me a heathen." He proclaims his separateness by contrasting himself to the heathen. He is obligated to 613 *mitzvot* while the heathen is obligated only to 7.[3]

The male Jew then recites the second benediction contrasting himself to the heathen male slave who is in service to a Jew. In order for him to remain in a Jewish home, the slave must undergo voluntary conversion, an act that renders him a "partial Jew," so to speak, in the sense that he becomes obligated to *mitzvot* that are not time oriented. Although he is not a full functioning Jew—if he wishes to become Jewish, the law requires that he undergo a second conversion when he is freed—he is, nevertheless, on a higher level of *kedushah* ("sanctity") than other heathens, by virtue of the fact that he now has more *mitzvot* to perform. The male Jew, of course, is on a still higher level in this regard, for he is obligated to observe the time-oriented *mitzvot* as well. In recognition of this status, he recites the benediction.

But what of the Jewish woman? How can she recite the second benediction? She, too, is obligated only to the *mitzvot* that are not time oriented. What makes her sanctity greater than that of the heathen female slave? First, we have already pointed out that a Jewish woman has full status as a Jew. Unlike the heathen slave who is not obligated to the time-oriented *mitzvot*, the Jewish woman is simply *exempt* from them. This means that she may observe these *mitzvot* if she so chooses—the only exception being *tallit* and *tefillin*, according to most authorities—but a heathen slave may not.[4] In point of fact, many women do observe these *mitzvot*. Second, there are seven time-oriented *mitzvot* that women *are* obligated to observe: being joyous on the festivals, *Hakhel*, that is, "gathering together to listen to the reading of portions of Deuteronomy," sanctification of the day of *Shabbat* and other holy days, eating *matzah* and drinking the four cups of wine on the first night of Passover, reading the *Megillah* on Purim, and lighting the Hanukkah lights.[5] Considering this, it is certainly in order for a female Jew to recite the second benediction, " . . . who has not made me a female slave."

The male Jew then recites the third benediction, contrasting himself to the Jewish woman, who is obligated only to the *mitzvot* that are not time oriented. But what should the woman recite? Should she say, " . . . who has not made me a man"? To some, this might seem appropriate enough, but considering the theme of these three benedictions, namely, obligation to *mitzvot*, it would surely be improper for her to do so. To praise the Almighty and thank Him for exempting one from *mitzvot* would be audacious. Some suggest that women say, " . . . who has made me a woman." While this formula is somewhat milder, being in the positive, it would not conform to the style of the other benedictions. Moreover, it is too general. It does not indicate the uniqueness of the Jewish woman, for a female gentile is also a woman. Others suggest " . . . who has made me a Jewish woman," but the original difficulty of *mitzvah* observance remains. What's more, by identifying herself as a Jewish woman, the two previous benedictions would be rendered superfluous for Jewish women. Finally, to phrase the benediction in the positive would still break the classic pattern of *havdalah*, which contrasts and tells what something *is not* rather than what it *is*. Truthfully speaking, positive statements of this nature would be inappropriate for both men and women for an even more important reason. Consider this:[6]

Man's posture before the Almighty is one of dependency and utter humility. In the *Ne'ilah* service for Yom Kippur, we recite the following:

> What are we? What is our life? What is our goodness? What is our righteousness? What is our helpfulness? What is our strength? What is our might? What can we say in Your presence, Lord our God and God of our fathers? Indeed, all the heroes are as nothing before You, the men of renown as though they never existed, the wise as if they were without knowledge, the intelligent as though they lacked understanding; for most of their doings are worthless, and the days of their life are vain in Your sight; man is not far above the beast for all is vanity.

Our sages considered this posture to be so important to the Jewish experience of prayer that they included this paragraph in the daily *Shaharit* service as well.

An astonishing question is raised in the Talmud concerning the creation of man: "Should man have been created or should he not have been created" (*Eruvin* 13b). Even more astonishing is the answer. In light of man's tendency to sin and his shameful record of evil, the Talmud concludes that it would have been better had man not been created.

Why did the sages in the Talmud come down so hard on man? Perhaps it was because man, with too few exceptions, has profaned rather than sanctified his soul. Rather than rising to the sphere of the angels, man has descended to the level of the beast, acting on instinct and impulse rather than on intellect and virtue. Indeed, since the beginning of history, man has brought more shame and dishonor to his existence than pride and praise. Better for such a being not to have been created, said the sages. Man being a *fait accompli*, however, let him engage in introspection daily, and repent his ways.

In light of man's poor record in history, it would be inappropriate for this benediction to be worded in positive terms. For, in truth, it would have been better, objectively speaking, if man had not been created—neither a man nor a woman, neither a Jew nor a gentile, neither a free man nor a slave. Having been created, however, the male Jew must express his thankfulness to the Almighty for not having placed his soul in the body of a gentile, who has only 7 *mitzvot* through which he can fulfill the Divine Will, or in that of a gentile slave who has more *mitzvot* but only by virtue of the fact that he is owned by a Jew. He is also thankful that his soul was not placed in the body of a Jewish woman, for although she is obligated to fulfill all the negative *mitzvot*, as well as the positive non-time-oriented *mitzvot*, and even some of the positive time-oriented *mitzvot*, she is not obligated to fulfill all. He is grateful for the opportunity, indeed, the responsibility to fulfill all 613 *mitzvot*. Yes, the Jew is thankful to God for the opportunity he was given to attain greatness, but due to his past record of accomplishments, a record that leaves much to be desired, he dares not express himself with the bold statement " . . . who has made me a Jew."

David Abudraham, the renowned sage of the fourteenth century, was the first authority to mention a special corresponding benediction for women. In his monumental work, *Abudraham HaShalem*, the benediction is worded as follows: "Blessed be You Lord our God, King of the universe, who has made me according to His Will."[7] While this benediction also breaks the positive formula of *havdalah*, the fact that the statement is indirect makes it somewhat more appropriate than the suggested formulas, and is as such the only alternative to silence. Now there is another thought to which this indirect statement may allude, but before we can discuss it intelligently, we must clarify why women are exempt from time-oriented *mitzvot*.

It is of the utmost importance that we keep in mind that the law ordains that women are *exempt* from fulfilling time-oriented *mitzvot*; they are not *prohibited*. If they choose to do so, they may fulfill all but three of the relevant time-oriented *mitzvot* and recite the appropriate benedictions as well.[8] In point of fact, many women observe the *mitzvot* of *shofar, lulav,* and *sukkah.* This should make it sufficiently clear that the Halakhah per se is not prejudiced against women, for had such been the case, it would have *forbidden* women to fulfill the time-oriented *mitzvot.* Nonetheless, it is true that women were exempted from the obligation to fulfill many of the positive time-oriented mitzvot. But why? We can only speculate on the reason for this exemption, and speculate we shall!

"Time is life!" Modern man has failed to take this principle seriously. Leisure time is often wasted on nonsense activities aptly termed "killing time." The Torah makes the Jew aware of time by obligating him to time-oriented *mitzvot.* But while these *mitzvot* are of crucial importance to males, they may not be that crucial for females, whose physiology, specifically their menstrual cycle and the *halakhot* that apply to it, make them consistently aware of time and teach them to sanctify it. Rabbi Emanuel Rackman, a contemporary scholar and theologian, writes:

> A careful examination of talmudic sources reveals that the law's differentiation between men and women was based on nature and natural function, and not on social or economic considerations. Now nature has not endowed man with any "built in" apparatus for measuring time. . . . Women, on the other hand, by the very nature of their physical constitution and the requirements of the law with regard to their menstrual periods, needed little more to make them aware of the sanctity of time.[9]

In light of Rabbi Rackman's statement, we turn to another contemporary talmudic scholar, Rabbi Aaron Soloveitchik, who made the following observation on this matter:

> One can readily see that Judaism not only accords to the woman an encomium of appreciation as an equal partner of man, but that it also recognizes the female as the gender which possesses innate

spiritual superiority as compared with the male gender. This out-
look can be deduced from a mere cursory glance at the Creation
in Genesis. It appears from Genesis that whatever was superior
was created later. . . . The human being was created after all the
animals. But in the human species, the male came first and then
the female gender.[10]

What is it that makes women superior to men? From where
do we learn of that superiority? asks Rabbi Soloveitchik. When
man was created, he was charged with two commandments: conquest and cultivation. These commandments are gifts from the
Almighty; without them, there can be no progress in the world. If
properly used, conquest can serve as a basis for progress; if improperly used it leaves disaster in its wake. But the Almighty
granted man another gift, says Rabbi Soloveitchik, "cultivation,"
that is, the ability to reach out to people through dedication and
perseverance. This is implied in the words, "And God took the
man and put him in the garden of Eden to cultivate it and to keep
it" (Genesis 2:15).

These two commandments represent two different approaches
to life. If one studies the Torah, says Rabbi Soloveitchik, and espe-
cially the Talmud and the Midrash, one comes to realize that only
in the tribe of Levi were the males given the mandate of cultivation; the rest of the males of Israel were involved with conquest.
The mandate of cultivation was given to *all* the women of Israel,
however. Furthermore, says Rabbi Soloveitchik, God created man
and woman different from one another not only biologically but
psychologically, emotionally, and spiritually as well. God imposed
more *mitzvot* upon the men because they are innately disposed
toward excessive and abusive conquest. He imposed time-oriented
mitzvot upon them and the obligation to be constantly involved
in Torah study to counteract this natural disposition. The words
"who has made me according to His Will" imply the superiority
of women, not their inferiority, says Rabbi Soloveitchik. For men
to be compassionate, good-hearted, and tolerant, they must

struggle against innate forces within their psyche, but women have a natural disposition toward compassion and consideration. "Women's character was molded by God in accordance with the eschatological goals that Almighty God reserved for the world. In the Messianic Era, every human being will be pursuing the gift of 'cultivation.' There will be no pursuit of 'conquest.'"[11] In recognition of her superiority, says Rabbi Soloveitchik, the woman thanks the Almighty for creating her according to His Will—the pattern He designed to be that of all mankind in the Messianic Era.

In light of what we have said, isn't it interesting that the Hebrew term for "womb"—that which is, biologically, the final uniqueness of womanhood—is *rehem*, from which the term *rahamim* ("mercy") is derived. And what greater testimony to the attributes of compassion, protection, and cultivation can we have than *Havah*, the name Adam gave to his wife indicating that she was the "mother of all living."

Women and Prayer

My dearest daughter,

I am so glad that you have the time to write, and that we are able to communicate on matters that are of ultimate concern to you. Truthfully speaking, these matters should be of concern to every Jewish man and woman. Perhaps they will be some day in the future. You question why women are not required to recite the entire service or to pray with a *minyan*, and you are disturbed by the fact that they cannot be counted in a *minyan* even when there are not enough men present. Many claim that this is another example of male chauvinism, and you would like to be convinced that it is not. So let me devote this letter to "Prayer": a brief discussion of the philosophy of prayer, a clarification of the halakhic obligations of women in the prayer service, and finally, why women may not be counted in a *minyan*.[1]

Judaism is not a religion that limits itself to mere excursions of the mind. It lays major emphasis on behavior, namely, commitment to a Divinely ordained and revealed plan for study, practice, and prayer. Each of these modes has a distinct purpose and goal; each is directed to a facet of man's soul. Study of the Torah engages man's intellect in the pursuit of Divine truths. Practice of the *mitzvot* engages his sovereign will for the purpose of endowing with meaning that which is usually an undirected and mundane existence. Prayer engages his heart or emotions and affords him the opportunity to come before the Almighty with praise, petition, thanksgiving, and even complaint, in response to what life has brought him.

To be sure, all three modes of performance are encounters with Divinity, but prayer is of a very special nature. While man can pursue both study and practice independently, prayer always requires the presence of the Almighty to render it meaningful—His "listening ear," so to speak. But can we assume the presence of the Almighty whenever we pray? Judaism asserts that we can, indeed, that we must. The Talmud teaches, "One who prays must see himself as if the *Shekhinah* ["Presence of the Almighty"] is before him, for it is said: 'I have put the Lord before me at all times' (Psalms 16:8)"[2] This teaches us that prayer is a dialogue rather than a soliloquy, an encounter between man and his Maker where both partners play an important role in the experience. Now some might contend that prayer can thus be likened to prophecy, but the definitive difference between the two must be kept in mind. In prophecy, God speaks and man listens; in prayer, man speaks and God listens.

Speech is a special gift from the Almighty, one of the major endowments peculiar to man for which he should be eternally grateful. For through speech, man is able to communicate his thoughts and vent his emotions to other human beings. Indeed, were it not for the power of speech, the joint effort and the community project would never have materialized, and the interaction between people would have been limited to primitive gestures.

Adam, the first man, recognized the Almighty as the Being to whom he owed his very existence. He felt the need to express his feelings of gratitude in words, and so he did. The song of thanksgiving attributed to Adam has been handed down to us by tradition through the generations as Psalm 92.[3] It opens with the words "It is good to give thanks to the Lord, and to sing praises to Your name O Most High." But early man had the desire to give more tangible expression to his feelings. Thus was born the ritual of sacrifice, a mode of worship practiced by Israel for many centuries. *Korban* ("sacrifice") derives from the root *karov*, which means "to draw near," and indicates that sacrifice was the medium through which Israel drew near to the Almighty.[4] Some contend that Adam brought sacrifices, but the first sacrifices recorded in the Torah were those brought by Cain and Abel. Abel recognized that all he had derived from God. In gratitude, he sacrificed the choice of his flock, reasoning that by doing so, he had earned the right to keep what was left. Cain, on the other hand, selfishly kept the best fruit of his crop for himself. He brought only those of inferior quality to the Almighty as an appeasement rather than an expression of gratitude, and reasoned that by doing so he would ensure successful crops in the future.[5]

Such reasoning could elicit only the following: "The Lord paid heed to Abel and his offering, but to Cain and his offering He paid no heed" (Genesis 4:5). It is not the quantity nor even the quality of the gift that matters; only the motivation and the sincerity of the giver is important.[6]

Sacrifice became the mode of worship for early man. Properly practiced, it is a legitimate form of worship and most admirable; indeed, the patriarchs offered sacrifices to the Almighty. But legitimacy does not preclude abuse. History testifies to the abominable practices in the pagan world: sexual aberrations and even human sacrifice. When the institution of sacrifice was legitimized for Israel at Sinai, however, it was cleansed of these impurities and directed to the One true God. To study the book of Leviticus is to be impressed and inspired by the rich symbolism of sacrifice as it was performed in the Tabernacle and later in the Holy Temple in Jerusalem; it is to be thoroughly convinced of the great impact that this institution must have had on the masses of the people.

The great reward promised to the nation of Israel with the erection of the Tabernacle and the institution of sacrifice as the mode of worship therein was that the *Shekhinah* would dwell in their midst. But this was also conditioned on their compliance with the word of the Almighty as preached in the Torah. They would become a kingdom of priests and a holy nation, but they had to guard themselves from sin, the defilement of body and soul. Since man is weak and prone to sin—as King Solomon so aptly put it, "There is not one good man on earth who does what is best and doesn't sin" (Ecclesiastes 7:20)—and much such defilement did occur, expiation was accomplished through the medium of sacrifice.

Although most of the rituals involving sacrifice may be performed only by the priest, the crucial ritual involved in the sin offering is performed by the sinner who brings the sacrifice. The ritual is called *semikhah* ("pressing of the hands"). The Talmud describes the process of *semikhah* as follows:

> How does one press the hands? The sacrifice stands to the north, with its face to the west, and he who presses the hands stands to the east, with his face to the west, and puts his two hands between the two horns of the sacrifice, and nothing may intervene between him and the sacrifice, and he confesses.[7]

Through the ritual of *semikhah*, the animal replaces the person; the sin as well as the punishment is transferred, symbolically of course, from the sinner to the animal. The sinner places his two hands upon the head of the live animal—perhaps he even feels its warm blood pulsating through its body—and he confesses his sin. It is as if he says to himself, "There, but for the grace of God, go I." One can only speculate as to the psychological impact this performance must have had on the sincere penitent: the cathartic soul-cleansing experience of one who sees himself reinstated to holiness.

I believe that it is sufficiently clear from what I have described thus far that the ritual of sacrifice was meant for man, not God. The Almighty needs nothing material from man. Indeed, He prefers for man to obey and not sin. By doing so, man would not be obligated to bring any offerings, for all other kinds of offerings that were brought by the individual were optional. This point is made quite succinctly by the prophet: "Does the Lord delight in burnt-offerings and sacrifices as much as obedience to the Lord's command? Surely obedience is better than sacrifice, compliance than the fat of rams" (1 Samuel 15:22). We must be very careful not to misconstrue the meaning of the statements made by the prophets about sacrifice. They spoke out against sacrifices that were brought perfunctorily, that is, without the proper motivation and without sincere repentance; they did not condemn sacrifice per se! The Almighty would not have condemned that which He Himself had ordained. Quite confirming of this point is a statement found in the Talmud in interpretation of the verse: "Guard your foot when you go to the house of God and be ready to listen: it is better than when fools give sacrifices; for they know not to do evil" (Ecclesiastes 4:17).

> What is the meaning of that which is written: "Guard your foot when you go to the house of God?" Guard yourself so that you do not sin, bring an offering before Me. "And be ready to listen"—be ready to the words of the sages; for if they sin, they bring an offering and repent. "It is better than when fools give sacrifices"—be not like the fools who sin and bring an offering without repenting. "For they know not to do evil [sic]"—If so, they are righteous! No, the meaning is be not like the fools who sin and bring an offering and know not whether they bring it for the good they have done or for the evil they have committed. The Holy One blessed be He says, "They are unable to discern between good and evil and they bring an offering before Me!"[8]

With the destruction of the Temple in Jerusalem (c. 70 C.E.), the institution of sacrifice came to an abrupt end. Prayer now became the mode of worship. In the words of the prophet: "Return O Israel to the Lord your God, for you have fallen because of your

sins. Take words with you and return to the Lord. Say to Him:
'Forgive all guilt and accept what is good; instead of bulls, we
will pay [the offering] of our lips'" (Hosea 14:2-3). The Talmud
teaches that the Almighty ordained this replacement of sacrifice
by prayer much earlier in history and revealed it to Abraham as
follows:

> Then He said to him: "I am the Lord who brought you out from
> Ur of the Chaldeans to give you this land as a possession." And he
> said: "O Lord God, how shall I know that I am to possess it?"
> (Genesis 15:7-8). Abraham said: "Master of the universe! Should
> Israel sin before You, will You do to them as You have done to the
> generation of the Flood and the generation of the Dispersion?" God
> replied to him: "No!" He then said to Him: "Master of the universe!
> Let me know whereby I shall inherit it." God answered: "Take Me
> a heifer three years old and a she-goat three years old. . . . " Abraham
> then continued: "Master of the universe! This holds good while
> the Temple remains in being, but when the Temple will no longer
> be, what will become of them?" God replied: "I have already long
> ago provided for them in the Torah the order of sacrifices and
> whenever they read it, I will deem it as if they had offered them
> before Me and I will grant them pardon for all their iniquities."[9]

According to one opinion in the Talmud, prayer was established
by the patriarchs. Abraham established *Shaharit*, the "Morning
Service"; Isaac established *Minhah*, the "Afternoon Service"; and
Jacob established *Arvit* or *Maariv*, the "Evening Service." Another
opinion posits that the sages ordained the services to commemorate the institution of the *Tamid* sacrifice, which was brought in
the morning and in the afternoon.[10]

What are the implications of this change in the mode of worship for the future? Was prayer meant to replace sacrifice permanently or was it a temporary decree due to the destruction of the
Holy Temple in Jerusalem? There is no doubt that according to
Jewish tradition the institution of sacrifice will return with the

rebuilding of the Temple in the Messianic Era. We consistently reaffirm this principle in our daily, *Shabbat,* and festival services. In light of this, the rationale for sacrifice postulated by Maimonides in his philosophical work *Guide of the Perplexed* is highly problematic, for it could lead one to the conclusion that this institution will never be reinstated. The difficulty here lies not only in the fact that such a contention is contrary to Jewish tradition—which would be reason enough for us to question such an interpretation of the words of Maimonides—but in the fact that it contradicts what Maimonides himself states in his halakhic work *Mishneh Torah.* Let me, therefore, present the relevant texts and attempt to resolve the apparent contradiction.[11] In the *Guide of the Perplexed* we read the following:

> On considering the Divine acts, or the process of nature, we get an insight into the prudence and wisdom of God as displayed in the creation of animals, with gradual development in their limbs . . . and we perceive also His wisdom and plan in the successive and gradual development of the whole condition of the individual. . . .

> Many precepts of the law are a result of a similar course adopted by the same Supreme Being. Namely, it is impossible to go from one extreme to another; it is therefore according to the nature of man, impossible for him to suddenly discontinue everything to which he has been accustomed. . . .

> God sent Moses to make a kingdom of priests and a holy nation . . . but the custom which was in those days general among men and the general mode of worship in which the Israelites were brought up, consisted of sacrificing animals in those temples which contained certain images, and burning incense before them. . . .

> It was in accordance with the wisdom and plan of God as displayed in the whole of Creation, that He did not command us to give up and discontinue all these manners of service, for to obey such a commandment would have been contrary to the nature of man who generally cleaves to that to which he is accustomed; it would

in those days have made the same impression as a prophet would make at present if he called us to the service of God and told us in His name that we should not pray to Him, not fast nor seek His help in times of trouble; that we should serve Him in thought, and not by any action. For this reason, God allowed these kinds of service to continue; He transferred to His service that which had formerly served as a worship of created beings and of things imaginary and unreal, and commanded us to serve Him in the same manner. . . .

By this Divine act, it was effected that the traces of idolatry were blotted out and the true principle of our faith, the existence and the unity of God, was firmly established; this result was thus obtained without deterring or confusing the minds of the people by the abolition of the service to which they were accustomed and which alone was familiar to them. . . .

As the sacrificial service is not the primary object, whilst supplications, prayers and similar kinds of worship are nearer to the primary object and indispensible for obtaining it, a great difference was made in the law between these two kinds of service. The one kind which consists in offering sacrifices, although the sacrifices are offered to the name of God, has not been made obligatory to us to the same extent as it had been made before. We were not commanded to sacrifice in every place, or to permit everyone who desires to become a priest and sacrifice. . . . All these restrictions serve to limit this kind of worship and to keep it within those bounds within which God did not think it necessary to abolish sacrificial services altogether. But prayer and supplications can be offered everywhere and by every person.[12]

In the *Mishneh Torah*, Maimonides writes the following:

King Messiah will arise and restore the kingdom of David to its former state and original sovereignty. He will rebuild the Temple and gather the dispersed of Israel. . . . Sacrifices will again be offered . . . in accordance with the commandments set forth by the law.[13]

And again:

> The statutes are the commandments whose reason is not known.
> . . . Our sages have said: My statutes are the decrees I have de-
> creed for you, and you are not permitted to question them. . . . All
> the laws concerning the offerings are in the category of statutes.[14]

If Maimonides held the institution of sacrifice to have been
merely a concession to Israel in order to wean them away from
idolatry, as some contend, it follows that he would likewise posit
that this institution would not be reinstated in the Messianic Era.
Yet, in the *Mishneh Torah*, he speaks of the rebuilding of the
Temple in the Messianic Era and with it the reinstatement of sacrifice. Moreover, by what right does Maimonides permit himself
to probe the rationale for sacrifice altogether when he categorizes
these laws as *hukkim*, namely, statutes that man is forbidden to
question, the reasons for them being unfathomable to man?

Before attempting a resolution, let me note that some authorities find no contradiction here at all. For even if Maimonides held
that the legitimization of sacrifice in Israel was a concession, it
would have no bearing whatsoever on the status of sacrifice in
the future. A careful reading of the *Guide of the Perplexed*[15] would
verify that Torah law does not stand or fall on man's rationaliza-
tions.[16] One could rightfully argue that since reasons are the product of human cognition, they carry no weight except to confirm
and reinforce the law that, as a Divine Code, is immutable.

A more explicatory approach to this problem is taken by a
contemporary talmudic scholar and theologian, the late Rabbi
Isidore Epstein.[17] In light of Maimonides' position on the *hukkim*,
says Epstein, it would seem that he had a twofold approach to
the institution of sacrifice: one in regard to the obligatory sacrifices, the other, markedly different, in regard to the voluntary
sacrifices.

The obligatory sacrifices are rational, says Epstein, for the Almighty does not decree purposeless acts, but the reasons for them are unfathomable by man.[18] Consequently, Maimonides contends that we are not permitted to rationalize them or even question them. But these sacrifices do have a purpose, namely, the expiation of sin. It was the obligatory sacrifices that Maimonides had in mind, says Epstein, when he wrote that sacrifices will be reinstituted in the Messianic Era. The voluntary sacrifices, on the other hand, were somewhat problematic. Epstein writes:

> Through their idolatrous origin and by their very nature, they were not without lurking dangers. Unlimited in their number, and unattended by confession and repentance which are fundamental to expiatory offerings, or by the mental preparation that is inseparable from other obligatory offerings, voluntary offerings were liable to become a source of inner injury to righteous life. . . . It was against the abuse of this type of sacrifice that the prophets launched their scathing denunciations. Yet, far from being suppressed by the Torah, they received, paradoxically enough, Divine approval. The only feasible explanation, in the opinion of Maimonides, was that they were to be considered in the light of a concession, because of their inestimable value as a road through which primitive Israel could travel, albeit slowly and gradually, from idolatrous superstition to the highest service to the One and only God.[19]

The logic is sound; the notion does not leave us with the uncomfortable feeling one usually experiences with forced apologetics. Nevertheless, there is nothing specific enough in the writings of Maimonides that corroborates Epstein's contention, and without such corroboration the resolution, while it is interesting, does not carry much weight.

It should be understood that, despite the lack of a definitive approach or resolution to the problem, the notion that Maimonides held the institution of sacrifice to have been abolished is untenable. The point is made by Rabbi David Hoffmann, the renowned German halakhist of the nineteenth century. Regarding the prayers recited daily for the reinstatement of the Temple service in the Messianic Era, he writes:

> Can those who eliminated these prayers from the liturgy claim support from Maimonides? We are far from thinking that it ever entered Maimonides' mind to teach that with the destruction of the Temple, the rite of sacrifice was permanently abolished. . . . Quite the contrary. It is apparent that Maimonides held that despite their having arisen amidst the customs of those early times, these forms of Divine service must be retained in the future as well, having received sanction from above.[20]

Hoffmann's words are inspiring, but let me present yet another attempt to resolve the dilemma regarding the position of Maimonides on this matter. We must subject Maimonides' position in the *Guide of the Perplexed* to more careful analysis. Since sacrifice was the mode of worship in early times, says Maimonides, the Almighty did not command Israel to discontinue this mode of worship and replace it with another, namely prayer, though prayer would be closer to what he terms "the primary object." Since the Almighty retained and sanctioned sacrifice, keeping it "within the bounds where God did not think it necessary to abolish the sacrificial service altogether," it certainly had meaning and significance at that time. If so, could it not likewise have significance in the Messianic Era when the Temple in Jerusalem is rebuilt? Although Maimonides did not indicate what significance or relevance sacrifice could possibly have in the future, perhaps I can offer an approach based on the analogy he brings to illustrate his theory. The analogy reads:

> He did not command us to give up and discontinue all these manners of service, for to obey such a commandment would have been contrary to the nature of man who generally cleaves to that to which he is used; it would in those days have made the same impression as a prophet would make at present if he called us to

the service of God and told us in His name that we should not
pray to Him . . . that we should serve Him in thought and not by
action.

Let us assume that the three modes of worship spoken of by
Maimonides, namely sacrifice, prayer, and contemplation, are in
ascending order to what he regards as the "primary object."[21] Let
us further assume that in a given generation there will always be
found some individuals to whom thought or contemplation is the
most meaningful mode of worship, for it would provide them with
the most profound religious experience. If this were not the case,
why would Maimonides mention contemplation at all? We must
likewise assume that in a given generation, there will always be
found others to whom sacrifice is the most meaningful mode of
worship despite it being farthest removed from the "primary
object." As the sages have explained, the types of offerings were
not chosen arbitrarily. On the contrary, they were very carefully
selected. The people of Israel were commanded to bring offerings from those things for which the heart longs, such as meat,
wine, and bread, so that their hearts would be more aroused as
they have recourse to them. The poor were obligated to bring flour,
over which their hearts and eyes were concerned the entire day.[22]
With the rebuilding of the Temple, all three modes of worship
could be functional, for each of them would be relevant to a portion of the population. Would it be presumptuous to posit that
Maimonides had this in mind as well?

Let me once more focus on the Maimonides analogy and probe
its widest implications. "He [God] did not command us to give
up and discontinue all these manners of service. . . . " Substitut-
ing what? Prayer, of course! Maimonides continues: "It would in
those days have made the same impression as a prophet would
make at present if he called us to the service of God and told us
in His name that we should not pray to Him . . . that we should

serve Him in thought and not by action." Does Maimonides not imply that prayer is to sacrifice what thought is to prayer?

Let me take the analogy still further. Just what impression would it make upon us if a prophet did, indeed, preach the substitution of thought or contemplation for prayer? Would such a person not be declared a false prophet? Surely Maimonides, who held that to pray is one of the 613 *mitzvot*,[23] would have considered him such. In point of fact, Maimonides implies that to abolish sacrifice, no matter what mode of worship is substituted, is biblically prohibited. Is this not the direction of the analogy?

From what I have said thus far, it is clear that Maimonides could not have postulated that the institution of sacrifice has been abolished. Therefore, he could not have proposed that the sole purpose of the Divine sanction of sacrifice was to wean Israel from idolatry. For unless one could make a convincing argument that the Jewish people are drawn to idolatry today, there would be no need for the institution of sacrifice to be reinstated. In point of fact, it is eminently clear that Maimonides was well aware of the value and significance of sacrifice as a legitimate mode of worship. Notwithstanding the fact that it is not very close to the "primary object," it has the potential of being a religious experience to some people. Had he felt otherwise, he would not have written: "The great principle of our Faith, the existence and the unity of God, was firmly established; the result was thus obtained without detering or confusing the minds of the people by the abolition of the service to which they were accustomed."[24]

No, we dare not underestimate the value of the institution of sacrifice, or underplay its role in ancient Israel. To study the talmudic and midrashic literature on this mode of worship is to be thoroughly impressed with the rich symbolism and the sophisticated meaning of the rituals and procedures. One can only wonder whether our prayer services today engender the feelings of awe and devotion in the hearts of the masses of the people to the extent that the institution of sacrifice had done in the days of the Temple in Jerusalem. Be that as it may, we must now return to prayer.

To pray is to make several presuppositions, the most fundamental of which is that God exists. To be sure, without God, prayer is an exercise in futility. The man of faith has no doubts on the matter of God's existence; he takes it as a given. He seeks no proof to confirm the tradition that has been handed down father to son and teacher to student, since the beginning of history, and he needs no rationale to justify his unqualified commitment to all that follows from this tradition. Suffice it to say that there is impressive evidence—from history, from tradition, and from the collective experience of the nation of Israel through the ages—to render the belief in the existence of God both reasonable and convincing to the objective mind.

The second presupposition is that man has a right to pray. Few of us ponder this thought; we just pray. But by what right do we pray? Is it not the height of audacity for man to confront the Almighty? Indeed, by what right does man address the Supreme King of Kings with his declamations of praise, petition, and thanksgiving? By what merit does he deem himself worthy of such a dialogue? One answer might be that the precedent for dialogue has already been set by the angels. As the prophet wrote: "And they called to one another and said: 'Holy, holy, holy, the Lord of Hosts; the whole earth is full of His glory'" (Isaiah 6:3). Man is simply following suit. And while there are differences of opinion, to be sure, on where man stands in comparison to the angels, rank is irrelevant here. Prayer is inspired and motivated by dependency, the common denominator of all creation. In this regard, angels are no different than human beings. If the angels have a right to confront the Almighty with praise, man has a right to do so as well. The patriarchs prayed and Moses prayed; the prophets of old prayed and the sages prayed, and the congregation of Israel in every generation has a right to follow their example.

All this notwithstanding, we pray because we must. Our condition is such that we cannot help but pray. The day-to-day experiences of life elicit man's response to the Almighty. At times, we encounter Him as the transcendent Creator who inspires awe and elicits praise and adoration. At other times, we encounter Him as the compassionate Father in heaven who inspires affection and evokes petition and thanksgiving. King David wrote: "A prayer of the lowly man who is faint and pours forth his plea before the Lord" (Psalms 102:1). Every human being feels lowly when he stands before the Lord in prayer. We are all alike in this regard. It is our creaturely needfulness that inspires prayer. We pray not because of what we *are* but because of what we *are not*. Thus it is not the sophistication of the prayer that is important but rather the sincerity of the one who offers it.

If the encounter with God in prayer is to have any meaning or purpose, we must presuppose far more than the existence of God and man's right to confront Him. We must posit that man is not just an insignificant speck of protoplasm in the vast and awesome universe, here today and gone tomorrow, no more worthy than a grain of sand or a blade of grass. We must aver that man is something special, of far greater significance to God than the brute creation. We must posit that God is concerned with man and interested in his well-being, more so than with any other living creature. In a word—providence! Not providence of a general nature as is extended to all other species, but personal providence that is extended to each and every member of the human species.[25]

But how do we know this to be the case? Not by *speculation* but by *revelation*. The revelation of the Torah on Mount Sinai in the presence of more than a million human beings, and the revelation of the Divine message to Israel through the prophets of later generations, indeed, the revelation of the Divine hand in history in our own day, are all manifestations of God's concern for mankind.

Our final presupposition is the efficacy of prayer. Does God answer man's prayers? If He does, prayer is certainly a worthwhile endeavor. If He doesn't, why pray? Perhaps prayer serves another purpose? A contemporary theologian and talmudic scholar, the late Rabbi Eliezer Berkovits, writes most incisively on this point. Prayer in its original form is not asking God for something, says Berkovits. It is a cry in pain. "It is an elementary outburst of woe, a spontaneous call in need. . . . It is the call of human helplessness directed to God. It is not asking but coming with one's burden before God. . . . This is the essence of prayer."[26] Above all else, to pray is to make the Almighty one's confidant; it is to unburden one's soul before the "eternal listener" of the cosmos. If only for this alone, it is a worthwhile endeavor.

But let us not beg the question.

Judaism, to be sure, postulates that God answers man's prayers. Biblical and postbiblical literature abound with examples of God's response to supplication. But should we expect Him to answer all our prayers? Indeed, are all prayers answerable? To expect an affirmative answer to all our prayers is both naive and heretical. It is naive because it is oblivious to the fact that at times God's Will may very well be determined by factors that are beyond His concern for man. As the prophet wrote: "For My thoughts are not your thoughts and My ways are not your ways, saith the Lord" (Isaiah 55:8). There is no basis for the assumption that the universe is anthropocentric. It is heretical because to expect God to fulfill all our requests is to designate Him as man's slave. Indeed, to entertain the notion that a negative response to our petition is even the slightest bit improper is sacrilege.

Consider the following: We petition God for things we believe to be beneficial. Many of our requests would undoubtedly be beneficial. But we cannot deny the distinct possibility that unbeknown to us some of the things we request would not be beneficial to us in the long run. For example: A positive response to a petition for a successful job interview when the candidate is not sufficiently qualified for the position could be disastrous to him, for if he gets the job and is discovered to be a poor worker, not only might he be fired, but he might be permanently black-listed, making it virtually impossible for him to secure a job in that field again. On the other hand, a negative response to such a petition might force him to face the reality that he is really un-qualified for the position and motivate him to seek additional training. A positive response to the death wish of a terminally ill patient who is in dire pain seems merciful; yet, if it happened on the eve of the discovery of a cure for his affliction, it would be cruel.

There is another problem in answering prayers. It is not at all inconceivable that the prayers of one person may conflict with those of another. At a particular time and place, the farmer may pray for rain while the vacationer prays for sunshine. Where they are both worthy and deserving, whose prayer should God answer?

All of the above notwithstanding, we know that God does, indeed, answer man's prayers. As we have already noted, both biblical and postbiblical literature testify to this. Many of us know from our own experience that God answers man's prayers. What we must keep in mind, however, is that the *why* and *when* of prayer efficacy are a Divine matter concerning which we have little if any understanding. Probing such questions leads mostly to disap-pointment and frustration and would, therefore, best be left to Divine providence.

The fact that even a single prayer is answered, however, poses a serious question. If man's prayers are successful, is he not altering the Divine Will? Yet, if God's Will were such that all things were unalterably determined, what purpose would His immanence in the world serve? If everything that was, is, and will be has been predetermined by God and there are no options open to man for change, human endeavor becomes futile and irrelevant. Judaism posits that man has a measure of freedom. Based on that freedom, he is either rewarded or punished for his actions. Indeed, main-stream Jewish thinking is decidedly nondeterministic. Berkovits contends quite logically: "If the Divine plan . . . allows a measure of importance to man's actions, why should it not be conceivable that the same plan may have a provision by which human suffering may be considered a matter of some importance?"[27]

Our sages were fully aware of the fact that prayer "imposes" upon God. Yet, they taught, "The Holy One blessed be He yearns for the prayers of the righteous."[28] Indeed, the Almighty wants to be imposed upon, for such impositions give Him the opportunity to manifest His goodness by showering His mercy upon the world.

We cannot overemphasize the fact that it is man's inadequacy rather than his intellectual or spiritual prowess that justifies prayer. Our sages taught that there is no self-importance before the Almighty.[29] The greater man's stature in this world, the greater the extent to which he must humble himself before his Creator.[30] Thus Jewish law decrees that the masses of Israel must bow four times during the Amidah ("Eighteen Benedictions") while the high priest must bow at the end of every benediction, and the king of Israel must recite the entire Amidah in a bowed position.[31] With this in mind, a point made by the late Rabbi Joseph B. Soloveitchik rings loud and true:

> The thrust of Halakhah is democratic from beginning to end. The Halakhah declares that any religion that confines itself to some remote corner of society, to an elite sect or faction, will give rise to destructive consequences that far outweigh any putative gains. A religious ideology that fixes boundaries and sets up dividing lines between people borders on heresy. If a religion declares that God is close to Reuben (on account of his lineage, profession or priestly role) and remote from Simon, it is gravely culpable. No person, according to the Halakhah, needs the aid of others to approach God. A person needs no advocates or special pleaders. Every person is insured by the Halakhah that whenever he will knock at the gates of heaven, they will be opened before him. And just as the Halakhah rejects the notion of human intercessors, so, too, it

rejects the notion of transcendental intercessors such as angels or seraphim.[32]

The desire of the Almighty to be imposed upon is a manifestation of His immanence, which is a crucial point in prayer. Though He is distant, he is also near. Rabbi Eliezer Berkovits writes:

> One cannot pray to the High and Lofty One . . . one cannot help but pray to the High and Lofty One who, breaking through the barriers of His infinitude, bends down to keep company with the lowly and the humble. Indeed, one may pray only because God wishes to be imposed upon. Notwithstanding His omnipotence, He considers our weakness; in spite of His omniscience, He does not despise our foolishness. . . . Man may pray because God invites him to bring his burden to Him that He may carry it along with Him.[33]

We have not yet resolved our problem. Theoretically, we may contend that God allows man to entreat Him because He recognizes man's creatureliness, but by what logic can we expect to alter God's Will? The matter is put quite succinctly by the fifteenth-century Spanish philosopher Joseph Albo, who writes:

> Either God has determined that a given person shall receive a given benefit, or He has not so determined. If He has so determined, there is no need for prayer. If He has not so determined, how can prayer avail to change God's Will that He should now determine to benefit that person, when He had not so determined before?[34]

To resolve the problem we must recognize that prayer as it is meant to be is much more than the mere recitation of words. It is an encounter with the Divine that results, ideally, in the transformation of man. One who turns to God in sincere prayer affirms thereby not only God's existence but His omnipresence and His omniscience as well. Moreover, he resolves to act accordingly. Were this not his intention, the gesture would be not merely ridiculous but offensive. By assuming the proper attitude in prayer, man is transformed; he becomes a better and more humble person to be sure, but more importantly, one who will effect a change in his life, as a result of the experience. "David" has been transformed into "Joseph," so to speak, a person not any different in body but altogether different in soul. The punishment decreed for David, the sinner, cannot be inflicted upon Joseph, the penitent. God's Will didn't change; the person changed.[35] Now he is seen in a new light, and he is judged by God from a new perspective. It is important to emphasize that this is not mere semantics. Sincere prayer can be an overwhelming experience; it can effect a complete turnaround in one's lifestyle and commitment.

With this in mind, a statement in the Talmud takes on new meaning: "Why is the prayer of the righteous compared to a pitchfork?" asks Rabbi Isaac. "As a pitchfork turns the sheaves of grain from one position to another, so does the prayer of the righteous turn the dispensations of the Holy One blessed be He from the attribute of anger to the attribute of mercy."[36] This is the power of sincere prayer!

The encounter in prayer serves primarily to establish a fellowship with God. Man rises toward heaven, so to speak, and God descends to meet him. Finity and Infinity meet in a symbolic handshake. This fellowship is depicted in the Torah with the words, "The Lord came down upon Mount Sinai, on the top of the mountain, and the Lord called Moses to the top of the mountain and Moses went up" (Exodus 19:20). Fellowship is among the most essential achievements of prayer.

There are many who ask: Why must we be bound by *Tefillat Hovah* ("obligatory prayer"), namely, a set service to be recited three times daily, composed of Psalms and litanies written centuries ago and addressed to problems and conditions that are totally irrelevant in today's society? Would it not be more appropriate and meaningful to reserve prayer for those special emotion-filled moments in our lives when personal experiences motivate us to reach out to God in praise, petition, or thanksgiving? Wouldn't prayer of this sort be more worthy than a lifetime of obligatory services?

These questions are not new, to be sure; they have been posed by many sincere and well-meaning people, and they are most deserving of an answer, at least an approach.

The contention that obligatory prayer generally lacks the sincerity and the luster of spontaneous prayer need not be challenged. In point of fact, the sages recognized the great value of spontaneity in prayer, and they encouraged us to engage in such noble worship whenever the need presents itself. But even more. They provided for spontaneous prayer in the *Amidah*. One may insert a personal prayer within any of the thirteen petitions with the single proviso that it be in consonance with the theme of that petition. Should one forget to do so at the appropriate time, he may insert the prayer, whatever the theme, in the last of the petitions, *Shema Koleinu,* ("Hear our voice") or in the prayer *Elokai N'tzor* ("O my God guard"), which concludes the *Amidah*.[37] Yet, to argue that prayer be left to special moments of excitement is to miss the whole point of obligatory prayer. For to limit prayer to such moments implies that the rest of life does not inspire feelings of awe or expressions of thankfulness. Dare we make such a statement, if only by innuendo? Is the fact that the sun rises and sets every day not worthy of our attention and thanksgiving? Is the fact that God has granted us the precious gift of life not worthy of our expression of gratitude? Are the many bounties in this world of which we so freely partake not sufficient reason for us to praise the Almighty? Are we to take all this and so much more for granted? Rabbi Johanan taught, "Would that man prayed all day long,"[38] and Rabbi Levi in the name of Rabbi Haninah taught, "For each and every breath that man takes, he is obligated to praise his Creator."[39]

Spontaneous prayer alone, however noble and sincere, is simply insufficient to fulfill man's obligation to address his Creator. Of course, to pray all day is a practical impossibility. The sages

therefore established the "service," the law that man pray three
times a day to fulfill his obligation as well as his personal need to
praise, petition, and thank the Almighty in response to the vicissitudes of life.[40] Obligatory prayer is addressed to the way of the
world and the ever present existential condition of man, while
spontaneous prayer, which by definition is of a personal nature,
is a reaction to the unique events in each person's life. One might
reasonably contend that obligatory prayer makes spontaneous
prayer permissible.

There is an interesting quality about obligatory prayer; it inspires a sense of fellowship with the greater community of Israel,
namely, past, present, and future generations. Whether or not it
is recited with a *minyan*, it is *tefillat haTzibbur* ("congregational
prayer"), for the language, the themes, and the words have been
recited by Jews the world over for more than a thousand years.
Consequently, prayer inspires a great sense of security. Perhaps
this is the rationale behind the following law: Whenever possible
one should pray with a *minyan*; if on a given day this is impossible, one should pray at the hour when the *minyan* is praying; if
this is also impossible, one should pray in the synagogue, where
services are held daily.[41]

We have already conceded that, for the most part, spontaneous prayer, being of a personal nature, is more heartfelt and more
stirring than obligatory prayer. Yet, one cannot help but wonder
whether anything can be done to improve the quality of obligatory prayer. Must the lack of specific urgency render obligatory
prayer a dull parrotlike mouthing of words? Must the daily recitation of the same prayers become an exercise in tedium? Not
necessarily.

Boredom is the result of improper praying, not the lack of
specific urgency or repetition. Our sages were very well aware of
the danger of obligatory prayer becoming routinized. "If man
makes his prayer a perfunctory act," says Rabbi Eliezer, "it is not
genuine supplication."[42] For prayer to be a religious experience,

it must be an expression of personal concern. "When you pray," says Rabbi Simon, "do not regard your prayer as a perfunctory act but rather as a plea for mercy and grace before God."[43]

But can we endow the obligatory service, the prayers we recite for all of Israel, with at least some sense of personal urgency? It is not impossible. We can do so by making the welfare of the Jewish people a matter of personal concern. Admittedly, this is easier said than done, but it is not mere wishful thinking. There is no doubt that taking upon oneself the *mitzvah* of "Love your neighbor as yourself" every morning before beginning to pray (a custom attributed to Rabbi Isaac Luria) would do much to facilitate this feeling in the hearts of the masses. To observe the pious in prayer, to see the look on their faces and to study their gestures, is to be convinced that they consider these obligatory prayers in behalf of the people of Israel a matter of personal concern and urgency. We must try our utmost to emulate them.

The role of *kavanah* ("concentration") in making obligatory prayer a religious experience is not to be underestimated. Our sages taught: "One who prays, should direct his heart to heaven."[44] Maimonides adds: "One must empty his heart from all other thoughts, and see himself as standing before the Divine Presence."[45] Finally, the *Shulhan Arukh* ("Code of Jewish Law") states:

> One who prays must concentrate on the significance of the words he pronounces with his lips, and see himself as if he is in the Divine Presence. He must remove all thoughts that trouble him so that his mind and attention remain pure and concentrated upon his prayers. Let him suppose that if he were in the presence of a mortal king, he would surely arrange his words well and concentrate upon them so that he should not stumble in his speech; all the more so, when he is in the presence of the Supreme King of Kings, the Holy One blessed be He.[46]

Our sages posited that proper *kavanah* has the power to lift man out of the finite world and propel him into heaven where he communes directly with the Almighty. It can endow the daily services with meaning, excitement, and the sense of urgency one feels in spontaneous prayer. But *kavanah* is not merely a matter of course. Would that we were all endowed with the ability to focus in on the prayers and concentrate on their meaning every time we confront God in obligatory prayer. We must make a concerted effort to induce *kavanah*. We must set the mood for prayer. It is of the utmost of importance that the place of prayer befit the occasion. The more awesome the structure, the more sophisticated the architecture, and the more lavish the decor, the greater the propensity for distraction, and it is well established that distraction is a major obstacle in the way of attaining proper *kavanah*. To expect the worshiper to be moved to prayer—an encounter with the Divine that is initiated through a feeling of lowliness and dependency—in a structure whose beauty and sophistication tend to inspire self-confidence and self-aggrandizement rather than dependency is unrealistic. Simplicity, not ostentation, must be the hallmark of synagogue design.

A *mehitzah*, the physical barrier required by Jewish law to separate the sexes in the synagogue during worship, is not only appropriate; it is essential to the attainment of proper *kavanah*. In our society, it is extremely difficult for men to fully vent their emotions in the presence of women, and one would venture to say that it is nearly impossible not to be distracted by the presence of women seated in the same synagogue pew not more than a few inches away. Of course, it should be clearly understood that regardless of these considerations, the Halakhah proscribes participation in a service where the sexes are not separated. "Togetherness" in worship is not at all a Jewish concept. In point of fact, it is totally discordant with the Jewish posture of prayer.

It would be a foolish mistake to disregard or underestimate the importance of music, specifically the *nusah* ("chanting patterns") of the service, to the attainment of proper *kavanah* in obligatory prayer. Music employed intelligently has the power to "move mountains." The cantor has this great power at his fingertips. A talented, properly trained cantor has the ability to stir the emotions of his congregants and make them feel the meaning and significance of the prayers. As such, it is of the utmost importance that the music follow the appropriate *nusah* and reflect the meaning of the words. The *nusah* announces the occasion. When one hears the *nusah*, he should immediately be put into the mood of the occasion. Many congregants are moved to sing along with the cantor. The weekday, *Shabbat*, festival, and High Holiday services each have *nus'haot* of their own. In the hands of a talented cantor, the basic *nusah* patterns can be expanded into beautiful *recitativi*, making the service a true religious experience. Indeed, even those who have only a minimal understanding of the prayers can thus experience the joy of *Hallel* on the festivals, the majesty of the *Musaf* on Rosh Hashanah, and the sacredness of the *Ne'ilah* on Yom Kippur.

Of course, to initiate this process, it is important to select a qualified cantor who will take it upon himself to create a meaningful service and who will inspire his congregants to be more attentive to his chanting, so that they experience the service as a true encounter with the Divine.

There is much to be done to improve the quality of obligatory prayer and to make the synagogue services more inspiring. The Mishnah teaches: "The pious men of old used to meditate an hour before prayer in order that they might concentrate their thoughts upon their Father in heaven."[47] Preparation for prayer is almost as important to the religious experience as the prayers themselves. To arrive at the synagogue shortly before the service begins, to study or meditate there for a while, and to contemplate the meaning and implications of an encounter with the Divine would make a marked difference in the way one prays and the way one feels at the conclusion of the service.

It may very well be that for the masses, obligatory prayer will never have the fervor and poignancy of spontaneous prayer. Nevertheless, obligatory prayer *can* be made into a religious experience.

Let me close this discussion on the philosophy of prayer with an interpretation of an intriguing discussion in the Talmud.

Rabbi Johanan said in the name of Rabbi Yose: How do we know that the Holy One blessed be He prays? Because it says: "Even them will I bring to My holy mountain and make them joyful in My house of prayer" (Isaiah 56:7). It is not said "their prayer," but "My prayer"; hence you learn that the Holy One blessed be He prays. What does He pray? Rabbi Zutra be Tovia said in the name of Rav: "May it be My Will that My mercy suppress My anger, and that My mercy may prevail over My other attributes, so that I may deal with My children in the attribute of mercy, and, on their behalf, stop short of the limit of strict justice." It was taught: "Rabbi Ishmael ben Elisha says: I once entered into the innermost part of the Sanctuary to offer incense, and saw *Akatriel Kah*, the Lord of Hosts, seated upon a high and exalted throne. He said to me, 'Ishmael My son, bless Me!' I replied, 'May it be Your Will that Your mercy may prevail over Your other attributes, so that You may deal with Your children according to the attribute of mercy, and may, on their behalf, stop short of the limit of strict justice!' And He nodded to me with His head."[48]

The perplexity of this talmudic adventure in symbolism begins with what on the surface seems to be a rather presumptuous if not absurd question, and the discussion becomes progressively more confusing with each statement that follows.

From where do we learn that the Almighty prays? Indeed, to whom would the Almighty pray? To Himself, of course, Rabbi Zutra tells us. But why? Prayer presupposes a need. Is there anything that the Almighty needs? It would seem so. Why else would He begin His prayer with the words, "May it be My Will?" Putting aside the problem that this line of reasoning poses regarding Divine omnipotence, what could the Almighty possibly need? The answer is found in the prayer. We must also address the matter of Rabbi Ishmael. What does his statement add to the discussion? Why is it included here?

God is the Supreme Being; He is the Eternal One. He lacks for nothing. By definition, He is omnipotent, omniscient, and omnipresent. For reasons beyond man's comprehension, God created the universe, which He has maintained to this day. As such the universe is totally and unalterably dependent upon Him. In the words of Maimonides:

> All existing things, whether celestial, terrestrial, or belonging to an intermediate class, exist only through His true existence. If it could be supposed that He did not exist, it would follow that nothing else could possibly exist. If, however, it could be supposed that all other beings were nonexistent, He alone would still exist. ... For all beings are in need of Him; but He, blessed be He, is not in need of them, nor any of them.[49]

Would it be presumptuous to postulate that the Almighty does in fact have a need—the need to manifest His goodness? The mystics and hasidic masters might put it this way: "God's purpose in creating the world is to benefit His creatures. True, if there were no creatures, no less of benefit or good would be experienced by anyone, but it is the nature of the All-good to have recipients for His bounty so that—as it were—He can fulfill Himself."[50]

Given such a need, can God not satisfy it by benefiting His creatures continuously? The answer is yes, but He chooses not to do so with man. Man is different. Having been endowed with freedom of will, man is to a great extent master of his own destiny. True, he is charged by the Almighty to do good, but he was given the freedom to do either good or evil, in consequence of which he reaps either reward or punishment. Judaism teaches that although the Almighty does, at times, intervene in the process of history, He does not interfere with man's decisions in the day-to-day events of life.

The hasidic masters say something very interesting. Man's deeds have a cosmic effect. Through his behavior, man initiates a chain reaction, so to speak, in the Supreme Being. When he is virtuous, he sends spiritual impulses to heaven, which causes the release of goodness into the world. It begins as purely spiritual goodness, much too sublime to affect the world. But it descends earthward through the ten *sefirot*[51] ("Divine emanations"), becoming increasingly more material in its descent, until it reaches *Shekhinah*, the lowest of the *sefirot*. It is through *Shekhinah* that good is delivered into the world. Man's wickedness, on the other hand, blocks the flow of Divine goodness; it is the cause of tragedy and destruction in the world.

As we have said: God is Good. His aim is to benefit both man and the world. This creates an interesting paradox: God wants man to be free. He wants him to choose the path of righteousness of his own accord so that he can be benefited by God. But by granting him freedom, God takes a gamble with man, for some people might choose the path of evil, bringing tragedy and suffering upon the world and thwarting the Divine "need" to manifest His beneficence. Had God withheld human freedom and with it the whole process of retribution, were God alone to determine man's actions, He could program man to do only good, and His need to benefit mankind could be fulfilled. Of course, had God withheld human freedom, man would be an entirely different creature. Lacking freedom of choice, he could not rightfully be judged on his behavior, and Divine beneficence under such conditions would be unearned.

This dilemma is implied in the talmudic discussion above. Man is free; God has granted him this blessing. God yearns for his beloved creature to choose the path of life and thus activate the process of Divine beneficence. Under ordinary conditions, God does not interfere with the release of goodness into the world, neither to augment it nor to diminish it. Precisely because He wants man to remain free, God has rendered Himself powerless to affect man's will directly (though there have been exceptions), and consequently, His need to benefit mankind is not always fulfilled.

We must take these ideas one step further. God created the world through the attribute of *din* ("strict justice"), referred to in the Torah by the Divine name *Elokim*. With the creation of man, however, there arose the need for *rahamim* ("mercy"), without which man could never have endured.[52] So mercy—an attribute God invokes with discretion, to be sure—was introduced into the world and referred to in the Torah by the Divine name *Havayah*, which we read *Hashem*. When man is introduced into the Torah narrative, God is referred to as *Hashem Elokim*, indicating that He treats man with justice tempered with mercy.

These ideas are expressed in the prayer of the Almighty: "May it be My Will that My mercy may suppress My anger, and that My mercy prevail over My other attributes, so that I may deal with My children in the attribute of mercy and, on their behalf, stop short of the limit of strict justice." In truth, strict justice should prevail in the world, not mercy. And strict justice would prevail were man perfectly righteous. Indeed, there would be no need for mercy, for justice would require that goodness alone prevail in the world. The trouble is that very few people even approximate perfect righteousness. The overwhelming majority of mankind survive on Divine mercy. Indeed, were the Almighty to exercise strict justice in the world, punishing man whenever he disobeys Him, the human race would have long perished. So God tempers justice with mercy, according to His own special formula, to be sure, and thereby preserves the world. He must prevail upon Himself to superimpose His attribute of mercy upon His attribute of strict justice, looking away from man's sin, thus easing his punishment. The rationale was put succinctly by King David: "As a father has compassion for his children, so the Lord has compassion for those who fear Him. For He knows how we are formed; He is mindful that we are dust" (Psalms 103:13-14).

How vivid an analogy! Just as a loving father disciplining his child allows himself to be overruled by compassion though he knows in his heart that justice should prevail, so it is with the Almighty. He allows Himself to be overruled by mercy because of His unbounded love for humanity and His need to shower them with goodness. This is the significance of God's prayer.

As we have already explained, man can give only one thing to the Almighty, namely, the opportunity to fulfill His need to be beneficent. Perhaps this thought was behind the words of Rabbi Ishmael. The *ketoret* ("incense offering") was brought by the high priest in the Temple to obtain atonement for what was probably the most common of human foibles—evil speech.[53] Rooted in jealousy and envy, evil speech is a regression to childlike behavior. It is a sign of weakness, lack of control, and the triumph of the emotions over the intellect. It undermines the dignity of man and taints the Divine image in which he was created. It betrays man's imperfection and his fallibility.

Is it not possible that while bringing the *ketoret* offering, Rabbi Ishmael had thoughts of God and man, that he contemplated man's weakness and God's compassion for him in recognition of that weakness? What else did Rabbi Ishmael experience at that moment? He perceived *Akatriel Kah*, the Lord of Hosts, seated on a high exalted throne. How interesting! On the one hand, he perceives the powerful and exalted image of God and His need to benefit mankind, and on the other, the weak and lowly image of idiosyncratic man, whose behavior more often than not casts him down into the muck of depravity. "Ishmael, My son, bless Me," comes the voice from above. Rabbi Ishmael thinks for a moment of the two images and the opportunity he is now being given to benefit both God and man, and he responds: "May it be Your Will that Your mercy prevail over Your other attributes, so that You may deal with Your children according to the attribute of mercy, and may, on their behalf, stop short of the limit of strict justice." How beautiful and how apropos was the gesture! Indeed, it even earned approval from heaven.

Let me now move to the obligations of women in prayer. Women are exempt from the obligation to recite prayers that are time oriented. From where does this law derive, and what are its parameters? The Mishnah teaches:

> Women, gentile slaves, and minors are exempt from reading the *Shema* and from donning the *tefillin*, but they are obligated to recite the *Amidah*, to affix a mezuzah, and to recite the Grace After Meals.[54]

It is quite clear that these three groups have a common denominator—time. Minors are not concerned with time. Slaves who are continually responsible to their masters by day as well as by night are oblivious to time. Women, while they are keenly sensitive to time, as we have explained, cannot be obligated to fulfill commandments that are limited to specific time periods, for Judaism holds them primarily responsible to home and family, a calling over which nothing may take precedence. It is because of this common denominator, *and for no other reason*, that minors, slaves, and women are grouped together in the Mishnah.

The Talmud teaches that the *Amidah* is an exception to the rule. While it is time oriented and women should be exempt, the fact that it is an appeal to the Almighty for compassion makes it obligatory for all. Every human being needs Divine compassion.[55]

The *Shulhan Arukh* rules that women are exempt from *Shema*, as stated in the Mishnah, but advises that they should recite the first verse as their acceptance of "the yoke of the kingdom of heaven."[56] Of course, it is not necessary for them to recite these prayers in the presence of a *minyan*.

The *Mishnah Berurah* adds:

> They are exempt from the benedictions that precede the *Shema*, for they, too, are time oriented, but they are obligated to recite *Emet*

V'Yatziv, and *Emet V'Emunah* [the benedictions that follow the *Shema* in the Morning and Evening Services], for the mitzvah of commemorating the redemption from Egypt applies in the morning and at night. Since they are obligated to recite the *Amidah*, they must also adjoin the benediction of redemption to it. Additionally, they must recite the *Pesuke D'Zimrah*, for it pertains primarily to the *Amidah* . . . and *Birkhot haShahar*. . . . We have enumerated what is obligatory to them. It is understood, however, that of their own free will they may choose to recite even the benedictions of the *Shema*.[57]

Now let me get to your question of women and the matter of *minyan*. Considering that women may recite all the services in their entirety if they so choose, why may they not be counted in a *minyan*?

Here again, ignorance of the process of Jewish law has led to misconceptions and misinterpretations. Once more, the cry "prejudice" is on the lips of the uninformed. Let me, therefore, trace the law to its roots and demonstrate that logic and the halakhic process rather than prejudice is what prompted the ruling that women *may not* be counted in a *minyan*.

By definition, a *minyan* is a quorum of ten adult Jewish males. This is deduced from several biblical verses. We read in the Book of Numbers that ten of the twelve spies who were sent by Moses to spy out the land of Canaan returned with a negative report. The people were disillusioned, and they expressed a desire to return to Egypt. This angered the Almighty, and He voiced His complaint to Moses and Aaron with the words: "How much longer shall that wicked community keep muttering against Me? I have heard the mutterings of the children of Israel which they keep muttering against Me" (Numbers 14:26-27). The second verse seems clearly to be redundant here, but as you know, there are no redundancies in the Torah. What then does this verse have to teach us? *Rashi* explains that the words *that wicked community* do not refer to the entire community of Israel but rather to the spies, who are designated here as a "wicked community." The Almighty chastised the community of spies who had returned from Canaan with an evil report about the land, for they had frightened the people and influenced them to express the desire to return to Egypt.

Since the term *community* here refers to the wicked spies, Joshua and Caleb, who had returned with a good report, would not have been included among them. Now we know that there were twelve spies in all, one from each of the tribes of Israel. Omitting Joshua and Caleb, we are left with ten adult Jewish males whom the Almighty referred to as an *edah* ("community").

Let us now proceed to a point of Jewish law. It is a positive commandment to sanctify God's name amidst the community of Israel. This principle is derived from the biblical verse, "You shall not profane My holy name; I shall be sanctified amidst the children of Israel, I am the Lord who sanctifies you" (Leviticus 22:32).

While ordinarily, life takes precedence over all *mitzvot*, the Talmud rules that there are three situations where despite the fact that one's life is being threatened, one must be prepared to submit to death rather than transgress the law. They are: murder, illicit sexual relations, and idolatry. In a situation where the threat takes place before the Jewish community, that is, in public, and the mass conversion of Jews is at stake, one must submit to death rather than transgress even a minor law.[58] This principle is called *Kiddush Hashem B'rabbim*, that is, "the public sanctification of God's name."

But the Talmud goes one step further. It designates all "holiness passages" recited in the prayer services, such as *Kaddish* and *Borekhu*, as public sanctification of God's name, necessitating the presence of the Jewish community.[59] What do the sages mean here by "community"? They could not possibly mean every Jew; it would be a practical impossibility to require the presence of every Jew at such times. What they require is the presence of the minimum number of Jews that can be called a community. But what is that minimum number?

Now, we must refer to the Oral Law. As you remember, there are thirteen principles of interpretation through which the Oral Law is derived from the Torah, that is, the Written Law. These principles have been transmitted through the generations and date back to Moses our teacher. The "second principle" is called *gezerah shavah*. It states: "From the similarity of words or phrases occurring in two passages, it is inferred that what is expressed in one, applies to the other." Now there are three biblical verses that we must consider, two of which we have already mentioned.

> 1. You shall not profane My holy name: I shall be sanctified *amidst* the children of Israel; I am the Lord who sanctifies you" (Leviticus 22:32).

> 2. How much longer shall that wicked *community* keep muttering against Me? I have heard the mutterings of Israel which they keep muttering against Me" (Numbers 14:26-27).

> 3. Separate yourselves from *amidst* this *community* and I will destroy them immediately" (Numbers 16:21).

From the identity of the term *amidst* in verses 1 and 3, the principle of *gezerah shavah* teaches us that the minimum number implied in verse 3 applies also to verse 1. What is that number? To determine it, we must refer to verse 2, where through the same process (the similar term being *community*) we derive that the minimum number of people that can be defined as a community is ten.

Now to answer your question: The minimum number, the gender, and the religion of the people required by Jewish law for the recitation of "holiness passages" is *ten adult Jewish males*. The halakhic construct having been derived from the aforementioned verses, it must conform to all the specifics of "community" implied therein. Just as the community of spies consisted of ten adult Jewish males, so, too, must the community or *minyan* needed to recite "holiness passages" consist of ten adult Jewish males. By definition, therefore, women and minors may not be counted in such a community or *minyan*.

It should be quite clear now, my daughter, that what is responsible for the exclusion of women in the *minyan* is not prejudice or male chauvinism but the halakhic process. To hold otherwise is not only incorrect, it is to engage in self-deception. And to suggest that the Halakhah notwithstanding, women should be included in a *minyan* today because of sociological considerations, as some have indeed suggested, is to undermine the validity of Halakhah and the significance of the halakhic process.

Women and Torah Study

My dearest daughter,

The first letter I received from you bemoaned the fact that as a female, you were not given a sophisticated Jewish education. You resented it, and you asked, "Isn't it a *mitzvah* for every Jew to study the Torah and Jewish law?" Technically speaking, the answer to your question is "No, it is not a *mitzvah* for every Jew to study Torah." Since my answer will undoubtedly confuse you, I shall devote this letter to an exposition of the whole matter of Torah study for women, referring to talmudic, posttalmudic, and finally present-day rabbinic sources, so that the issue becomes clear in your mind.

As in most issues regarding women and Judaism, misinformation and misinterpretation have been responsible for negative impressions and incorrect conclusions. We will, therefore, examine the issues carefully to determine whether Judaism obligates women to study Torah, that is, the Written Law, as it does men, and whether women may be taught the Written and/or the Oral Law by men or by other women if it is not a *mitzvah* for them to study it on their own. Last, we will address the issue of whether women *may* study Torah on their own if they have the desire to do so, albeit that they are not obligated.

What is the source for the *mitzvah* of Torah study and to whom does the *mitzvah* apply? There are two biblical verses:

1. To study—

> And Moses summoned all Israel and said to them: "Hear O Israel
> the ordinances and the social laws that I shall speak to you, and
> you shall study them and keep them to practice them." (Deuter-
> onomy 5:1)

2. To teach—

> And you shall teach them to your children [lit. "sons"] speaking of
> them when you are sitting at home and when you go on a jour-
> ney, when you lie down and when you rise up. (Deuteronomy
> 11:19)

The Talmud delineates this *mitzvah* as follows:

> Our Rabbis taught: The father is bound with regard to his son to
> circumcise him, redeem him and teach him Torah. . . . How do we
> know it? Because it is written, "And you shall teach them to your
> sons." And if his father did not teach him, he must teach himself,
> for it is written, "And you shall study." How do we know that the
> mother has not the duty to teach her children? Because it is writ-
> ten *v'limaditem* ("and you shall teach") which can also be read
> *u'lemaditem* ("and you shall study"). Hence, whoever is com-
> manded to study is commanded to teach. And how do we know
> that she is not bound to teach herself? Because it is written, "And
> you shall teach," "And you shall study," the one whom others are
> commanded to teach is commanded to teach oneself; the one
> whom others are not commanded to teach is not commanded to
> teach oneself. How then do we know that others are not com-
> manded to teach her? Because it is written, "And you shall teach
> them to your *sons*," but not your daughters.[1]

The entire discussion in the Talmud concerns obligation. It is
obligatory upon a father to teach his son Torah; and it is obligatory upon a son to study Torah himself if his father does not teach

him. A mother is not obligated to teach her son Torah; neither is she obligated to study Torah herself. The question arises as to whether others may teach her. On this matter, there are differing opinions in the Talmud.

The case in point is that of a *sotah*, that is, a married woman who is suspected of being unfaithful. Despite repeated warnings not to fraternize with a particular man, she is found alone with him, a fact to which two witnesses testify. Did she commit adultery with him? Since no one witnessed the act itself, it cannot be determined by man whether she is guilty or not. In the time of the Temple, the woman was brought to the high priest, who tested her with the "bitter waters." If she is innocent, says the Talmud, nothing will happen to her when she drinks; if she is guilty, the telltale signs will appear:

> She had scarcely finished drinking when her face turns green, her eyes protrude and her veins swell; and it is exclaimed: remove her that the Temple not be defiled. If she possesses merit, it causes the water to suspend its effect upon her. Some merit, suspends the effect for one year, another for two years, and another for three years. Hence, declared Ben Azzai: man is under obligation to teach his daughter Torah, so that if she has to drink the waters of bitterness, she may know that merit suspends its effect. Rabbi Eliezer says: whoever teaches his daughter Torah, teaches her *tiflut*.[2]

It is clear from this Mishnah that in the case of an adulteress who has some redeeming merit—for example, she had readily escorted her sons to the house of study or had encouraged her husband to pursue his Torah studies in a distant city despite the fact that it meant much time spent away from home—her punishment would be suspended for a period from one to three years. Had she studied Torah, she would be aware of this halakhic principle and would not doubt the efficacy of the waters. On the contrary, it might motivate her to repent her sin. Ben Azzai, therefore, deemed it obligatory for a father to teach his daughter Torah.

Rabbi Eliezer, on the other hand, disparaged the practice. We must make note of the fact that if he is none other than Rabbi Eliezer ben Hyrcanus, as most authorities contend, his wife was the sister of Rabbi Gamliel of Yavne, a woman quite well educated in Torah.[3]

Now the precise words of Rabbi Eliezer were, "One who teaches his daughter Torah teaches her *tiflut*." But what is *tiflut*? According to one opinion, it is "subtlety";[4] according to another, it is "triviality";[5] according to still another, it is "immorality."[6] What is the rationale here? Since mastery of Torah demands the unqualified dedication of one's time and effort, women—whose primary responsibilities are to the home and family—are not predisposed to such demands. Consequently, the Torah knowledge they would acquire would be superficial. Now superficial knowledge in any discipline is dangerous, all the more so in Torah, for such superficiality could lead to inadvertent violation of biblical or rabbinic law. In the realm of family purity, an area of Jewish law where women's practical judgment might be heavily relied upon, superficial knowledge could lead to immorality.[7] Perhaps this is the objection of Rabbi Eliezer.

Let me make one further point. The relationship between teacher and student is primarily an intellectual one, as compared to the relationship between father and child, which is primarily an emotional one. Consequently, the proper rapport for Torah study between father and son would be difficult enough to attain. In many families the proper rapport would be even more difficult to attain between father and daughter. Better not to teach at all than to teach improperly. Let us also keep in mind that Rabbi Eliezer referred to a father teaching his daughter. Perhaps even Rabbi Eliezer would not have objected to women being taught by other women. Whatever the rationale, I want you to note that the language of Rabbi Eliezer seems more expostulatory than prohibitive.

It is extremely important to understand what is meant by

"Torah" in this context. Is it the Oral Law, the Written Law, or both? Ben Azzai clearly meant both, for one would not know the principle of "suspension of punishment" from the Written Law alone. If the Oral Law would be permissible to Ben Azzai, all the more so the Written Law.[8]

Now let us examine the ruling of the *Shulhan Arukh* on this matter.

> A woman who studies Torah is rewarded, but the reward is not as great as a man's reward, for she is in the category of one who *does but was not commanded to do.* Yet, though she earns reward, our sages ruled that a man should not teach his daughter for, generally, women are not predisposed to Torah study, consequently, Torah becomes trivial [in their eyes] due to their shallowness in understanding it. . . . To what are these words addressed? To the Oral Law. With regard to the Written Law, however, it should not be taught to her, but if one does, it would not be considered as if one taught her *tiflut.*

> *Rema:*

> Nevertheless, women are required to learn the laws that apply to them. A woman is not required to teach her son Torah. However, if she encourages her son to study Torah, she receives reward.[9]

What conclusions can we draw from the material we have seen so far? Though a woman may not be taught Torah, there is nothing wrong with her studying Torah on her own. In point of fact, women have been doing so throughout Jewish history. Some of them became noteworthy Torah scholars. The Talmud mentions Beruriah, the wife of Rabbi Meir, and Ima Shalom, the wife of Rabbi Eliezer ben Hyrcanus. History records the scholarly wife of Rashi and that of his grandson *Rabbenu Tam.*

The reward for women engaged in Torah study is less than that earned by men. But why? It can be compared to a man who performs a *mitzvah* from which he is exempt. One who is obligated to do a *mitzvah* must do so whether he personally finds the task pleasant or unpleasant, spiritually rewarding or tedious. He must perform the *mitzvah* simply because he was commanded by the Almighty to do so. When he fulfills his obligation, he demonstrates his dedication and commitment, and he is rewarded accordingly. On the other hand, one who is exempt from a *mitzvah* but nevertheless chooses to fulfill it is doing so because it gives him some sort of personal satisfaction. While the latter is still admirable and deserving of reward, it is not quite like the former.

While women are not obligated to study Torah, they are required to know the laws that are relevant to them. These include family purity, *kashrut*, *Shabbat*, *Yom Tov*, the negative commandments, and much more.

One Torah authority offers an important qualification on this issue that puts the matter into proper perspective. Commenting on the words of the *Shulhan Arukh* "because women are not generally predisposed to Torah study," he writes:

> But where she teaches herself, it is clear that she is not one of the majority of women. It is, therefore, written that she is rewarded if she studies it properly, namely, that she does not look upon Torah study as triviality. But her father is not permitted to teach her Torah lest she look upon it as triviality, for he does not know what is in her heart.[10]

Considering the multiplicity of laws that a woman must know and their complexity, how can she rely on teaching herself? And according to the opinion that women may be taught the Written Law but not the Oral Law, we must ask the obvious, "Is it possible to comprehend the Written Law without the Oral Law?"

The ruling of many of the later authorities is to permit teaching Torah to women, both the Written Law and the Oral Law, on those matters that pertain to them, but to discourage in-depth analysis of the law. This is the position of the renowned Rabbi Judah HaHasid, who writes:

A man is obligated to teach his daughters the mitzvot, namely, the final decisions of the Law. The statement, "He who teaches his daughter Torah, it is as if he teaches her triviality," refers to in-depth study, i.e., the significance of the mitzvot and the secrets of the Torah. . . . But he must definitely teach her the practical application of the mitzvot: she must learn the laws in order to observe them. In the time of King Hizkiah [eighth century B.C.E.], both the men and the women were well versed in the law, even the laws of sacrifice and purity. . . . An unmarried man, however, should not teach young girls. . . . A father should teach his daughter and wife.[11]

It is understood, of course, that the obligation referred to above is a practical one; women are not obligated to study *Torah Lishmah* ("Torah for its own sake").

What of the laws that are relevant to women, of which Rabbi Judah HaHasid and Rabbi Moses Isserles [*Rema*] spoke? Is there any basis for teaching women these laws in depth? Rabbi Joseph Saul Nathanson, the nineteenth-century halakhic master, makes an interesting observation.[12] After dismissing the issue in its entirety, he concludes that the statement of Rabbi Eliezer concerned the Oral Law alone. The ruling in the Talmud is that a father is not obligated to teach his daughter Torah. This means that there is no obligation, says Rabbi Nathanson, but it is certainly permissible. More importantly, he says, in the time of King Hizkiah women were taught the laws of kosher slaughter and the laws of the sacrifices in depth, for, being involved in these rituals, they needed the knowledge for practical purposes. Consequently, says Rabbi Nathanson, it would be permissible to study whatever laws are relevant to them in depth—the Written as well as the Oral Law.

What remains, therefore, is to ascertain and clarify what laws would be relevant to women in our generation, and to see how this question has been handled by more current responsa.

Let us examine two statements made by Rabbi Israel Meir HaKohen, the renowned rabbinic authority for Ashkenazic Jewry of the last generation, also known as the *Hafetz Hayyim*. The first is a commentary on the words of Rabbi Eliezer, "Whoever teaches his daughter Torah, it is as if he teaches her *tiflut*."

> It is clear that this applied only in past times when everyone lived in the place of his ancestors and the tradition to act in the ways of one's ancestors weighed heavily on every person. As it is written: "Ask your father and he will tell you . . . " (Deuteronomy 32:7). Under such conditions, one could say that she should not study Torah but rely on her upright parents to teach her proper conduct. But today, due to our many sins, parental influence has become very weak; most people no longer live where their ancestors lived, and many women are exposed to a secular education. It is unquestionably of great merit, therefore, to teach women Bible, Prophets, the Writings, and the ethical treatises of our sages [which is Oral Law] . . . to authenticate our holy faith within their minds. For if not, they are prone to stray completely from the way of God, Heaven forbid, and become totally uprooted from our religion.[13]

What is clearly evident from these words is that society changes— for better or for worse—and we must determine in each generation how best to preserve and foster adherence to Judaism. In a society such as ours, it is important to teach Torah to women; indeed, in some circles, it is a necessity. The statement of Rabbi Eliezer, as the *Hafetz Hayyim* points out, is simply not meant for our times. In the same vein, when the first *Bet Yaakov* school for girls was organized, the *Hafetz Hayyim* wrote:

> When I heard that some pious and God-fearing men offered to establish a *Bet Yaakov* school in our city, to teach Torah, fear of God and ethics to the girls of our brethren the House of Israel, I said of this noble venture, "May God give them strength." For in our times, when heresy abounds and freethinkers of all sorts lie in wait to entrap the souls of our brethren the House of Israel, such a project is a noble venture. It is required of every God-fearing person to enroll his daughter in this school. All the apprehension and doubts that one may harbor because of the prohibition of

teaching one's daughter Torah, are totally inapplicable in today's times.[14]

Some years ago, an interesting conversation took place between the Rebbe of Belz and the Rebbe of Lubavitch at the main Lubavitch headquarters in Brooklyn, New York. Among the issues that were discussed was the matter of women and Torah study, and the following statements were made:

> Rebbe of Belz: If so, the Rebbe opines that girls may study Mishnah and *Gemara*.
>
> Rebbe of Lubavitch: Chapters of the Mishnah are law; no doubt that they may study it. And concerning *Gemara*, when I was asked, I said that they should study those sections that are relevant to the halakhot necessary for them in their lives such as the sections of the *Gemara* relevant to blessings, Shabbat and the like.
>
> Rebbe of Belz: What then is included in the category of *tiflut*?
>
> Rebbe of Lubavitch: My understanding of the matter is that those things that they already know [from nontraditional or secular studies] would fall under the category of *tiflut*. We have the choice or opportunity to set the matter straight.

There is no question, indeed it is eminently clear from the sources that I have quoted to you, that in our day it is permissible—and perhaps even obligatory—to teach women Torah, the Written as well as the Oral Law, in those areas of Halakhah that are relevant to them. The revered rabbinic decisor of our time, the late Rabbi Dr. Joseph B. Soloveitchik, of blessed memory, once remarked that this would include most of the Talmud. Indeed, it was he who gave the opening lecture in Talmud at Stern College for Women in New York City, when it was introduced into the curriculum.

The Written and
the Oral Law

My dearest daughter,

I want you to know that your thirst for Jewish knowledge is most gratifying to me as a parent, and I thank the Almighty that our relationship is such that we can study and discuss traditional Judaism calmly and in a sophisticated manner. You ask me to explain how Halakhah works, and you are interested in knowing how the halakhic decisors arrive at the positions they take on contemporary issues. You are confused with what is subsumed under the rubric "Oral Law," and you want some background on its historic development. So let me devote this letter to "Halakhah," namely, the halakhic method and a brief sketch of the history of halakhic literature.

The Talmud relates the following story:

> A certain heathen once came before Shammai and asked him, "How many Torahs do you have?" "Two," he replied, "the Written Torah and the Oral Torah." "I believe you with respect to the Written Torah, but not with respect to the Oral Torah; make me a proselyte on condition that you teach me the Written Torah only." But he scolded him and repulsed him in anger. When he went before

Hillel he accepted him as a proselyte. On the first day, he taught him *alef, bet, gimmel, dalet*; the following day, he reversed the order to him. "But yesterday you did not teach me thus," he protested. "Must you then not rely upon me? [said Hillel] Then rely upon me with respect to the Oral Torah as well."[1]

The most fundamental principle in a discussion of the development of the Oral Law is "integrity." We must rely upon the wisdom and the integrity of our sages in having faithfully transmitted those laws that came down from Moses but are not specifically mentioned in the Torah, and the hermeneutical laws for interpreting the Torah. For unless we can trust both their wisdom and their integrity, the body of Jewish law and the halakhic method will crumble.

The Bible consists of twenty-four books in which are depicted events in history commencing with Creation and ending in the early part of the Second Jewish Commonwealth, a span of almost 3,500 years. Canonized by the Men of the Great Assembly [fifth century B.C.E.] as *Kitve haKodesh* ("Holy Scripture"), these works are the foundation of Jewish law and tradition. They are most commonly referred to as *Tanakh*, an acronym for *Torah, Neviim, Ketuvim* ("Pentateuch, Prophets, and Writings"). Let me note, however, that the works differ considerably in rank. The Pentateuch was revealed by the Almighty to Moses *Mi'pi haGevurah*, namely, in the most direct manner possible, or in the words of Nahmanides, "like a scribe who copies from an ancient book."[2] It ranks highest in authority. The Prophets rank second, and the Writings, which according to the sages were written through *Ruah haKodesh* ("Divine Inspiration"), rank third.[3]

The Pentateuch, also referred to as *Torah she'bikhtav* ("the Written Law"), records history from Creation to the death of Moses in the year 2488;[4] it is the source of the 613 commandments. Just before he died, Moses committed all this material to writing.[5] He wrote thirteen duplicate scrolls; one for each of the tribes of Israel and the remaining scroll to be placed in the Holy Ark for posterity.[6]

The Prophets consists of: *Neviim Rishonim* ("Former Prophets") and *Neviim Aharonim* ("Latter Prophets"). The Former Prophets is essentially narrative, and covers the period from the death of Moses to the end of the First Jewish Commonwealth, a span of almost a thousand years. The Latter Prophets is mainly a compendium of prophecies but also includes events in the lives of the prophets. It begins with the prophecies of Isaiah, who prophesied at the end of the reign of King Uzziah, and ends with the writings of Ezra and Nehemiah, who were the leaders of the people when they returned from Babylonia to Judea in the fifth century B.C.E. The Latter Prophets covers approximately 270 years, from 760-520 B.C.E.

The Writings consists of eleven separate works that cover almost the same period as the Prophets. Some of these works are essentially historical, while others compose what is known as the "Wisdom Literature," and still others are essentially religious poetry and prayer.

With the exception of one verse in Jeremiah and parts of Daniel and Ezra, which are in Aramaic, the *Tanakh* was written in Hebrew. Again, with few exceptions, these works were admitted into the canon as *Kitve haKodesh* in the early part of the Second Commonwealth. Our Hebrew text was established as the authoritative one by the scholars of the *Messorah*, specifically the tenth-century scholar Aaron ben Asher, who vocalized and accented the text to facilitate reading and comprehension. The messorites also reaffirmed the division of the text into *parshiyot petuhot u'setumot*, that is, major and minor paragraphs, as well as its breakdown into verses. All of this had been handed down by the Almighty at Sinai as tradition to Moses, our teacher.[7] (I want to bring to your attention that the division of the text into chapters in the thirteenth-century Vulgate edition of the Bible, which was adopted by the Hebrew Bibles in the sixteenth century, is not of Jewish origin.)

For various reasons, the authors of these books did not always edit and publish their works.[8] What follows is a list of *Kitve haKodesh* and their compilers.

Books of the Bible and Their Authors

Section of Bible	Book of Bible	Author
Pentateuch	Genesis	Moses
	Exodus	Moses
	Leviticus	Moses
	Numbers	Moses
	Deuteronomy	Moses
Prophets		
Former prophets	Joshua	Joshua
	Judges	Samuel
	Samuel	Samuel
	Kings	Jeremiah
Latter prophets		
Major (3)	Jeremiah	Jeremiah
	Ezekiel	Men of the Great Assembly
	Isaiah	King Hizkiah and His Court
Minor (12)	Hosea	Men of the Great Assembly
	Joel	Men of the Great Assembly
	Amos	Men of the Great Assembly
	Obadiah	Men of the Great Assembly
	Jonah	Men of the Great Assembly
	Micah	Men of the Great Assembly
	Nahum	Men of the Great Assembly
	Habakkuk	Men of the Great Assembly
	Zephaniah	Men of the Great Assembly
	Haggai	Men of the Great Assembly
	Zechariah	Men of the Great Assembly
	Malachi	Men of the Great Assembly

Writings	Psalms	King David and Others
	Proverbs	King Hizkiah and His Court
	Job	Moses
	Song of Songs	King Hizkiah and His Court
	Ruth	Samuel
	Lamentations	Jeremiah
	Ecclesiastes	King Hizkiah and His Court
	Esther	Men of the Great Assembly
	Daniel	Men of the Great Assembly
	Ezra-Nehemiah	Ezra
	Chronicles	Ezra

The Written Law was revealed to Moses together with the Oral Law, but while the former was written down in its entirety by Moses before he died, the latter remained as oral tradition for many years thereafter. Regarding the Oral Law, the Torah charges: "All this which I command you, that shall you observe to do; you shall not add to it nor diminish from it" (Deuteronomy 4:2). Moses taught the Oral Law to the seventy elders of the people, to Aaron, Eliezer and Pinhas the priests, and to Joshua, his attendant. Thus began a chain of tradition that was faithfully transmitted through the generations by the wisest men of the nation, from Moses to the present day.[9]

Understandably, the traditions were written down. The prophets, and later the sages, recorded the traditions and interpretations that they had heard from their teachers. They also recorded the new material that had evolved in each generation, which had not been received through tradition but rather had been deduced through the "Thirteen Hermeneutical Principles,"[10] and had officially been adopted by the court as law. This written material was only for their personal use, that is, so they they would not forget the laws and traditions. They could not teach the Oral Law from a written text, however; the material had to be taught orally.[11] The Talmud warns: "The words which are transmitted orally, you are not at liberty to recite from writing."[12]

It was in the second century that Rabbi Judah HaNasi ("the Prince") saw that the number of students of the law was diminishing, and that the wickedness of governments led many Jews to emigrate to distant countries. It was a time of crisis, and such times demand expedient measures. As the undisputed head of the Sanhedrin, the highest court of the land, he gathered all the traditions, interpretations, and expositions of every portion of the Written Law that had either come down from Moses or had been deduced by the courts in succeeding generations, and he redacted the material in the form known to us as the "Mishnah."[13] The Mishnah would serve as the authoritative text to be studied and mastered by all.

The chain of tradition was transmitted from teacher to student as follows:

Student	Teacher
Rav Ashi	Rava
Rava	Rabbah
Rabbah	Rav Huna
Rav Huna	Rabbi Yohanan, Rav, and Samuel
Rabbi Yohanan, Rav, and Samuel	Rabbi Judah HaNasi
Rabbi Judah HaNasi	Rabbi Simon (his father)
Rabbi Simon	Rabban Gamliel (his father)
Rabban Gamliel	Rabban Simon (his father)
Rabban Simon	Rabban Gamliel the Elder (his father)
Gamliel the Elder	Rabban Simon (his father)
Rabban Simon	Hillel (his father) and Shammai
Hillel and Shammai	Shemaya and Avtalyon
Shemaya and Avtalyon	Judah and Simon
Judah and Simon	Joshua ben Perahyah and Nittai of Arbel

Joshua and Nittai	Yosi ben Yoezer and Joseph ben Yohanan
Yosi and Joseph	Antigonos
Antigonos	Simon the Righteous
Simon the Righteous	Ezra
Ezra	Barukh
Barukh	Jeremiah
Jeremiah	Zefaniah
Zefaniah	Habakkuk
Habakkuk	Nahum
Nahum	Joel
Joel	Micah
Micah	Isaiah
Isaiah	Amos
Amos	Hosea
Hosea	Zechariah
Zechariah	Yehoyadah
Yehoyadah	Elisha
Elisha	Elijah
Elijah	Ahiyah
Ahiyah	King David
King David	Samuel
Samuel	Eli
Eli	Pinhas
Pinhas	Joshua
Joshua	Moses
Moses	Almighty God

Concerning the above sages, Maimonides comments:

All of the above-mentioned scholars were the greatest men in their respective generations; some were heads of schools, others exilarchs, and still others, heads of the Great Sanhedrin; and with them were their contemporaries in each and every generation numbering in the thousands, even ten thousands, who heard the Oral Law being expounded together with them, or received it from them.[14]

There were other compilations, those made by students of Rabbi Judah HaNasi. Rav compiled the *Sifra* and the *Sifre*, which were explanations of the principles of the Mishnah. Rabbi Hoshiah and Bar Kappara compiled the *baraitot*, which were the legal discussions that had been omitted by Rabbi Judah HaNasi for a variety of reasons. Many of these discussions are found in a work known as the *Tosefta*. The *Tosefta* also contains an aggadic treatise similar in style and content to the *Pirke Avot* (Ethics of the Fathers), called *Avot D'Rebbi Natan*. Rabbi Yohanan compiled the *Talmud Yerushalmi* ("Jerusalem Talmud") in the land of Israel in about the fourth century. Ravina and Rav Ashi compiled the *Talmud Bavli* ("Babylonian Talmud") in the fifth century.[15]

The two talmudic works are expositions of the text of the Mishnah. They elucidate its complexities and survey the legal precedents that had been established by the courts from the days of Rabbi Judah HaNasi until the time of the redaction or completion of these talmudic works.[16] We also derive from them, as well as from the *Sifra* and *Sifre*, what is forbidden and what is permitted, what is clean and what is unclean, what is a penal violation and what bears no penalty at all. All of these matters were transmitted from teacher to student stemming from Moses, who received them from the Almighty at Sinai. From these sources were also derived the *gezerot* and *takkanot* ("decrees instituted by the prophets and sages of each generation to protect the laws") as well as the customs and bylaws that either had been formerly introduced in various generations by their respective authorities or had come into use with their sanction. These works also contain laws that had not derived from Moses, but that the courts of a particular generation had themselves derived from the Torah by applying the hermeneutical principles.[17]

The sages of the mishnaic period also composed other works that expounded on the Torah. Rabbi Hoshiah wrote an exposition on Genesis, Rabbi Ishmael compiled the *Mekhilta*, a work on four of the books of the Torah [Exodus, Leviticus, Numbers, Deuteronomy], and sages of a later generation compiled various midrashic collections. All of these were edited before the compilation of the *Talmud Bavli*, however, thus making Ravina and Rav Ashi the last of the sages to edit the Oral Law, issue edicts, enact statutes, and establish customs; their decisions were accepted by all of the Jewish people wherever they lived.[18]

After the tenure of the court of Rav Ashi, the people became dispersed among countries that were at great distances from each other, and the study of Torah was neglected. It was therefore decreed that every court founded during the posttalmudic era could issue edicts or establish customs either for its own citizens or for those of other countries, but its authority was not extended to all the Jews due to the great distances between countries. Moreover, the citizens of one country could not be forced to accept the customs of another country, nor could the courts of one country enforce upon their citizens edicts issued by another country. It was also decreed that where one court or rabbinic authority interpreted a law in a particular way that another court held to be contrary to the Talmud, the more reasonable of the two opinions was to be accepted as correct, regardless of whether it was an earlier or later opinion.[19]

These rules applied only to customs or edicts that arose during the posttalmudic era. Those that appear in the Talmud, however, are binding upon all Israel at all times and in all places, for they were the consensus of all or a majority of the sages in the Talmud, who received their interpretation as tradition dating back to Moses our teacher.[20]

It cannot be overemphasized that the Oral Law is indispensable to the proper understanding of the Written Law. Indeed, without the interpretations of the Oral Law, the Torah or Written Law is often confusing—at times, even contradictory. Several examples will suffice to illustrate this:

According to the Torah, the duration of the enslavement of the Israelites in Egypt was 430 years.[21] Yet, if we calculate the years from the sojourn of Jacob in Egypt until the word of God came to Moses informing him that the redemption had finally arrived, they total only 350 years, a discrepancy of 80 years. The Oral Law resolves this discrepancy by bringing the tradition that the enslavement actually began when the Almighty said to Abraham, "Your offspring shall be slaves in a land not theirs . . . " (Genesis 15:13), which was at the "Covenant of the Parts." If we calculate the years accordingly, the 430-year period is correct.[22]

In Deuteronomy 10:22 we read: "Your ancestors went down to Egypt, seventy persons in all." Now, if we review the given list of persons who went with Jacob to sojourn in Egypt, it totals only sixty-nine persons. Who was missing? The Oral Law teaches us that the seventieth person was Yoheved, the mother of Moses, who was born upon the arrival of the family in Egypt. For this reason, she is not mentioned at the onset of the journey.[23]

We also find verses in the Torah that are vague and would have remained obscure were it not for the Oral Law that elucidates their meaning. Note the following:

On the festival of Sukkot, we are charged, "And you shall take the fruit of *hadar* trees . . . " (Leviticus 23:40). The term *hadar* is usually rendered "goodly." But many trees are "goodly." Which fruit is to be taken? The Oral Law points out that *hadar* also means "that dwells" and explains that what is meant is a tree upon which the fruit "dwells" from one year to the other. That fruit is the *etrog* or citron.[24]

In Exodus 21:5-6, concerning the laws of slavery, we read: "But if a slave declares, 'I love my master and my wife and my children; I do not wish to be freed,' his master shall take him before God, he shall be brought to the door or the doorpost, and his master shall pierce his ear with an awl; and *he shall then remain his slave forever.*" Are these last words to be taken literally? Is he to remain a slave for the rest of his life? The Oral Law explains that it means only until the Jubilee year. This is supported by the verse, "And you shall sanctify the fiftieth year and proclaim release throughout the land for all its inhabitants" (Leviticus 25:10).[25]

These are but a few examples of the role of the Oral Law in clarifying the text and elucidating the *mitzvot*. It is important to emphasize here that these interpretations were not created by the sages; they were handed down by tradition, father to son and teacher to student. This principle is fundamental in Judaism. The point is made quite succinctly by the renowned nineteenth-century talmudic scholar Rabbi Zevi Hirsch Chajes in his work on the history of Halakhah, *Mevo laTalmud*.[26] Note the following:

> We are thus led to recognize that even without the above-mentioned methods of exegesis these precise interpretations were already known as ancient traditions transmitted orally from Sinai, for otherwise could such a law as "taking the fruit of a goodly tree" have been given to Moses in general terms without instructing him in detail regarding the nature of the fruit and in what manner he should carry out the command? ... Such explanatory details, therefore, must have been given clearly to Moses, in connection with every precept, and this in spite of the fact that the Rabbis endeavored to deduce them from Scripture by means of the exegetical rules.[27]

The great sage Hillel the Elder taught that there are seven principles through which the Oral Law can be derived from the Written Law. About a century later, Rabbi Ishmael expanded the seven principles into thirteen. It is important to clarify that he did not add to Hillel's seven; he delineated them more fully. Just as the seven were included in the thirteen, so were the thirteen included in the seven. These principles were handed down from Moses, who himself knew not only the principles but all the Oral Law that is derived through them from the Written Law as well as all facets of the law that would be so derived by any sage in the future. What Moses did not know, however, was how each and every one of these laws is alluded to in the Torah. This was left for the sages of future generations to discover through the hermeneutical principles.[28]

The thirteen hermeneutical principles were employed by the sages in two ways: to find biblical support for laws that were transmitted as tradition, and to derive details of the law from Torah texts. In the former case, the reasoning was sometimes somewhat strained, but the sages persisted, for these supports were primarily mnemonic devices. As Rabbi Chajes writes: "In view of all this, one should not be astonished at some of the homiletic expositions employed in support of clear and definite halakhot, even if the literal meaning of the passages used appears to be far removed from the halakhot of which they are intended as proof, because their main purpose was only to assist the memory in preserving halakhot transmitted orally and already practiced."[29]

Some *mitzvot* are mentioned generally in the Torah, but the details are omitted. The Oral Law supplies the details. Note the following:

The *mitzvah* of *shehitah* ("ritual slaughter") of animals is derived from the verse "If the place where the Lord has chosen to establish His name is too far from you, you may slaughter any of the cattle or sheep that the Lord gives you as I have instructed you; and you may eat to your heart's content in your settlements" (Deuteronomy 12:21). Although the process of ritual slaughter is etymologically deduced from the term *v'zavahta* ("you shall slaughter"), the details of the law, for example whether the trachea and the esophagus must both be severed and other such details, were handed down by Moses.[30] The *mitzvah* of dwelling in the *sukkah* ("hut"), or taking the *lulav* ("palm branch") on the festival of Sukkot, or the *mitzvah* of sounding the *shofar* on Rosh Hashanah, are mentioned only generally in the Torah. The details of these laws have come down to us from Moses as tradition.[31]

On the other hand, there are practices that have no relationship at all to a biblical text. They have simply come down to us as *Halakhah LeMosheh MiSinai*, that is, a Sinaitic tradition dating back to Moses. One such practice would be the beating of the *aravah* ("willow") on Hoshanah Rabbah, the seventh day of the Sukkot celebration. Another would be the practice of the courts of setting aside two burial places for criminals who were executed, one for those who were executed by strangulation, the other for those who were executed by burning. These laws have no biblical sources; they are traditions.[32]

The role of reason and logical inference is often underestimated, particularly by those who are unfamiliar with talmudic texts and the halakhic method. Some would go so far as to imply that reason and logic play no role whatsoever in the determination of Jewish law. Of course, such a contention is totally unfounded and clearly a sign of ignorance. Indeed, there are many *halakhot* that are deduced exclusively from reason, and one can state reliably that reason is as authoritative as that which is supported by the written text.[33] For example:

In *Sanhedrin* 74a, the following point is made: "Just as one must rather be slain than commit murder, so also must the betrothed maiden rather be slain than allow herself to be violated. And how do we know this of murder itself? It is common sense. Even as one came before Rabbah and said to him, 'the governor of my town has ordered me: Go and kill so and so, if not I will kill you.' He answered him, 'Let him rather kill you than that you should commit murder; who knows that your blood is redder? Perhaps his blood is redder.'" The law here is clearly based on common sense or reason.

The point is made even more succinctly in *Ketuvot* 22a, where with regard to testimony the Talmud states that "the mouth that forbade is the mouth that permits"; if we rely on a witness to testify regarding a prohibition, we should rely on him as well for the reverse. Rabbi Assi brings biblical proof to substantiate the principle, and the Talmud asks, "Why is biblical proof necessary? It stands on reason."

Last, the expression "If you wish, I can say that this follows from reason, and if you wish, I can say that it follows from the Bible" is a common one in the Talmud.[34]

I have spoken to you of the Torah as a source for the Halakhah, but you must also recognize that the Prophets and the Writings are sources for the Halakhah as well. In point of fact, that which is derived from the Prophets and the Writings is considered as authoritative as that which is derived from the Torah.[35] Again, to cite some examples:

In *Yevamot* 4a, it is asked from where in the Torah we derive the exegetical principle that we deduce laws from the proximity of biblical texts. In response, the verse, "They find support forever to the end of time" (Psalms 111:8) is quoted. Though the text is from the Writings, it is employed as if it were from the Torah.

In *Hullin* 17b, the question is asked, "From where in the Torah do we learn that it is necessary to examine a knife [for nicks] before it can be used for ritual slaughter?" In response, the verse "And slaughter here and eat" is quoted. Here again, the verse is not from the Torah but from the Prophets.[36]

Because it is the law that no prophet is permitted to introduce a new law, that is, one that is not found in the Torah, one might ask, "By what right did the sages derive laws from the Prophets or the Writings?" The answer is found in *Sanhedrin* 22b, in a discussion on what disqualifies a person from serving as priest in the Temple. In response, a verse from Ezekiel is quoted. "But before Ezekiel came, who stated it?" asks the Talmud. "It must have been a tradition," is the response, "and then Ezekiel came and found support for it in the Torah." Clearly what is implied here is that it was not the prophet who initiated these laws. He had no authority to do so. He must rather have had a tradition to which he gave textual support.[37]

I have thus far spoken to you of the Written Law and the Oral Law. Concerning the latter, I have delineated the various categories, and I have illustrated them. Before moving to the next category, however, I want you to note the following caveat made by Rabbi Zevi Hirsch Chajes:

> All those legal decisions of the Mishnah or the Gemara which come under the above-mentioned categories, whether they were inferred from the interpretation of unintelligible passages or as a result of the elucidation in detail of the implications of the precepts of the Torah and the manner of their observance; whether they were deduced by means of the exegetical rules which were received by way of tradition or whether they were suggested by common sense; or again, whether they were based on the words of the prophets— they are all as authoritative as those derived from clear statements in the Torah, and he who transgresses any of them, is liable to punishment as he who breaks any of the laws of the Torah.[38]

We come now to the *takkanot* and the *gezerot* of which you asked. These were laws enacted by the prophets and later by the sages, as precautionary measures to safeguard the Written Law. The term *takkanot* refers to enactments pertaining to the positive laws while *gezerot* refers to those pertaining to the negative laws. The enactments are found in the Talmud and in the *baraitot*; as man-made laws, they are designated *d'rabbanan* ("of rabbinic origin"), and do not carry the authority or incur the same punishment as biblical laws. In cases where there are differing opinions as to what the ruling should be, if a biblical law is involved we rule according to the more stringent view; if it is a rabbinic law we rule according to the more lenient view. Nevertheless, it is important to note that the rabbinic laws are implied in the positive *mitzvah* "You shall act in accordance with the instructions given to you and the ruling handed down to you" (Deuteronomy 17:11), in the sense that we are obligated by this biblical law to abide by all the decisions made by the Sanhedrin. But in addition to transgressing this positive *mitzvah*, those who do not abide by the decisions of the Sanhedrin transgress the latter part of the verse, "You must not deviate from the verdict that they announce to you either to the right or to the left," which is a negative *mitzvah*.[39]

Rabbinic enactments of this nature date back to Moses our teacher, who himself enacted many *takkanot* and *gezerot*, among which are: marriage festivities for a virgin should last for seven days; the layman is obligated to inquire as to the laws of the festivals as they approach and the teacher is obligated to instruct in these laws; and the mourning period for the dead is seven days. Moses was also responsible for the formulation of the first of the benedictions of *Birkat haMazon* ("Grace After Meals").

Joshua formulated the second benediction of *Birkat haMazon*. He and his court put down ten rules for dividing the land of Canaan among the tribes of Israel. Pinhas, the grandson of Aaron the priest, formulated the *gezerah* forbidding the use of wine prepared by idolaters, for fear that such wine might have been used by them for worship. Boaz initiated the use of the Divine name *Shalom* in greeting one's fellow man. The court of King David formulated the *gezerah* forbidding *yihud*, that is, being alone with an unmarried woman in a closed room. According to some authorities, he also ordained the recitation of one hundred benedictions daily. Solomon, his son, enacted the law of *eruv*, through which one is permitted to carry from one's house into the courtyard on *Shabbat*. The prophets who lived during the Babylonian exile established the four fast days to commemorate the tragedies that had befallen the Jewish people at that time. Daniel prohibited oil that was prepared by idolaters from being used as food, and Nehemiah forbade discussing business matters on *Shabbat* as being contrary to the spirit of the day. Ezra enacted ten *takkanot*, among which were: public reading of the Torah at the *Shaharit* service on Monday and Thursday mornings and at the *Minhah* service on *Shabbat*, holding court on Mondays and Thursdays, and requiring women to cleanse their bodies and comb their hair before immersing in the *mikvah*.[40]

The *gezerot* were, at times, motivated by a high incidence of chicanery among the masses—they would do things that were forbidden and claim that they had done them in a permissible way. To prevent such abuses in the law, the sages forbade such things even when they were done in a permissible way. For example:

It was found that in the Sabbatical year, when the land was to lie fallow, some people would work the land, claiming that they were merely picking up bits of wood or grass, which is permissible. The sages, therefore, forbade removing anything from the land, even large rocks or boulders that were actually permissible and would not come under the prohibition of working the land were it not for this *gezerah*.[41]

Bathing was originally permitted on *Shabbat*, with the stipulation that the water be heated before the onset of the day. But the bathhouse attendants took advantage of the law by heating up the water on *Shabbat* and claiming that it had been done the day before. The sages therefore forbade taking hot baths on *Shabbat* altogether.[42]

Some *gezerot* were enacted by the sages for *mar'at ayin*, that is, appearances, in order to avoid suspicion. A person might do something that conforms with the law, but in a way that might arouse suspicion that he had done it unlawfully. A case in point would be where a gentile is contracted on a yearly basis to do work for a Jew. Though the laws of *Shabbat* do not apply to a gentile, he is forbidden to work for his Jewish employer on *Shabbat* because those who see him working may think that his employer hired him specifically to work on *Shabbat*, a practice that is prohibited.[43]

There were *gezerot* that had been formulated because of potential danger to one's health, such as drinking water that had been left uncovered overnight[44] and eating the flesh of an animal that had swallowed a deadly poison.[45]

It is important for you to know that insofar as the laws handed down by Moses at Sinai are concerned, there was never a controversy among the sages. This is not always the case, however, with regard to the laws derived from the Torah through the hermeneutical principles. When there was unanimity among the sages, there was no problem; when there was a difference of opinion, the majority opinion became the law, and it was binding upon all the people. Now I want you to note the following point very carefully. The fact that the law followed the majority opinion was not necessarily to say that the majority were always of the *correct* opinion on the matter; they may or may not have been correct in their opinion. It was not a matter of being correct but rather one of practicality or principle. To avoid chaos, a definitive ruling for all the people had to be made, and the Torah had given the formula for such a definitive ruling, namely, "majority rule." The principle of majority rule applied to differences of opinion regarding *takkanot* and *gezerot*, and customs as well, that is, whether a particular one of them should be enacted or discontinued.[46]

During the tenure of the Sanhedrin, there were no controversies among the people regarding the law. When a question arose in the community, the local court was consulted and ruled. If it was unable to rule, the inquirer and representatives of the court went to Jerusalem, where they presented their question to three courts, if necessary, the last of which was the Sanhedrin. If the Sanhedrin did not know the law, it would discuss the matter immediately, and when either a unanimous decision or one based on majority rule had been reached, the inquirer would be informed.[47]

It is important to note that the sages were avid students of human nature, on the basis of which they made certain presumptions about man vis-à-vis the society in which he lives. For example: it is presumed that an object in one's possession belongs to him. The burden of proof that the object does not belong to that person falls upon the plaintiff. Another presumption is that no one pays his debts before they are due. Should a borrower claim that he had paid his debts before the due date, the burden of proof falls upon him. These presumptions are based both on reason and on experience; they are grounded on neither the Written Law nor the Oral Law, but were recognized nevertheless by the sages as bona fide principles upon which to base their rulings.[48]

Some principles by which the sages operated were drawn from natural law, that is, the physical world. For example:

1. Blood is forbidden to the Jewish people by biblical law. The sages knew that it is an inherent property of salt to draw blood. They therefore ruled that meat should be salted to render it permissible as food.

2. A substance that is in the process of discharging material from its pores cannot simultaneously absorb that substance or any other substance. Therefore, if a piece of meat that is in the process of discharging its blood is touched by another piece of meat that is in the same process, neither is rendered unfit for Jewish consumption.

3. A piece of meat discharging its own blood also discharges any blood it may have previously absorbed from another source.

4. A neutralized forbidden substance can under certain conditions "revive itself" and thus render itself unfit for Jewish consumption.

5. Blood on the surface of meat cannot be removed through the salting process. It must be washed.

Many of the laws of *kashrut* are based on these principles.[49]

I believe that in this letter I have given you much food for thought. Study it carefully and assimilate it. As you can see, Jewish law is quite sophisticated, and it takes a great disciplined mind to become a decisor of Jewish law. Indeed, there are only a few true decisors in every generation.

In my next letter, I shall discuss the various "Codes."

The Codes

My dearest daughter,

I am glad to hear that you have settled into a routine at the university, and that you have been able to allot sufficient time to letter reading and writing. You tell me that the sophistication of Jewish law is awe inspiring, and that you have gained even greater respect for it than you had before. This pleases me greatly. I have not forgotten your query on how the rabbinic authorities come to halakhic decisions on the pressing issues of the day, and I will go through the halakhic method with you in this letter. But first, I must complete my discussion on the development of Jewish law with a brief survey of the "Codes."

The sages who arose after the period of the redaction of the Talmud were known as *Geonim*. They lived in the lands of Israel, Babylonia, and Spain. Although no complete commentary on the Talmud from the *Geonim* has come down to us, we do have their comments on chapters of particular tractates, and even some on complete tractates. We also have what is known as Responsa literature, that is, letters they wrote to people who sought their expertise regarding matters of Jewish law or Jewish philosophy, or simply, the elucidation of difficult passages from the Talmud. There were *Geonim* who compiled treatises on juridical decisions and timely matters of crucial concern, so that even one who is not a Talmud scholar can become acquainted with the literature.[1]

From what I have said thus far, it is sufficiently clear that with the dispersion of the Jewish people and the neglect of the study of the Torah, the masses were in desperate need of a "code of practice" to unify them and to prevent the laws from being forgotten. Note the words of Maimonides:

> In this age, when afflictions have greatly intensified, the pressure of the hour weighing heavily upon everyone, when the wisdom of the wise has perished, and the understanding of our prudent men is hidden, all commentaries, treatises and responsa that the Geonim compiled which they considered to be clear texts are perplexities in our day, and only a select few comprehend the subject matter thereof; not to speak of the Talmud itself, both the Bavli and the Yerushalmi, the Sifra, Sifre and the Tosefta, which require a broad understanding, a soul endowed with wisdom and lengthy reflection, whereafter one can learn from them the correct practice as to what is forbidden and permitted, and the other rules of the Torah.[2]

The first Code to have been written during the period of the *Geonim* was the *Sheiltot*, literally, "Problems," by Ahai Gaon. Compiled in the land of Israel in the eighth century, and written in "question and answer" form, the work consists of 191 discourses that elucidate the *mitzvot* by bringing brief summaries of the material that pertains to them from the Talmud. The subject matter is arranged according to the weekly *parshiyot* ("Torah portions"). Regrettably, the work has come down to us in incomplete form and covers only 145 of the 613 *mitzvot*.

Somewhat similar to the *Sheiltot* in form is the *Halakhot Gedolot* ("Large Collection of Laws") by Simon Kaira, also written in the eighth century. This work deals with the *mitzvot* as well, and it is a compendium of Jewish law. The author was the first to give us a precise list of the 613 *mitzvot*. Of particular interest is his systematic arrangement of the material by subjects. Aside from demonstrating his erudition, the work facilitated the comprehension and mastery of the material, for in the Talmud, material on a particular subject is often dispersed among several tractates. The Code was a practical one in the sense that the author omitted all material that has become temporarily obsolete with the destruction of the Temple in Jerusalem.

The next Code of importance for our purposes in this brief survey of the literature is the work of Isaac Alfasi entitled *Halakhot*, simply, "Laws." Better known to the student and scholar as *Alfasi* or the *Riff*, an acronym for the author's name, the Code was written in the eleventh century as an abridgement of the Talmud. The author followed both the order and the text of the Talmud in his work; he simply extracted the laws and omitted the discussions, thus creating a "code of practice." When he recorded a difference of opinion among the sages, he always indicated according to whom the law had finally been determined. When additional interpretations of new laws had been added by the *Geonim*, he mentioned them. Like the *Halakhot Gedolot* that preceded it, the *Riff* omitted all halakhic material that was not currently operative, such as the laws of sacrifice and the laws of purity, both of which applied only in the days of the Temple.

By far the most important Code of its time, the *Mishneh Torah*, was written by Maimonides in the twelfth century. It is a work I have made reference to many times in my letters. The *Mishneh Torah* was a summary of the vast literature of the Oral Law that had developed from the time of Moses our teacher until Moses Maimonides. Writing in his own chosen order, in a concise and exacting style and in a lucid mishnaic Hebrew, Maimonides created what his contemporaries and the sages that followed him would agree was a masterpiece of halakhic literature. He took difficult and involved legal concepts and put them into language that even a layman can understand. But that was not all. He gathered material that is scattered throughout the Talmud and put it under categories and subcategories that greatly facilitated both study and reference. Unlike the *Halakhot Gedolot* and the *Riff*, the *Mishneh Torah* covered the entire scope of Halakhah, the purpose of which was to obviate the necessity for any other book on Jewish law. As Maimonides writes: "Therefore, I call this treatise *Mishneh Torah* ("Second to the Torah") for a man should first read the Written Law and then read this book, and he will know the Oral Law and will not need any other book."[3] Ironically, this was one of the few things that some of the great rabbinic scholars that followed him held against his work.

The *Mishneh Torah* won wide acceptance among world Jewry, but there were those who objected to the fact that Maimonides had not indicated his sources. Many commentaries were written on the *Mishneh Torah* for the express purpose of tracing the *halakhot* to their sources in the Talmud with the clear intent of establishing thereby the integrity of both Maimonides and his work. To the present day, the *Mishneh Torah* is recognized by the entire Jewish community, those of Ashkenazic background as well as those of Sefardic background, as one of the foremost sources of Jewish law. As was said of him by the great minds of his day, "From Moses [our teacher] to Moses [Maimonides] there was none like Moses."

In the thirteenth century, the renowned sage Rabbi Asher ben Yehiel compiled a Code of Jewish Law for the Franco-German community where he had spent most of his life. Like the *Riff*, its predecessor, the work of Rabbi Asher is most often referred to as the *Rosh*, an acronym for his name. Like Rabbi Alfasi before him, Rabbi Asher also extracted the law from the discussions in the Talmud and recorded it. He included the decisions of Rabbi Alfasi in his work, but he did not always agree with those decisions. Where such was the case, he indicated it. Most importantly, this Code was not limited to concise legal decisions like that of Rabbi Alfasi; it incorporated interpretations and halakhic decisions from the sages of France and Germany as well. Like some of his predecessors, Rabbi Asher included only those *halakhot* that were relevant in post-Temple times.

There were other Codes written in the thirteenth and fourteenth centuries such as *Sefer haManhig* by Rabbi Abraham ben Natan of Lunel, a rather short work dealing primarily with synagogue ritual, and *Toldot Adam v'Havah* by Rabbi Yeruham, a student of Rabbi Asher, which was written in a more popular form. But it is not until the Code of Rabbi Jacob ben Asher that we come upon another major compilation.

The work of Rabbi Jacob ben Asher was called *Sefer haTurim* ("The Book of Rows"), an allusion to the four rows of stones that were set into the breastplate worn by the high priest during the Temple service. The work was divided into four parts: the *Tur Orah Hayyim* ("Path of Life") included all the laws that pertain to the Jew in his daily routine, from when he awakens in the morning until he retires at night, as well as the laws of *Shabbat*, festivals, and holidays; the *Tur Yoreh De'ah* ("Teacher of Knowledge") included the laws of *kashrut*, ritual purity for women, and mourning, among others; the *Tur Even haEzer* ("The Helping Stone") included the laws of family matters such as marriage, divorce, and levirate marriage; and the *Tur Hoshen Mishpat* ("Breastplate of Judgment") included the civil laws of Judaism.

The *Sefer haTurim* is a concise Code that, for the most part, follows the halakhic decisions of Rabbi Asher, the author's father. Where the opinions of others are brought, Rabbi Jacob frequently offers his own opinion on the matter, but he leaves the final decision to the student. The *Sefer haTurim* was widely accepted in its time, and it served as the forerunner for what was to become the definitive halakhic Code for all Jewry—the *Shulhan Arukh*.

In the sixteenth century, Rabbi Joseph Karo, the renowned Spanish kabbalist and halakhic master, composed a Code, the preparation of which took a major portion of his life. It was called the *Bet Yosef* ("House of Joseph"). Although some would consider the *Bet Yosef* a commentary on *Sefer haTurim*, it was a Code in and of itself. The sages of the day seemed to have been disappointed with the *Sefer haTurim*, in that the author, like Maimonides in his *Mishneh Torah*, had not indicated his sources. Some felt that other important opinions should have been included. Although he had originally intended to append his work to Maimonides' *Mishneh Torah*, Rabbi Karo subsequently chose the *Sefer haTurim*. Since that work had included other opinions of the law, he felt that it would be more appropriate. Some time later, Rabbi Karo abridged the *Bet Yosef*, his *magnum opus*, and called it the *Shulhan Arukh* ("Set Table"), a work he had intended to be used by younger students in preparation for the study of his major work.

The *Shulhan Arukh* followed the divisions and categories of the *Sefer haTurim*, but it subdivided the sections even further, into paragraphs, making it easier to use for reference purposes. The language of the work, like that of Maimonides, was lucid mishnaic Hebrew, rendering it accessible to scholar and student alike. Rabbi Karo based his halakhic decisions on three authorities: Rabbi Alfasi, Maimonides, and Rabbi Asher, the latter being the only one of the three who took the Franco-German [Ashkenazic] halakhic authorities into consideration in his work. I want you to note, however, that where Rabbi Alfasi and Maimonides differed with Rabbi Asher, Rabbi Karo decided the law according to the former. Consequently, the *Shulhan Arukh* was a Code geared more for the Sefardic than the Ashkenazic communities.

To put the final touch of authority on the *Shulhan Arukh* that would make it the definitive halakhic work for world Jewry, it was necessary to incorporate the Franco-German or Ashkenazic practices. This task was undertaken by Rabbi Moshe Isserles. Most commonly referred to as *Rema*, an acronym for his name, this sixteenth-century sage was known as the foremost Ashkenazic halakhic authority of his time. Recognizing the *Shulhan Arukh* for the masterful halakhic work that it was, he chose to append his comments to it rather than compile a halakhic Code of his own.

Where a halakhic decision brought by Rabbi Karo agreed with
the Ashkenazic practice, he voiced his concurrence with the words
hakhi nahug ("this is the common practice"), or *v'khen anu nohagin*
("such is our practice as well"). But where it did not agree, he
appended the Ashkenazic practice and indicated its source. He
paid special attention to customs, warning the reader not to deviate from the customs of the community or town in which he
lived. *Rema* called his work *Mapat haShulhan* ("The Tablecloth").
Considering that his work was on the *Shulhan Arukh* and subsequently appended to it, the name is most apropos.

It would be beyond the scope of this letter to discuss all of the
other Codes, and commentaries on the *Shulhan Arukh* from the
sixteenth through the eighteenth centuries, but I would be remiss
if I were not at least to mention the four important Codes of the
nineteenth century.

From Hungary came the *Kitzur Shulhan Arukh* by Rabbi Solomon Gansfried, an abridged version of the work by Rabbi Karo.
It follows the order of the *Shulhan Arukh* and covers all four of its
parts: *Orah Hayyim, Yoreh De'ah, Even haEzer, Hoshen Mishpat.*
Because of its clear and forthright style, the work won popularity
with the masses, the Hungarian community in particular.

From Poland came three Codes. The first is a work by Rabbi
Abraham Danzig that also follows the order and arrangement of
the *Shulhan Arukh*, but covers only the first two parts: *Hayye Adam*
on *Orah Hayyim* and *Hokhmat Adam* on *Yoreh De'ah*. The second
is *Arukh haShulhan*, the masterful compilation by Rabbi Yehiel
Mikhel HaLevi Epstein, who was the undisputed master of
Halakhah in his day. This work is a unique contribution to
halakhic literature. Not only does it summarize the laws of the
Shulhan Arukh, as others do, but it provides the student with a
concise summary of the talmudic and selected posttalmudic literature on each topic, in lucid mishnaic Hebrew. Those who study
this work cannot help but be impressed by this halakhic giant
whose wealth of knowledge was matched only by his love for the

Jewish people and his concern for the justification of *Minhage Yisrael*, that is, the customs of the Jewish people. Last, we must mention the Code of Rabbi Yisrael Meir HaKohen, the *Mishnah Berurah*, which is a running commentary on the first part of the *Shulhan Arukh*, the *Orah Hayyim*. Its lucid style and its clarity of expression makes this work popular among laymen and scholars alike. The last of the halakhic Codes, the *Mishnah Berurah* has become to many the definitive halakhic text for our time.

And now, in response to your request to see how the halakhic method works, and how the halakhic masters reach their decisions on modern halakhic problems, I will take you on an adventure in halakhic reasoning.

To what extent are human beings self-determined and to what extent is their destiny determined by the Almighty? What role does their genetic makeup, their sovereign will, and the environment in which they live play in their destiny? While these questions have given birth to a wealth of fascinating literature, a definitive answer is still forthcoming. Truthfully speaking, man may never know the answer, for in all likelihood it is beyond the realm of his intellectual capabilities. While some consider such questions to be moot, queries to be left to the philosophers to pursue merely as an intellectual exercise, we must recognize that whether we realize it consciously or not, we take a stand on this matter every day of our lives. We don't just leave things to God, we make conscious decisions to determine what happens to us. We try to preserve our health, and we consult with a physician when we are ill. But is this posture most of us take for granted halakhically valid?

The knowledge that you have acquired from our discussion of the Written and the Oral Law has given you sufficient background to follow a halakhic discussion intelligently, and I am ready to pursue the halakhic method with you and demonstrate how the law is determined by our rabbinic decisors. Follow my words carefully, and I am sure that you will find this pursuit an exhilarating adventure in logic and reason.

In this halakhic discourse, I shall respond to the following questions:

1. Is the pursuit of medicine, or for that matter any of the healing arts, halakhically valid?

2. Does the Halakhah posit that our health and our life span are at least to some extent in our own hands, contrary to the idea that these things are exclusively in the hands of the Almighty and we may take no action whatsoever to improve our health or to extend our life span?

If the latter must be answered in the negative, the former must be answered in the negative as well, for to engage in the healing arts when it is forbidden to seek healing is, at the very least, to become an accessory to a transgression.

In point of fact, most of us today feel very positive about the healing arts, and we have the "gut feeling" that despite the fact that many practitioners leave much to be desired in the realm of medical ethics, the profession of medicine is not only permissible according to Jewish law, it is honorable. On the other hand, we must recognize that there is an incontrovertible logic to the posture of the Karaites and the Christian Scientists who contend that man has no right to intervene in the Will of God; that if, for whatever reason, God brings illness upon an individual, even life-threatening illness, that individual must accept the condition willingly. Needless to say, Jewish law is not determined by "gut feelings," nor is logic, as important a role as it plays in the halakhic process, the sole determinant of the law. Nevertheless, were it not for the fact that there are biblical verses that clearly give permission to the physician to heal, it would be difficult for a religious person to argue against the position of nonintervention.

The halakhic decisors, certainly the mainstream of Jewish thinkers from early times to the present, do posit that the practice of medicine is permissible and that it is commendable as well. Let me present some of the source material upon which they base their position.

The Midrash relates the following story:

> It happened that Rabbi Ishmael and Rabbi Akiva were walking with someone in the streets of Jerusalem, and they came upon a sick person. He said to them: "My masters, how may I be cured?" They said to him: "Do such and such and you will be cured." He said to them: "Who smote me?" They answered: "The Holy One blessed be He." He said: "Are you involving yourselves in a matter that is not of your concern? He smote me and you heal? Are you not transgressing His Will?" They said to him: "What is your occupation?" He said: "I am a tiller of the ground; here is the sickle in my hand." They said: "Who created the vineyard?" He said: "The Holy One blessed be He." They said: "And you involve yourself in a matter that is not of your concern? He created it and you cut the fruit?" He said to them: "Do you not see the sickle in my hand? Were I not to go out and plow, cover and fertilize and weed it, nothing would grow." They said to him: "Fool that you are, have you never heard what is written, 'Man, his days are like the grass,' just as the tree will not grow if it is not weeded and plowed, and once it begins to grow, it will not live if it is not watered and fertilized, so it is with the body. The drugs and medication are like the fertilizer, and the physician is like the tiller of the ground."[4]

It is interesting to note that the apparent lesson from the analogy, namely, just as the grass in the ground must be nurtured in order for it to survive, so, too, must man's body be nurtured, was not picked up by the classical Bible commentators. What they saw here was rather an allusion to man's frailty and his short life span. By likening the physician to the tiller, and the drugs and medications to fertilizers, it is also apparent that the sages recognized disease and illness as the pitfalls of living. Of course, this does not preclude the possibility of an illness or disease having been inflicted by the Almighty upon a particular person as punishment for his sins, nor would it deny the possibility that a Di-

vine decree may render a person chronically ill and unrespon-
sive to even the most heroic efforts of expert practitioners.

The most authoritative and, therefore, the most compelling
source for the law is the Torah. In attempting to determine the
halakhic position on any matter, the Torah is the first source to
probe. Thus we read: "And if men quarrel and a man smites his
fellow man with a stone or with his fist, and he does not die but
becomes bedridden: if he rises again and walks with his cane, then
shall he who smote him be freed: only he shall pay for the loss of
his time, and shall cause him to be thoroughly healed" (Exodus
21:18-19). The last phrase of this verse, namely, "cause him to
be thoroughly healed," draws the following comment from *Rashi*:
"As is translated by *Onkelos*, 'he shall pay the physician's fee.'"
Now the fact that medical expenses must be paid implies that a
physician is consulted, and *ipso facto* that the physician has the
right to heal. Logic notwithstanding, the Talmud spells it out:
"Rabbi Ishmael said, 'to be thoroughly healed' from here we learn
that permission was given to the physician to heal."[5] The *ba'ale
haTosafot* (a school of French and German rabbinic scholars who
lived from the twelfth through the fourteenth century) went still
further in their clarification of the law. On the talmudic phrase
"permission was given" they commented:

> And should one ask: "Would this not be known from the word
> *v'rapo* which means "he shall be healed?" [Why then is the double
> verb *v'rapo yirape* written?] The answer is: [Had only the single verb
> been written] I would have said that the obligation to heal applies
> only to a wound or illness inflicted by man, but [intervening in]
> one inflicted by heaven would imply interfering with God's decree.
> The double verb is used to teach you that this is not so.[6]

We certainly have here an unqualified positive position on the
right of the physician to heal. But we cannot stop here. We must
discover whether or not this ruling is upheld in other sources.

From the Tosafists we move to Maimonides. One would certainly expect Maimonides, a physician, to take a positive position on the right to heal and be healed. Of course, he does, but the fact that he does not include Exodus 21:19 in his enumeration of the 613 commandments is quite puzzling. While many explanations have been offered for this apparent omission, the simplest and perhaps the most likely explanation is that the words "he shall be thoroughly healed" teach us that a physician has the *right* to heal rather than the *obligation*.[7] It is Deuteronomy 22:2 that obligates the physician to heal, according to Maimonides. The verse concerns the obligation to return a lost animal to its owner and reads: "And if your brother be not near to you, and you do not know him, then you shall bring it home to your house, and it shall be with you until your brother requires it, and you shall restore it to him." The last letter *vav* in the Hebrew word *v'hashevoto* is superfluous and would render the phrase literally "and you shall restore him to him." But the Torah is never superfluous. The additional *vav* must be there to teach us something. The Talmud clarifies that it is to teach us that at times it is necessary to restore not only one's animal or other belongings but one's health as well, if one has the ability to do so. This is the significance of the additional *vav*.[8] Maimonides, therefore, posits the following:

> A physician is obligated from the Torah to heal the sick of Israel. This is included in the meaning of the phrase "and you shall restore it to him," which means to heal his body. This means that when one sees his fellow man in danger and can save him by personally helping him, by spending money or using his knowledge [to help him], he must do so.[9]

Literally, if one is capable of helping another human being by restoring his health, he is biblically obligated to do so. We are now ready for the ruling in the *Shulhan Arukh*, where we read the following:

The Torah gave permission to the physician to heal, indeed, it is a positive commandment in the category of saving a life. One who refuses to do so is considered a shedder of blood, even if there is another physician who can do so, for a patient is not necessarily healed by every physician. However, one should not practice medicine unless he has mastered it, and one should not treat if there is a greater one than he present, for that, too, would be considered bloodshed.[10]

Now there is a difficulty here. If the physician has merely been given the permission to heal, why is it called a positive commandment, which indicates that it is obligatory? Isn't this a contradiction? The difficulty was picked up by the seventeenth-century Polish talmudic scholar Rabbi David HaLevi, who makes the following point: True healing is the positive result of a petition to God for mercy. Most of us are not deserving of such mercy, however. When we are ill, we must rely on a physician to heal us. The Almighty approves of this practice; He has given the physician the ability to heal. This is implied in the term "permission." Since man must resort to this method of healing rather than relying on prayer alone, the physician is biblically obligated to heal.[11]

It is quite clear from the sources I have brought thus far that according to Jewish law the art of healing is not only permissible to the physician when the opportunity presents itself, it is obligatory. In light of this, a statement found in the Talmud regarding physicians is most disturbing. In *Kiddushin* 82a we read: "The best of physicians will inherit Gehenna. . . . " Is this not an unqualified condemnation of medicine? How is this possible? It seems to fly in the face of everything we have said. While some dismiss the statement as mere subjective opinion, others take it quite literally. An interesting rationale is offered by Rabbi Hanokh Zundel in his commentary *Etz Yosef*. One who is considered by the community to be "the best of physicians" faces a difficult challenge, says Rabbi Zundel. He may become so impressed with himself that he will refuse to consult with others and rely totally on his own judgment even in situations where he is not sure of what the appropriate treatment or procedure should be, and by doing so endanger the life of his patient. Such a physician will surely inherit Gehenna, says Rabbi Zundel; this is what the Talmud meant.[12]

Nahmanides also qualifies the statement made in the Talmud. Note his words: "The statement is made to denigrate their ways, that is, their negligence and their insolence, but not to intimate that the practice [of medicine] is prohibited."[13]

It is important to take into consideration that in talmudic times, medicine was quite primitive. To put oneself in the hands of a physician, even a competent one, was dangerous. With the advances made in medicine in the last century, however, the sages of old would surely have insisted that the sick consult with a physician for treatment. Indeed, even in the eighteenth century, the renowned Rabbi David Azulai wrote:

> Nowadays we must not rely on miracles. The sick person is obligated to conduct himself with the natural order by calling a physician to heal him. In fact, to depart from the general practice by claiming greater merit than many saints in previous generations who were cured by physicians is almost sinful on account of both the implied arrogance and the reliance on miracles when there is danger to life. . . . Hence one should adopt the ways of all men and be healed by physicians.[14]

We are now able to answer the questions we posed at the beginning of this adventure in the halakhic method. The pursuit of medicine or for that matter any of the healing arts is certainly permissible for both the physician and the patient. If this was true in talmudic times when medicine was quite primitive, it is certainly true today. Indeed, we are obligated to consult a physician when we are sick because saving a life, particularly if it is our own, takes precedence over all the *mitzvot* in the Torah. If a physician is present and he knows what to do, he is obligated to heal, unless one greater than he is there as well. But a word of caution to the physician is certainly in order. One should not allow himself to be overwhelmed by his medical accomplishments and his reputation. A little humility can do much for both the patient and the physician.

This is the halakhic method. Step by step, the *posek*, that is, "halakhic decisor," goes through the sources, from the Torah to the *Shulhan Arukh*, and he looks for precedent. Then he puts it all together in his mind and makes his decisions. Sometimes the ruling is black on white; most other times, however, he must use his judgment and experience to come to what he believes is the right conclusion. The Halakhah is flexible; it is meant to live by. There is no situation, nor will there ever be one, that cannot be addressed by the Halakhah. This is the beauty and the timelessness of Torah.

SEVENTH LETTER

The Ten Commandments
—Man and God

My dearest daughter,

I am glad to hear that you are slowly but surely beginning to emerge from your state of confusion regarding the tenets of Judaism, that you now feel more comfortable with your status as a Jewish woman, and that you are truly awed by the sophistication of the halakhic method. You ask me how you can convey to your friends, who are open minded enough to listen to the message of Judaism but whose knowledge of the Bible is limited to the Ten Commandments, the indispensable role played by the Oral Law in understanding the Written Law. Let me help you by devoting this letter to an exposition of the Ten Commandments according to the Oral Law. You can then use my letter to demonstrate how much more there is to know about these laws than one can discover from the text of the Written Law itself and thereby justify the role of the Oral Law.

Let me begin with a little background material. It was in the third month after the Israelites had left Egypt that they entered the wilderness of Sinai and encamped there in front of the mountain. Moses went up the mountain, and the Lord called out to him, saying:

Thus shall you say to the house of Jacob and declare to the children of Israel: "You have seen what I did to the Egyptians, how I bore you on eagles' wings and brought you to Me. Now then, if you will obey Me faithfully and keep My covenant, you shall be My treasured possession among all the peoples. Indeed, all the earth is mine, but you shall be unto Me a kingdom of priests and a holy nation."[1]

Moses summoned the people and told them God's word, to which they responded, "All that the Lord has spoken we will do" (Exodus 19:18). He returned to God with their answer, whereupon he was instructed to sanctify the people that day and again on the following day, for on the third day God would descend upon the mountain. The people would hear God's word to Moses, and this would inspire them to trust Moses and to obey him. Moses was instructed by God to set boundaries for the people around the mountain to keep them from ascending it, or even touching it, lest they suffer the punishment of death.[2] He brought God's word to the people, and they obeyed. Then . . .

On the third day, as the morning dawned, there was thunder and lightning, and a dense cloud upon the mountain, and a very long blast of the shofar; and all the people who were in the camp trembled. Moses led the people out of the camp toward God, and they took their places at the foot of the mountain. Now Mount Sinai was all in smoke, for the Lord had come down upon it in fire; the smoke rose like the smoke of a kiln, and the whole mountain trembled violently. The blare of the shofar grew louder and louder. As Moses spoke, God answered him in thunder.[3]

Moses led the people to their positions: the masses at the foot of the mountain, the priests a bit higher, Aaron the high priest higher still, and Moses above them all. Then God summoned Moses and told him to warn the people once more not to attempt to ascend the mountain lest they perish. He told Moses to go down for Aaron, but to instruct the rest of the priests to remain in their positions below. Again Moses returned to the people with God's word. Then God revealed the Ten Commandments to the assembly of Israelites who had surrounded the mountain.

Following the revelation, God told Moses to ascend even higher on the mountain.[4] There he would be given the tablets of stone upon which the commandments would be inscribed. Moses remained on the mountain for forty days and forty nights, and the rest of the 613 commandments were revealed to him, all of which derive from the original ten.[5] Then God gave Moses the stone tablets to bring to the people below. The tablets were inscribed with the Ten Commandments on both their surfaces. Miraculously, they were able to be read from both sides. The work was God's work; the writing was God's writing.[6]

Suddenly, God told Moses to descend the mountain, for the people had sinned. A golden calf had been constructed, and they shouted, "This is your God, O Israel, who brought you from the land of Egypt."[7] God threatened to destroy the people, but Moses pleaded with Him on their behalf, and He renounced the punishment. Moses then descended the mountain, tablets in hand. As he approached the camp and witnessed the calf and the dancing, his heart filled with rage. He hurled the tablets to the ground and smashed them. He then took the calf and burned it. He ground the ashes to a fine powder, strewed it upon the waters, and forced the people to drink. Turning to Aaron, he inquired as to the cause of this horrendous sin. Aaron explained that the people had panicked because Moses had tarried so long on the mount. They had demanded a god to lead them, and the molten calf was the result.

Seeing that the people were out of control, Moses gathered the Levites and ordered them to pass throughout the camp and slay the sinners: brother, kinsman, and neighbor alike. The next day, Moses went before the Almighty to ask forgiveness for the people. "And yet, if you would only forgive their sin," he said, "if not, erase me from the record which You have written" (Exodus 32:32). God told Moses that only the guilty ones would be erased from His record. He instructed him to take the people to Canaan, and informed him that in God's place the people would now be led to the land by an angel. He put a plague upon the remaining sinners as punishment for their sin.

Unhappy with the Divine decree, Moses returned once more before God's Presence. "Unless You go into the land," he said, "do not make us leave this place. For how would it be known that I have gained Your favor, I and Your people, unless You go with us, that we may be distinguished, I and Your people, from every people on the face of the earth" (Exodus 33:15). Impressed with Moses' plea, the Almighty acquiesced. God then said to Moses:

Carve two tablets of stone like the first, and I will inscribe upon the tablets the words that were on the first tablets, which you shattered. Be ready by morning, and in the morning come upon Mount Sinai and present yourself there to Me, on top of the mountain. No one else shall come up with you, and no one else shall be seen anywhere on the mountain; neither shall the flocks and the herds graze at the foot of this mountain. [Exodus 34:1-3]

So Moses did what God had commanded. He ascended Mount Sinai bearing the tablets of stone. And the Torah tells us, "And the Lord came down in a cloud." He passed before Moses and proclaimed His attributes:

The Lord, the Lord, a God compassionate and gracious, slow to anger, rich in steadfast kindness, extending kindness to the thousandth generation, forgiving iniquity, transgression and sin; yet He does not remit all punishment, but remembering the sins of the fathers for their children and children's children to the third and fourth generation. (Exodus 34:6-7)

God promised Moses that He would perform miracles for Israel the likes of which had not been performed for any other nation, and that He would drive out all the nations that had inhabited the land of Canaan. He commanded the nation of Israel that when they entered the land they should tear down the idolatrous shrines, and He warned them that they were to make no treaty with the inhabitants of the land. "And the Lord said to Moses: 'Write down these commandments, for in accordance with these commandments, I make a covenant with you and with Israel'" (Exodus 34:27). And Moses stayed with the Almighty on the mountain for forty days and forty nights. "He ate no bread and he drank no water; and he wrote down on the tablets the terms of the covenant, the Ten Commandments" (Exodus 34:28).

The tablets upon which the Ten Commandments were inscribed are referred to in the Torah as *Luhot haEdut*[8] ("The Tablets of the Testimony") and *Luhot haBerit*[9] ("The Tablets of the Covenant"). In the Torah, the commandments themselves are called *Aseret haDevarim*,[10] literally "The Ten Words"; and in the Talmud they are called *Aseret haDibrot*, usually translated as "The Ten Commandments."[11] As has been already noted, the first tablets were broken by Moses. The text of these commandments, however, was preserved; it appears in Exodus 20:1-14. The text that appears in Deuteronomy 5:6-18 is the one that was inscribed on the second tablets.[12]

The two versions of the Ten Commandments are essentially the same.[13] I will put them side by side here for comparison and highlight the differences in my discussion.[14]

Exodus 20:2-14	Deuteronomy 5:6-18
I	**I**
I am the Lord your God who brought you out of the land	I am the Lord your God who brought you out of the land

of Egypt, the house of bondage.

II

You shall have no other gods
beside Me. You shall not
make for yourself a sculptured image, or any likeness
of what is in the heavens
above, or on the earth below,
or in the waters under the
earth. You shall not bow
down to them or serve them.
For I the Lord your God am a
God demanding His exclusive
rights, remembering the sins
of fathers for their children,
for the third and for the
fourth generation of those
that hate Me, and showing
love unto the thousands of
those that love Me and of
those that keep my com-
mandments.

III

You shall not swear falsely by
the name of the Lord your
God; for the Lord will not
clear one who swears falsely
by His name.

of Egypt, the house of bondage.

II

You shall have no other gods
beside Me. You shall not
make for yourself a sculptured image, or any likeness
of what is in the heavens
above, or on the earth below,
or in the waters under the
earth. You shall not bow
down to them or serve them.
For I the Lord your God am a
God demanding His exclusive
rights, remembering the sins
of fathers for their children,
for the third and for the
fourth generation of those
that hate Me, and showing
love unto the thousands of
those that love Me and of
those that keep my com-
mandments.

III

You shall not swear falsely by
the name of the Lord your
God; for the Lord will not
clear one who swears falsely
by His name.

IV

Remember the Sabbath day and keep it holy. Six days you shall labor and do all your work, but the seventh day is a Sabbath of the Lord your God; you shall not do any work—you, your son or daughter, your male or female slave, or your cattle or the stranger who is within your gates. For in six days the Lord made heaven and earth and sea, and all that is in them, and He rested on the seventh day; therefore the Lord blessed the seventh day and He made it holy.

IV

Observe the Sabbath day and keep it holy as the Lord your God has commanded you. Six days you shall labor and do all your work, but the seventh day is a Sabbath of the Lord God: you shall not do any work—you, your son or your daughter, your male or female slave, your ox or your ass, or any of your cattle, or the stranger in your gates, so that your male and female slave may rest as you do. Remember that you were a slave in the land of Egypt, and the Lord your God freed you from there with a mighty hand and an outstretched arm; therefore the Lord your God has commanded you to observe the Sabbath day.

V

Honor your father and mother that you may long endure on the land that the Lord your God is giving you.

V

Honor your father and mother that you may long endure on the land that the Lord your God is giving you.

VI

You shall not murder.

VI

You shall not murder.

VII

You shall not commit adultery.

VIII

You shall not steal.

IX

You shall not bear false witness against your neighbor.

X

You shall not covet your neighbor's house: you shall not covet your neighbor's wife, or his male or female slave, or his ox or his ass, or anything that is your neighbor's.

VII

You shall not commit adultery.

VIII

You shall not steal.

IX

You shall not bear worthless witness against your neighbor.

X

You shall not covet your neighbor's wife. You shall not crave your neighbor's house, or his field, or his male or female slave, or anything that is your neighbor's.

The commandments on the tablets were 10, but these 10 allude to all 613 commandments in the Torah. This was implied by Rabbi Ishmael when he said: "The general laws were stated at Sinai, and the details were stated at the Tent of Meeting."[15] Indeed, the text itself hints at this, for the sum total of letters on the first tablets is 613.[16]

The Midrash teaches us that the Ten Commandments are symbolic of the "Ten Sayings" through which God created the world, intimating, perhaps, that Creation and the Torah, representing respectively the natural realm and the ethical realm, are complementary rather than antithetical to each other. Just as there would be no world were it not for the "Ten Sayings," the world could not exist without the Ten Commandments.[17]

Let no one think that the order of the Ten Commandments is simply random, the Midrash tells us. They are divided into two sets of five: the first five commandments are meant exclusively for the Jewish people; the remaining five are meant for the rest of mankind as well.[18] Even more: the commandments were written on two tablets, five on one tablet and five on the other, and they are cross-matched: one to six, two to seven, three to eight, four to nine, and five to ten. Seen in this way, they teach the following five lessons in Jewish ethics:[19]

The first commandment is "I am the Lord your God . . . " and opposite it, "You shall not murder." This is to teach you that if one sheds blood it is considered as if he diminished, as it were, the image of the Almighty, for man was created in the image of God. The second commandment is "You shall have no other gods . . . " and opposite it, "You shall not commit adultery." This is to teach you that whoever commits the sin of idolatry is considered unfaithful to the Almighty. The third commandment is "You shall not swear falsely . . . " and opposite it is "You shall not steal." This is to teach you that whoever steals will eventually swear falsely when he is called upon in court to take an oath that he had not stolen the item in question. The fourth commandment is "Remember the Sabbath day and keep it holy . . . " and opposite it, "You shall not bear false witness . . ." This is to teach you that whoever desecrates the *Shabbat* connotes by his actions a denial of the fact that the Almighty created the world in six days and rested on the seventh. Finally, the fifth commandment is "Honor your father and your mother . . . " and opposite it, "You shall not covet . . . " This is to teach you that whoever covets will beget a son who will dishonor his parents, and will honor one who is not his parent. For to covet that which is not ours, whether it is the spouse of another or his material possessions, is an indication of misdirected feelings and honor. By coveting, the parents impart an improper lesson to their children. Responding in kind, the children will also display their feelings of affection to another.

In the Jerusalem Talmud, it is stated that Rabbi Levi contends that in the *Keriat Shema*, that is, the three-paragraph recitation at the morning and evening services, there is an allusion to each of the Ten Commandments, as follows:

The opening words, "Hear O Israel the Lord our God the Lord is One," allude to "I am the Lord your God" and "You shall have no other gods beside Me." The words "and you shall love the Lord your God" allude to "You shall not swear falsely," for one who truly loves God will not swear falsely in His name. The words "so that you remember My commandments and do them" allude to "Remember the Sabbath day and keep it holy," for *Shabbat* is likened to the whole body of commandments. The words "so that you and your children may long endure" allude to "Honor your father and your mother so that you may long endure." The words "you will quickly perish from the good land" allude to "you shall not murder," for he who kills will himself be killed. The words "you shall not follow the desires of your heart and your eyes" allude to "You shall not commit adultery," for the heart and the eyes are the agents for this weakness in man. The words "you shall gather in your grain" allude to "You shall not steal," for we are permitted to gather in only that which belongs to us. The words "I am the Lord your God" are combined with the first word of the benediction that follows, that is, "true," so that it reads "I am the Lord your true God"; this alludes to "You shall not bear false witness." Rabbi Abin taught that the truth referred to here is the truth of His being the Sovereign of the world and its Creator. "If you testify falsely against your fellowman," says the Almighty, "I consider it as if you testified falsely against Me, saying that I did not create heaven and earth." The words "you shall write them on the doorposts of your house" allude to "You shall not covet the house of your neighbor," for your concern should be with your own house, not with that of your neighbor.[20]

How many commandments did the Israelites hear? There is a difference of opinion on this matter. Rabbi Joshua ben Levi contends that they heard the first two commandments while the "Rabbis" contend that they heard all ten.[21] Did the people actually hear the words of the commandments or was it a muffled sound? Maimonides, in his *Guide of the Perplexed*, devotes an entire chapter to this question.[22] It is clear, says Maimonides, that what Moses experienced at Sinai was categorically different from what was experienced by the rest of the Israelites, for he alone was addressed by the Almighty, and for this reason, the second person singular [thou] is used in the Ten Commandments.[23] Only Moses heard the words; the people heard a mighty sound. This is implied in what was said to the masses: "You heard a sound of words" (Deuteronomy 4:12).

Now there is a statement in the Talmud, says Maimonides, to the effect that Israel heard the first two commandments in the same manner as Moses heard them, that is, directly from the Almighty, unlike the manner in which they heard the rest of the commandments, which was through the mouth of Moses.[24] This is because the existence of God and His unity—the themes of these commandments—can be arrived at through reason, and whatever can be attained through reason is known by the prophet in the same way as by any other person. The rest of the commandments are of an ethical and moral character; they do not put forth truths that can be attained by the intellect.[25] Nevertheless, says Maimonides, the people of Israel heard only mighty sounds for the first two commandments; Moses interpreted them in intelligent words.[26] The sounds they heard terrified them, and they requested of Moses that he alone communicate the rest of the Ten Commandments to them.[27]

Many people have the impression that the Ten Commandments are the most important Torah laws, and the remaining 603 are of secondary importance. That this impression is false is alluded to in the following talmudic discussion:

Mishnah: The deputy high priest said to them [the other priests], "Say one benediction," and they said the benediction and then recited the Ten Commandments. . . .

Gemara: Outside the Temple, people also wanted to do the same, but they were stopped on account of the insinuations of the heretics. [*Rashi:* that the Ten Commandments were the only valid part of the Torah] . . . Rabbah bar Bar Hanah wanted to institute this in Sura, but Rabbi Hisda said to him that it had long been abolished on account of the insinuations of the heretics. Amemar wanted to institute it in Nehardea, but Rabbi Ashi said to him that it had long been abolished on account of the heretics.[28]

Let me now go to the text of each commandment and give you an idea of how it is interpreted by the Oral Law. The whole text is introduced with the following words:

And God [E-lohim] spoke all these words saying:

The sages comment on the apparent redundancy here. Surely the term *saying* is superfluous. Considering that there are no redundancies in the Torah—the Almighty is never redundant in His words—what does this word teach us? It comes to teach us that the Almighty reviewed the text several times to Himself, "saying" it to Himself, as it were, the sages tell us, before He presented it to Israel. All the more so man! Prepare yourself in the reading and in the interpretation of the Torah, and be secure in your understanding of the Torah, before attempting to teach it to others.[29]

What is the significance of the fact that the name *E-lohim* appears in this verse, considering that the Tetragrammaton, which is the ineffable four-letter name of God we refer to as *Hashem*, is the name that appears in the Ten Commandments?

The names of the Holy One blessed be He are symbolic of His attributes. *E-lohim* symbolizes strict justice while the Tetragrammaton symbolizes the attribute of mercy. Rashi explains:

Since there are chapters in the Torah of such a character that if a person observes the commands contained therein he will receive a reward and if he never observes them at all he will not receive punishment on their account, one might think that the Ten Commandments are also of such a character: therefore, Scripture expressly states *E-lohim* spoke—God who is Judge, exacting punishment.

The sages saw still more in the introductory verse. What is the significance of the phrase "all these words"? they asked. It is to teach you that the Almighty first declaimed all the Ten Commandments simultaneously, says the Midrash, an act not only beyond man's capability but beyond his comprehension as well. He then revealed each commandment separately.[30]

What is the meaning of this midrashic statement? Surely the Almighty did not perform this miracle merely to demonstrate His omnipotence. Not at all. It was rather to convey to man the holistic nature of the Ten Commandments, to demonstrate to him that they are not an incidental sum of mutually unrelated precepts, but constitute an organic unity that is indivisible as surely as it is immutable. We must see them as an intrinsic totality. They are not ten separate commandments but rather one commandment that has ten aspects. The social norms are inseparable from the theological norms, the Midrash tells us. The set of laws between man and God and those between man and his fellowman were both legislated by the Almighty. To pick and choose between them is not only forbidden; it is absurd, for secular social morality is simply not viable.[31]

But what is the message conveyed by this Divine gesture? Perhaps it is the following. Just as there are two aspects to the revelation—the incomprehensible, namely, the simultaneous declamation of all ten commandments, and the comprehensible, namely, the revelation of each commandment separately—similarly, the significance of these commandments is twofold. They have reasons that were Divinely ordained, and they have a practical purpose. It may very well be that the Divine reasons for the commandments are incomprehensible to man. Consequently, man is charged to accept them on faith alone, just as he is charged to accept the incomprehensible fact that the Almighty declaimed all Ten Commandments simultaneously. But there is also the other aspect of the commandments, their practical purpose. This is definitely within man's intellectual capacity both to probe and to comprehend. For unlike the man-made taboos of primitive religions that are designed to appease vengeful deities, the commandments were given by God *to* man and *for* man. Indeed, all the commandments are for man and they all have an effect upon him. Not only do the ethical and moral norms that guide man's relationship with his fellowman have a profound effect upon his personality and shape his perspective on life in general, but the laws between man and God do so as well. As such man must willingly accept upon himself the responsibility to study all the *mitzvot* and thus become a better Jew and a better person in society. And now, on to the commandments.

I. I am the Lord your God who brought you out of the land of Egypt, the house of bondage.

There is a difference of opinion among the sages as to whether or not this verse is counted as one of the 613 commandments. Indeed, can one be commanded to believe? Maimonides would respond in the affirmative, for in the *Mishneh Torah*, he lists this verse as the first of the 613 commandments.

> The most basic of all principles and the pillar of wisdom is to know that there is a First Being who brought every existing thing into being. All existing things, whether celestial, terrestrial, or belonging to an intermediate class exist only through His true Essence. If it could be supposed that He did not exist, it would follow that nothing else could possibly exist. If, however, it was supposed that all other beings were non-existent, He alone would still exist. . . .

For all beings are in need of Him, but He, blessed be He, is not in need of them. . . . This Being is the God of the universe, the Lord of all the earth. . . . To acknowledge this truth is an affirmative precept, as it is said, "I am the Lord your God."[32]

If we accept this verse as one of the 613 commandments, perhaps it should be translated a bit differently. We would not read it "I am the Lord your God" but rather "I am *to be* the Lord your God." More is implied by this modification than meets the eye. To accept these words as a *mitzvah* is to take upon oneself the duties that are involved in considering God our King, namely, to recognize Him as the providential and beneficent Being to whom we owe ultimate commitment of body and soul.[33] Even more: as our sages say, "For each and every breath that man takes, he is obligated to praise his Creator."[34]

One cannot help but wonder why the Almighty chose to speak of Himself as the Redeemer of His people from bondage in Egypt. One would have thought that a more appropriate appellative would be "the Creator of heaven and earth." And yet, what greater assurance of God's concern could have been given to the "generation of the lawgiving" than the fact that He had intervened in the historical process and had redeemed them from Egypt? Indeed, our sages comment: "One cannot compare hearing to seeing."[35] It is one thing to have been taught of the providential acts of God in the universe; it is quite another to have experienced them personally. Moreover, the redemption from Egypt was a confirmation of Creation. Great miracles were performed at the time of the redemption, supernatural events that were witnessed by the whole nation of Israel. These events attest to *creatio ex nihilo* ("creation out of nothing"), for in an eternal universe the laws of nature would be permanently fixed; there could be no change, no supernatural event.[36] As such the phrase "who brought you out of the land of Egypt" has two advantages. First, it grounds the belief in God and the commitment to His Kingship to an event that the people of Israel knew to be true from their own experience, one that they handed down faithfully father to son through the generations. Second, it implies Creation, which is one of the most fundamental beliefs of Judaism.

Our sages have taught that the measure of Divine providence manifested upon the Jewish people is greater than that which is manifested upon the rest of mankind. Consequently, the Almighty is more demanding of the people of Israel in terms of *mitzvot*. Providence is manifested upon the nations of the world in proportion to their obedience to the seven Noachide commandments.[37] Nothing more is required of them. If they observe these laws, they are entitled to a share in the World to Come. Having been allotted a greater proportion of providence, the nation of Israel has been charged with 613 commandments. This greater calling is implied in the words "I am the Lord *your* God." I am more particularly yours, says the Almighty, therefore you must serve Me more than any other nation.[38]

> **II. You shall have no other gods beside Me. You shall not make for yourself a sculptured image, or any likeness of what is in the heavens above, or on the earth below, or in the waters under the earth. You shall not bow down to them or serve them. For I the Lord your God am a God demanding His exclusive rights, remembering the sins of fathers for their children, for the third and for the fourth generation of those that hate Me, and showing love unto the thousands of those that love Me and of those that keep My commandments.**

Did monotheism precede polytheism or did man develop from a polytheistic society to a monotheistic one? Much hangs in the balance here. Indeed, regarding this issue, the believer can be distinguished from the nonbeliever. To contend that it was God who found man, that in the dawn of Creation God revealed Himself to man in order to establish His existence in man's mind in no uncertain terms, is to contend that monotheism preceded polytheism, which is to assume the position of the believer. But to contend that primitive man, beset by confusion and fear of the environment in which he lived, a world that he could not possibly even begin to understand, invented a multiplicity of deities to explain his world, worshiping them to appease them and obtain thereby peace of mind, and to contend further that his refinement of these beliefs evolved into monotheism is to assume the position of the disbeliever. The Torah teaches that it was, indeed, God who found man through the act of revelation.[39]

When and why did idolatry begin? Maimonides posits that it was in the time of Enosh, the grandson of Adam, and he proposes the following rationale:

The wise men of the generation of Enosh wanted to find favor in the eyes of the Almighty and they reasoned as follows: Since the Almighty created the stars and honored them by setting them into the heavens to guide the world, they deserve to be honored and praised by man, for it is God's Will that man honor those whom God has honored. So the people built temples wherein they offered sacrifices to the stars, praising and glorifying them, thus hoping to please the Almighty and to be rewarded accordingly. In the course of time, there arose false prophets who asserted that God had revealed to them that a particular star, or at times, all the stars, should be worshiped. The prophet would construct an image of that star, which he claimed was revealed to him by God, and he would instruct the people to worship that image. Such images were constructed in temples, under trees, and on mountain tops. The prophet would bow down to them and worship them. He would tell the people that the images conferred benefits or caused injuries, and that it was for their own good that they fear and worship these images. Some of the prophets claimed that the image itself had instructed them how it wanted to be worshiped. Gradually, the practice of idolatry spread throughout the ancient world. The great name of God was forgotten, and monotheism, for all intents and purposes, was forgotten as well.

Only a few individuals of the generation still maintained the belief in One God. They were Methusaleh, Noah, Shem, and Ever. It was not until the time of Abraham that a major attempt was made to bring people back to monotheism.[40]

Let me now focus on some of the specifics of this commandment. The second commandment follows logically from the first. Having been charged to accept the Almighty as our God, we are now given to understand that He demands exclusivity. He refuses to share allegiance with some other force or discipline.[41] We are forbidden to commit ourselves to one whom others have designated as a god, even if our intention is to worship both. Indeed, even to entertain the notion that there exists another Supreme Being is to transgress this commandment.[42]

Not only is the worship of strange gods forbidden, but to make images that are intended for worship is forbidden as well. It makes no difference whether one makes the image himself or hires someone to make it for him, the one who initiates the action is culpable.[43] It is important to take note of the fact that while both terms *likeness* and *image* are mentioned, neither is superfluous. "Sculptured image" refers to a three-dimensional representation while "likeness" implies a two-dimensional one. Both are prohibited.[44] The qualifying phrase "in the heavens above" is meant to include the sun, moon, stars, signs of the zodiac, and even representations of angels. The phrase "on the earth below" is meant to include rivers and seas, mountains and valleys, and the like.[45] The Talmud adds that although prostration before an image is forbidden even where it is not being practiced as worship, prostration before a human being out of fear or respect is permissible.[46]

I have chosen the Hirsch rendering of the term *kana* as "demanding His exclusive rights" rather than the more common rendering "jealous," for the sake of clarity, and because of the negative connotation of "jealous" in popular usage. I have also chosen to render the phrase *poked avot al banim* as "remembering the sins of fathers for their children," which is likewise the

Hirsch rendering, because the common rendering "who visits the sins of the fathers upon their children" is not only harsh sounding but imprecise. On this last phrase, Rabbi Hirsch makes the following comment:

> Does it mean that God remembers the sins of the parents when children, grandchildren, and great grandchildren hate Him? That when children, grandchildren, and even great grandchildren continue on the path of sin, God thinks back to the first step which the parents took, considers that the sin has not yet been embedded throughout many generations, that the return is still possible, and He tries, by educating them in the school of suffering, to lead the children, grandchildren, or even the great grandchildren back again to Him; but if return is not achieved until into the fourth generation further generations perish in their sin? . . . Does it mean that God carries over the sins of fathers to children, grandchildren and great grandchildren? That instead of destroying the parents on account of their sins, God waits till the fourth generation, perhaps grandchildren or great grandchildren will rectify the guilt of the parents, and only then, if there is no betterment, does He allow the generation to perish in their continued guilt? Whatever the real truth of this measure of God's rule may be . . . there lives a God who judges men according to their deeds, whom nobody can evade and who allows nobody to evade Him.[47]

The matter of punishing the children for the sins of their fathers is discussed in the Talmud. "Why do the righteous suffer and the wicked prosper?" asked Moses of the Lord. "The righteous man who prospers is the son of a righteous man and the one who suffers is the son of a wicked one," answered the Almighty. Moses then pointed to a contradiction between the words "visiting the sins of the fathers upon the children," in the Book of Exodus, and the words in Deuteronomy, "neither shall the children be put to death for the sins of the fathers," whereupon the Lord responded: "The first verse deals with children who continue in the same course as their fathers, and the second deals with children who do not continue in the course of their fathers." The Talmud then explains: "You must therefore say that the Lord said to Moses, 'The righteous man who prospers is a perfectly righteous man; the righteous man who suffers is not a perfectly righteous man.'"[48] Most importantly, it should be noted that the sin of idolatry is the only sin for which retribution is visited upon the children, and then, only when they walk in the ways of their fathers.[49] This matter needs further elaboration, and perhaps I will discuss it with you in some future letter.

III. You shall not swear falsely by the name of the Lord your God; for the Lord will not allow the one who takes His name in vain to go unpunished.

An oath is a very serious matter in Judaism. It should be limited to very special circumstances, and even then it should be exercised with extreme caution. Of course, what is spoken of here is an oath made with the use of God's name. Such an oath constitutes submitting oneself, the whole of one's existence, to the Almighty, that is, to His punishing judgment if the oath is not fulfilled.[50] It means placing oneself under the Divine power that intervenes in earthly affairs, and calling that power down upon oneself if this oath is not carried out. An important explanation is made here by Rabbi Samson Raphael Hirsch:

> It is clear that in an oath, the two phases of our acknowledgement of God are jointly expressed—His watching over all our deeds and His power of ordering our fate. An oath in the name of God implies both, and by the actual submission of our whole future under God's power of deciding our fate, wishes to prove the truth of our statements and the honesty of our actions. Hence, conversely, a false oath is the most direct denial of God in the most contemptuous manner.[51]

Only two of the Ten Commandments speak of the punishment for disobedience: the prohibition of idolatry and the prohibition of swearing falsely. This indicates that swearing falsely in the name of God is a serious sin with grave consequences. The Talmud teaches that with all other negative transgressions that do not incur the death penalty at the hand of man or God, the sinner is forgiven if he repents his sin; he is held guiltless by the Almighty. But even the advent of Yom Kippur does not bring atonement to one who swears falsely; he must first endure some suffering.[52] One can readily understand the seriousness of swearing falsely in God's name. Such an oath is not merely a sign of disrespect; it is a statement. The person who swears falsely is really saying one of two things: that God does not exist, and as such, an oath in God's name is meaningless, or that God, even if He does exist, is powerless and therefore irrelevant to that person's life.

The oaths referred to here are *shevuot sheker* ("false oaths") and *shevuot shav* ("useless oaths"). False oaths are those that relate to the past or future and pertain to human behavior. For example: swearing falsely that one has not eaten a particular food or that one would not go to a particular place. Useless oaths are of four kinds: those that contradict known truths, such as swearing that the color white is black; those that confirm that which for obvious reasons needs no confirmation, such as swearing that the earth is the earth; those that nullify a *mitzvah,* such as swearing that one will not don *tefillin*; and last, those that promise the impossible, such as swearing that one will fast for an entire year. One who takes an oath in the name of the Almighty in any of these ways has transgressed the third commandment.[53]

One would have expected this commandment to read like the first two, that is, the Almighty being the implied speaker rather than Moses. As it stands, it confirms the statement in the Talmud that only the first two commandments were communicated by God directly to Israel, the others having been told to them by Moses. Moreover, it establishes that the Almighty wanted the people of Israel to know directly the themes of the first two com-

mandments, namely, His existence, His Oneness, and the prohibition of idolatry.[54]

> **IV. Remember the Sabbath day and keep it holy. Six days you
> shall labor and do all your work, but the seventh day is a Sab-
> bath of the Lord your God: you shall not do any work—you, your
> son or your daughter, your male or female slave, or your cattle,
> or the stranger who is within your gates. For in six days the
> Lord made heaven and earth and sea and all that is in them,
> and He rested on the seventh day; therefore the Lord blessed
> the seventh day, and He made it holy.**

The version of this commandment found in Deuteronomy reads
somewhat differently. I must point out to you, however, that with
the exception of the change there from *Remember* to *Observe*,
which I will explain presently, the variants are inconsequential.
Mark the words of Nahmanides:

> It would not have been proper for Moses to change God's words
> from a positive commandment to a negative commandment. There-
> fore our sages were careful to point out that both these words were
> uttered by the Almighty simultaneously. The change in the sec-
> ond commandment from "or any likeness" to "any likeness" and
> all such similar changes in the Ten Commandments, do not mat-
> ter, for it is all one.[55]

Our sages understood the term *remember* to imply the positive *mitzvot* of *Shabbat*, while *observe* implies the negative *mitzvot*.
This is what Nahmanides meant. The fact that both words were
uttered by the Almighty simultaneously has some important implications. As you know, Jewish law obligates women to obey all
the negative commandments, and all the positive commandments
that are not time oriented. Moreover, the positive commandments
that are linked thematically to negative ones, such as the commandment that adjures eating *matzah* on Passover and the one
that prohibits eating or maintaining leaven, are also obligatory

upon women. In the case of *Shabbat*, women are obligated to proclaim its sanctity, a positive, albeit time-oriented, commandment. This is because "Remember" and "Observe" were uttered simultaneously, obligating all those who must observe *Shabbat*, namely, to follow its negative commandments, to also remember it, which is to follow its positive commandments.[56]

The rationale for *Shabbat*, according to the text in Exodus, is that God created the world in six days and rested on the seventh. *Shabbat* teaches Creation. The rationale is different in Deuteronomy. Predicated on the fact that God took the people of Israel out of the land of Egypt, the rationale is redemption.

Let me elaborate a bit on these two themes. *Shabbat* teaches two principles: the natural and the supernatural. In six days God created heaven and earth, and on the seventh day, He desisted, as it were, from creative activity. No new species has been created in the world since that time. *Shabbat* thus symbolizes the creation of nature, the laws of which have been fixed for all time. But God did not limit His beneficence to the natural; He brought the supernatural into the world, that facet of providence that is predicated upon man's behavior and the Divine promise of retribution. True, *olam keminhago noheg* ("the world pursues its natural course"), but the Almighty intervenes in that pursuit if and when He finds it necessary to do so. Such was the situation in Egypt that brought the redemption.[57]

These two aspects of *Shabbat* are alluded to in the words "therefore the Lord blessed the seventh day and he made it holy." The holiness of the day is its uniqueness, the fact that God, as it were, desisted from creative activity; its blessedness consists in the fact that on this day the Almighty initiated the supernatural in the world. Blessing implies the extraordinary, that which is more than the expected or the normal. As such it alludes most appropriately to a measure of Divine beneficence that is over and above nature, that supersedes its laws in accordance with man's behavior. This aspect of *Shabbat* is associated with the redemption from Egypt

because that event was the greatest manifestation of God's intervention in both the natural and the historical process ever witnessed by man.[58]

Our sages tell us that we must articulate the greatness and the
uniqueness of *Shabbat* when it begins and when it departs. This
mitzvah, expressed through the two rituals *Kiddush* and *Havdalah*,
should preferably be fulfilled over a cup of wine, for wine arouses
the senses and stimulates the emotions, creating an air of joy and
happiness in the day.[59]

The Talmud teaches that on *Shabbat* eve, Rabbi Hanina would
don his finest robes and go out to greet *Shabbat* with the words,
"Come let us go forth to welcome the *Shabbat* Queen."[60] Preparation for *Shabbat* should not be limited to *Shabbat* eve, however;
it should be anticipated all week long. We should count the days
of the week with *Shabbat* in mind, labeling them *rishon b'Shabbat,
sheni b'Shabbat*, that is, first day of *Shabbat*, second day of *Shabbat*,
and so forth, days leading up to *Shabbat*.[61] The Talmud also speaks
of Shammai the Elder, who, in a sense, ate in honor of *Shabbat*
every day of his life. When he would find a wholesome animal,
he would buy it, saying, "This one will be in honor of *Shabbat*." If
he would find a better one subsequently, he would save that one
for *Shabbat* and eat the first one. Hence, what he ate during the
week had originally been dedicated to *Shabbat*. Hillel the Elder
was guided by another principle: "all one's deeds should be for
the sake of heaven." He did not find it necessary to reserve an
item for *Shabbat* until a better one was found because he felt as-
sured that he would always find something good for *Shabbat*.[62]

From earliest times, the Jew dedicated his *Shabbat* to the study
of Torah. It is a day to visit great people and study with them. In
ancient times, it was the prophets, later in history it was the sages.
This practice is hinted at in the verse, "And you shall call the
Shabbat a delight" (Isaiah 58:13)—a spiritual delight![63]

I want you to note that the commandment does not read "Make
the seventh day a *Shabbat*," but rather "Remember the day of

Shabbat." *Shabbat* is not being introduced here as a new institution, for it has existed in the world since Creation. Rabbi Samson Raphael Hirsch comments:

> Remember reminds us of the ancient memorial which God established right at the beginning when He first set man up to be His representative as "servitor and guardian" of the world. It was to insure this recognition [of God as the Ruler and Guide of our actions], the forgetting of which has been the sole cause of the downward path along which the development of human history was leading the world, and the consequent necessity for the election of Israel to be God's herald in leading it upward again.[64]

The Midrash points out that some of the laws of *Shabbat*, the pattern for which had already been set in Egypt, were introduced at a place called Marah, before the revelation of the Ten Commandments.[65] The phrase that appears in Deuteronomy, "as the Lord your God commanded you," may refer to Exodus or perhaps to what transpired at Marah, or perhaps even to Egypt. It is important for you to note here that the fact that *Remember* and *Observe* were uttered by the Almighty simultaneously belies the contention that all the Almighty wants of us on *Shabbat* is to commemorate it as a day of remembrance in our hearts. It involves all the laws that pertain to *Shabbat*, the negative commandments as well as the positive ones, and all of the Oral Law that comes with them. Indeed, *Shabbat* can have significance only when man, like God, regards *Remember* and *Observe* as one.[66]

I believe that I have given you enough material for one letter. Study the material carefully. Show it to your friends and discuss it with them. I will focus on the second part of the Ten Commandments in my next letter.

The Ten Commandments —Man and Man

My dearest daughter,

I am most pleased to hear that you have gained a new respect for Judaism, and that you now realize that the Oral Law is indispensable to a proper understanding of the Written Law. Your friends, you say, are satisfied that I have demonstrated this clearly with regard to the commandments that relate to man vis-à-vis God, but they would also like to see how it would apply to the commandments between man and his fellowman. This is understandable, and as I promised you, I will do so in this letter.

We have completed the laws that pertain to man in his relationship with God. With the fifth commandment we begin the laws that pertain to man and his fellowman, and it is a most fitting beginning, for the relationship between parents and children is in many ways similar to the relationship between God and humanity.

V. Honor your father and your mother, that you may long endure on the land which the Lord your God is giving you.

Parents are God's partners in bringing children into the world, and just as God has commanded us to honor Him, so has He commanded us to honor our parents. Though the Torah has not specified how we should honor our parents, we can deduce this from some of the things that are expected of us in our relationship with God. For example: one should acknowledge his true father and mother as parents, and not give other human beings this role in his life; one should not serve his parents for an ulterior motive like the wealth he expects to inherit from them or any other material benefit he may derive from his familial relationship; one is forbidden to swear in vain or falsely by the life of his parents.[1]

In Leviticus 19:3 we read: "You shall each revere his mother and his father and observe My Sabbaths; I am the Lord your God." The *mitzvah* to honor one's parents is linked to *Shabbat*, from which we derive two important lessons. First, it teaches us that although it is a *mitzvah* to honor our parents, this *mitzvah* does not take precedence over *Shabbat*. Namely, if our parents tell us to violate *Shabbat*, we must disobey them; they have no right to ask this of us for they, too, are obligated to observe the laws of *Shabbat*. In point of fact, had the phrase "and observe My Sabbaths" not been put there specifically to teach us this lesson, it would be superfluous, for the third commandment already charges us to observe *Shabbat*. Second, it teaches us that parents are held in highest esteem in the Jewish religion, for were it not for this verse, we would have presumed that honoring parents supersedes even *Shabbat*.

Since one of the reasons we are charged to honor our parents is that they are our progenitors, the Almighty rewards those who observe the *mitzvah* accordingly and grants them long life. But even more. In the Deuteronomy text we find the phrase "that you may fare well" appended to this *mitzvah*. There are always those in society who believe that the evil in the world far exceeds the good; they abhor life, which they find to be a continuous battle against the currents. They resent their parents for having brought them into this world. Honor your parents, the Torah tells us, and life will be better for you because of it.[2]

I have already noted that honoring parents is likened to honoring God.[3] One who curses God is executed; so it is with one who curses his parents.[4] Financial support of parents is one of the obligations of honoring them;[5] its importance surpasses even honoring God. Let me give you an example. The Talmud teaches that a person is obligated to honor God with the wealth that God has graciously given him, but the poor are released from this obligation. Not so with regard to children and parents. If parents need financial support, their children are required to provide it even if they must go begging from door to door in order to do so.[6]

Many illustrations of how parents must be honored by their children are brought in the Talmud. Let me note just three:

1. Our Rabbis taught: What is fear and what is honor? Fear means that one must neither stand in his father's place nor sit there, nor contradict his words, nor tip the scales against him. Honor means that one must give him food and drink, clothe and cover him and lead him in and out.[7]

2. It was taught: if one's father is unwittingly transgressing a *mitzvah* in the Torah, he must not say to him, "Father, you are transgressing a biblical *mitzvah*," but rather "Father, it is thus written in the Torah."[8]

3. Eliezer ben Mattia said: if my father orders me, "Give me a drink of water," while I have a *mitzvah* to perform, I disregard my father's honor and perform the *mitzvah*, since both my father and I are bound to perform the *mitzvot*. Issi ben Judah maintained: if the *mitzvah* can be performed by others, it should be performed by others while he should bestir himself for his father's honor.[9]

I have already noted the two reasons given for the commemoration of *Shabbat*: "Creation" and "Redemption." Regrettably, insofar as the nations of the world are concerned, the message of Creation has fallen on deaf ears. What's worse, it led early man to polytheism, as I have explained. It took redemption, the classic example of God's concern, to reverse the process and bring man back to monotheism. Indeed, redemption and Creation are historic truths, but how are such truths preserved through the generations? Note the words of Rabbi Samson Raphael Hirsch:

> The knowledge and acknowledgement of historical facts depends solely on tradition, and tradition depends solely on the faithful transmission by parents to children and on the willing acceptance by children from the hands of their parents. So the continuance of God's whole great institution of Judaism rests entirely on the theoretical and practical obedience of children to parents, and honor to parents is the basic condition for the eternal existence of the Jewish nation.[10]

Parents are not only the progenitors of their children; they are their children's link with the past—the Torah and Jewish history. The child receives the tradition from his parents and in turn transmits that tradition to his own children. As such, Judaism rests on the faithful transmission of its tradition from one generation to the next. Honor to parents sustains and encourages the integrity of this system of tradition. It is considered of such importance that it was included in the Ten Commandments.[11]

VI. You shall not murder.

No civilized human being would contest the validity of this commandment and its importance. Upon it rests not only the integrity of society but its very survival. Our sages warn: "For this reason was man created alone, to teach you that whoever destroys a single soul of Israel, Scripture imputes guilt to him as though he had destroyed a complete world."[12] Moreover, "whoever sheds blood is seen as diminishing the image and likeness of God."[13] In this commandment, the Almighty Himself pleads with man, saying:

> Now I have commanded you to acknowledge in thought and in deed that I am the Creator of all, and to honor parents because they joined Me in your formation. If so, guard against destroying the work of My hands and spilling the blood of man, whom I have created to honor Me and to acknowledge Me in all these matters.[14]

The seriousness of the crime of murder is further emphasized in the Talmud with the statement: "In every other law of the Torah, if a man is commanded, 'transgress and suffer not death,' he may transgress and not suffer death, excepting idolatry, incest, and murder."[15]

The intended victim of a murder is compared in the Talmud to a betrothed maiden. Just as a betrothed maiden must be saved from dishonor even at the expense of the ravisher's life, so in the case of intent to commit murder, the victim must be saved even at the expense of the potential murderer's life. The potential murderer is also compared to a betrothed maiden. Just as a person must allow himself to be slain rather than commit murder, so must a betrothed maiden allow herself to be slain rather than acquiesce to being violated.[16]

According to Jewish law, the punishment for murder is death by execution. One must be certain that the accused is guilty of this horrendous crime, however, before sentence is passed. The crime must have been properly witnessed, and the accused must have been appropriately warned that the act he is about to commit is in violation of Jewish law. He must acknowledge at that time his awareness of the law and his intent to commit the crime despite the consequences. The law is so exacting on these matters that the sages were prompted to remark that if the court sentenced one person in seventy years to the death penalty, it was considered a brutal court.

In recognition of the preciousness of a human life and the unparalleled viciousness of murder, Judaism teaches the law of "pursuit." When one person is in pursuit of another with the clear intent to kill, and he does not relent after being warned that such an act is contrary to Jewish law and is punishable by execution, every Jew is duty bound to save the victim if it is within his power to do so, even if the pursuer must be killed in the process. This obligation applies even though no crime has yet been committed and even though the pursuer is a minor, for in such a situation, the intended victim cries out to the Almighty to help him, and we must act as the Almighty's agents.[17] Needless to say, all that is possible must be done to avoid bloodshed; killing the pursuer is a last resort.

A wider application of the law of pursuit is in the case of a woman giving birth in a life-threatening situation. Where it has been medically determined that this crisis has been caused by the fetus, it may be aborted in order to save the woman, for under such circumstances, the fetus would be considered a pursuer.[18] Active or even passive euthanasia, however, is prohibited by Jewish law and would be considered an act of murder. Under those circumstances, we have no right to presume to act as agents of the Almighty. Indeed, the Talmud teaches that a dying person is regarded as alive in all matters. One may not close his eyes, for by doing so he is shedding blood. Rabbi Meir said: He can be compared to a flickering candle. If a person touches it, it will go out. Likewise, if one touches the eyes of a dying person, it is considered as if he took his life.[19]

Jewish law condemns the murder of any human being. The closer the relationship to the victim, the more culpable is the murderer. But no one is closer to a person than he is to himself. One who commits suicide, therefore, commits perhaps the most horrendous of all crimes. Severe punishment in the World to Come is ordained for a person who commits suicide.[20]

VII. You shall not commit adultery.

Even a casual reading of the story of Creation will draw one's attention to the recurring phrase "after its kind," and arouse one's curiosity. The words first appear in the text on the third day, with the creation of vegetation, and subsequently with the creation of all other forms of life in the sea and on the land. A little thought, and the message rings out loud and clear: it is the Divine Will that the diverse kinds in nature retain the characteristics with which they were endowed and not cross over their natural boundaries. This point is reinforced with the law of *kilayim* ("diverse kinds") in the vegetable and animal realms. Note the following:

> You shall not let your cattle mate with a different kind; you shall not sow your field with two kinds of seed; you shall not put on cloth from a mixture of two kinds of material. (Leviticus 19:19)

> You shall not sow your vineyard with a second kind of seed, else the crop—from the seed you have sown—and the yield of the vineyard may not be used. (Deuteronomy 22:9)

I have already explained to you the meaning and significance of *havdalah* in Judaism, how it assigns importance to each creation. The rationale for the prohibition of adultery may very well be based on three considerations: *havdalah*, purity, and honor. Although this commandment proscribes all illicit sexual relations, it refers primarily to adultery.[21] Licentiousness marks the beginning of the breakdown of society, just as honoring family ties is the foundation upon which society is built. The Almighty has programmed all other living things to breed *within their own kind*. He expects human beings to do so as well, to be faithful and to honor one another; for by virtue of the marriage contract between them, they have been designated "their own kind," to the exclusion of all other human beings.

From one perspective, adultery is akin to theft, for the adulterer steals the woman's affection from her husband, to whom it would normally be directed. From another, it is akin to being an accessory to assault, even murder, for there is no telling what action a jealous husband may take. Moreover, should a child result from this illicit union, it will suffer much pain and misery brought on by the thoughtlessness and lust of its parents.[22]

Where the adulterer and the adulteress had both been duly warned of the prohibition against such behavior, they incur the death penalty; where they had not been duly warned, the death penalty is not incurred. In the days of the Temple in Jerusalem, the commission of adultery by virtue of ignorance of the law obligated the transgressor to bring a sin offering.

VIII. You shall not steal.

To what kind of theft does this commandment refer, property or abduction?[23] The Talmud deduces that since the context here is capital offenses, this commandment must likewise refer to such an offense. (This is one of the hermeneutical principles of which I spoke to you in a previous letter. It is called *davar halamed me'inyano*, namely, an interpretation deduced from the text or from subsequent terms of the text.) Abduction is the only kind of theft that carries the death penalty, and then, only where it was properly witnessed and where the perpetrator brought the victim into his home and forced him to work, or sold him into slavery. Considering the horrendous nature of this offense, the severe penalty it holds needs no apologetics.

While the Talmud concludes that this commandment refers to abduction, some of the sages are of the opinion that every kind of theft, namely, robbery, fraud, and all other manner of deceit, is alluded to as well. This is true notwithstanding the fact that these offenses are mentioned specifically in the Torah. Thus we read: "You shall not steal. Neither shall you deal deceitfully with one another . . . you shall not oppress your neighbor. You shall not commit robbery" (Leviticus 19:11-13).[24]

In a sense, taking property that belongs to another person, which certainly includes abduction, is idolatry. For if God grants a person wealth and he is robbed of that wealth, the thief is imposing his will over the Will of God, and if one enslaves a person whom God has given freedom, he, too, defies God. Moreover, total disregard of the rights or property of man, who is the only creature that is created in the image of God, is clearly a manifestation of self-deification.

What could be the rationale for theft in the eyes of the thief? Self-gratification, of course. Let me elaborate a bit on this. To know the motivation of the thief, we must probe the meaning and the parameters of what is known in Judaism as the *yetzer hara* ("evil inclination").

The Midrash teaches: "Were it not for the evil inclination, man would not build a home, marry, have children, or engage in business."[25] On the surface, the words of the Midrash are perplexing. Is it sinful to desire these things? Doesn't every normal human being pursue these pleasures? It is my contention that what is meant by the evil inclination here is the "life force" of the human being, namely, the driving power within him that is responsible for all his accomplishments. I believe that *Rashi* had this definition in mind when on the words in Genesis 8:21, "for the imagination of man's heart is evil from his youth," he commented, "From the moment the embryo bestirs itself to emerge from its mother's womb, it is given the evil inclination."

The evil inclination is given this name because of its potential rather than its nature. Given free rein in man, it will stop at nothing to attain its goal of total satisfaction, even where that would mean harming others physically, taking away what rightfully belongs to them, or violating their rights. Some might liken this drive to what is called in psychoanalysis the "id." Harnessed and sublimated, however, this inclination in man, given to him by none other than the Almighty Himself, can inspire him to actualize his intellectual and spiritual potential, and thus bring him ever closer to conformity with the Divine Will and to the fulfillment of the Divine charge given to him to "master the universe." But how can this be accomplished? Only one way—observance of the *mitzvot*.

The Talmud teaches us that the *mitzvot* are the means to the perfection of man's "life force." Indeed, through the *mitzvot*, the *beast* is transformed into the *human being*, who is the last of God's works, and thus the quintessential creature of Creation.[26]

Theft, fraud, and deceit are indications of an evil inclination that has run amok. Such violations of the Torah, when left unpunished, can lead only to more serious violations and eventually to self-destruction. Where there are witnesses to the offense, the accused must make restitution. Depending upon the property in question, the thief can be made to pay double the value of the stolen article or merchandise, even four times its value. Where he is unable to do so, the court is permitted to sell him into slavery and use the money to make restitution. This ruling applies only to men, however; women were never sold into slavery for such an offense. It is important to take note of the fact that where the accused repents, confessing to the theft of his own free will, double restitution is not imposed upon him. Last, it is forbidden by this commandment to accept stolen property.

IX. You shall not bear false witness against your neighbor.

The Hebrew verb *la'anot* means "to answer." It indicates a response to either a statement or an event that preceded it. The opening words of this commandment are *lo ta'aneh*; they refer to testimony in court. Addressed to a potential witness, the commandment warns him of his responsibility. You, if you are a false witness, says the Torah, shall not bear witness against your fellowman.[27] Jewish law differentiates between one who witnessed an event and gave false testimony regarding it, and one who did not witness the event at all and gave testimony of any kind whatsoever regarding it. The former is termed "false testimony"; the latter, "a false witness." The commandment as it appears here refers to both situations.[28]

In the Deuteronomy text, the phrase is "worthless witness"

instead of "false witness," thus emphasizing the prohibition against giving testimony on a matter where one was not present. The law thus prohibits relying on circumstantial evidence or hearsay in giving testimony.[29] You remember, of course, that according to tradition the words *sheker* ("false") and *shav* ("worthless") were uttered by the Almighty simultaneously.[30] Perhaps this was to emphasize the gravity of both transgressions.

It is important to take note of the fact that the term *neighbor* rather than *brother* appears in both versions of this commandment. This indicates that the law applies not only to testimony given by one Jew against another, but by a Jew against a gentile as well. In addition, had the term *brother* been used, one might have erred, thinking that legitimate testimony by a relative is permissible in a Jewish court, that only false testimony would be prohibited.[31] Last, although this commandment is addressed primarily to witnesses with regard to testimony, it includes talebearing and slandering as well.[32]

X. You shall not covet your neighbor's house; you shall not covet your neighbor's wife, or his male or female slave, or his ox or his ass, or anything that is your neighbor's.

To *covet*, as it appears here, does not mean simply to "desire" but rather to take action upon that desire. Maimonides rules, therefore, that when one lusts after something that belongs to another and badgers that person until he finally agrees to sell that object to him, he has transgressed this commandment. This is true even where the price paid for the object was more than adequate.[33] The law also applies in the following situation: David covets the wife of Joshua. He induces Joshua to divorce his wife so that he can now marry her. By doing so, David has transgressed the tenth commandment.[34]

The text in Deuteronomy substitutes the verb *crave* for *covet* regarding all things except the wife of one's neighbor, where *covet* is used. To *crave* means simply to "*desire*." The necessity for both terms is explained quite succinctly by Rabbi Samson Raphael Hirsch. He points out that coveting is necessary to teach you that even if your intention is to acquire an object legally, you may not covet; craving is necessary to teach you that the sin starts at the moment of craving, even the desire for something that does not belong to us is prohibited.[35]

Now, one might ask, "How is it possible for a person not to crave for something that is beautiful and desirable? Wouldn't such a prohibition be contrary to human nature?" The answer is, "Absolutely not!" Every society has its mores. Living in a society means accepting its mores and abiding by them. One who is raised with these mores from childhood will not lust, much less take action, to attain that which is accepted as forbidden. All the more so must this be the case with regard to the prohibitions in the Torah, for they are not man-made mores but rather absolute truths created by God and given to man. People must be taught to regard all things belonging to others as private property. To crave for these things or to covet them is simply unacceptable behavior.[36]

Let me qualify this commandment somewhat and note that not all forms of coveting are forbidden by Jewish law. The Talmud teaches: "The jealousy of scribes increases wisdom."[37] To covet an individual's tenacity in Torah study or in the observance of *mitzvot*, where such coveting inspires one to do the same, is not only permissible, it is exemplary, and it earns great reward from the Almighty.[38]

Let me conclude this letter with one more thought to ponder. The Torah was revealed to human beings. It addresses human needs and aims to correct human foibles. It is not meant for angels.

The more one studies the Torah, the more he learns, and the more he realizes how much more still remains for him to learn, for Torah study is a lifelong endeavor. Nevertheless, more than study is expected of the Jew. The Torah proclaims: "Hear O Israel the laws and norms that I proclaim to you this day! Study them and observe them faithfully!" (Deuteronomy 5:1). We must put what we learn into practice. Indeed, the *mitzvot* must become the basis of our lifestyle. Still more: it is of the utmost importance that we recognize that just as the Tablets of the Testimony were two, held together as one—the laws between man and God and the laws between man and his fellowman—so must our allegiance to them be indivisible. *To be a good Jew is not merely to observe the* mitzvot *between man and God, nor is it merely to observe those between man and his fellowman; it is to observe both with equal vigor and with equal dedication.*

Last, the Midrash teaches:

> When the Holy One blessed be He spoke to Israel, each and every one of them said: "The commandment is addressed to me personally, for it is not written, 'I am the Lord your God' but rather 'I am the Lord *thy* God.'" The commandments were perceived by every member of Israel, each according to his ability.[39]

Let no one say, "The Torah is too difficult for me; its pursuit is for scholars; its observance is for saints." The Torah was given to every Jew. No Jew is so wise that there is nothing that the Torah can teach him; no Jew is so simple that there is nothing he is capable of learning from it. Indeed, the Torah itself says this most beautifully:

> Surely this instruction which I enjoin upon you this day is not too baffling for you, nor is it beyond reach. It is not in the heavens that you should say, "Who among us can go up to the heavens and get it for us and impart it to us, that we may observe it?" Neither is it beyond the sea that you should say, "Who among us can cross to the other side of the sea and get it for us and impart it to us, that we may observe it?" No, the thing is very close to you, in your mouth and in your heart to observe it. (Deuteronomy 30:11-14)

The Concept of God

My dearest daughter,

I have waited until now to discuss the topic of God because I feel that despite all we shall say on this matter, in the final analysis, the belief in God is rooted in one's heart rather than in one's mind. Ultimately, it is a spiritual awareness rather than a rational argument that brings one to accept the existence of God. For this reason, I wanted first to uproot the bad feelings you had with regard to the role of women in Judaism and engender within your heart a feeling of awe for the Torah and a healthy respect for the system of Jewish law. From what you have written to me in your last letter, I can see that this has been successfully accomplished.

A brief preface before we move to the topic. Having enrolled in your first course in philosophy, you say that you are intimidated, and feel very much inadequate and alone in your meager effort to defend the existence of God to a class of agnostics, particularly when an atheist professor stands at the helm. I must tell you that I, too, took an introductory course in philosophy in a secular university, and was similarly intimidated. After a few sessions, there ensued the inevitable discussion on "God." Knowing that I am a religious person, my professor challenged me. He asked me if I believe in God, and when I answered in the affirmative, he countered, "Then convince me. What proof is there that

God exists?" Somewhat taken aback by the question, I answered timidly, "Quite frankly, I don't have any proof. I always took it for granted that God exists." Irritated by my naivete, he ended the conversation with, "Really, I thought you *yeshivah* boys were thinkers. Apparently, I was in error." Needless to say, I was very embarrassed, and annoyed with both myself and the professor. I went home and began to ask questions. I came to class the following session armed with material. Though I never succeeded in convincing either my professor or my fellow students, they did gain a new respect for me when I confronted them with the following question: "By what arrogance do you and all other atheists dare to assume that reality is limited to what you can see, hear, touch, and comprehend?" And now to the topic of my letter—"God."

The great twelfth-century philosopher and halakhic giant Moses Maimonides opens his *opus magnum*, the *Mishneh Torah*, with the words:

> The foundation of foundations and the pillar of wisdom is to know that there is a First Being who brought every existing thing into being. All existing things whether celestial, terrestrial or belonging to an intermediate class, exist only through His true existence.[1]

Even one who is not very adept in rabbinic literature is cognizant of the fact that precision is the hallmark of Maimonides' works—precise terminology and precise phraseology. Nuances in language are not just coincidental in his writings or merely a matter of style. Whatever Maimonides writes has halakhic or philosophical significance. As such it is intriguing that in the *Mishneh Torah* he refers to the above principle with the words, "to *know* that there is a First Being," while by contrast, in the *Sefer haMitzvot* he refers to it as the *mitzvah* to *believe* in the existence of God. Of course, many have attempted to resolve this apparent contradiction. Let me attempt to do so as well.

Sefer haMitzvot enumerates the 613 commandments of the Torah and discusses each one briefly. The first commandment is to accept the existence of the Supreme Being with resolve and with unqualified commitment. Without God there would be no Torah, no commandments. Indeed, without God there would be nothing, as Maimonides implies in his statement above. Parenthetically, proofs for the existence of God would not only be irrelevant here; they would be counterproductive, for what is expected is a gesture of faith, namely, the belief in that which has not been proved definitively. Based on that belief, commitment to unqualified obedience is demanded. This is not at all meant to imply that Maimonides disapproved of or rejected the various proofs for the existence of God, for he himself employed them in his philosophical treatise, *Guide of the Perplexed.*[2] What it does imply is that philosophical proofs—when they accomplish their purpose, so that what was formerly accepted on faith alone is now accepted because it has been proved to be irrefutably true—would undermine the reward due to the faithful. For one cannot compare commitment based on faith to commitment based on reason. The former is an act of courage, the latter, simply good practical judgment. For this reason, Maimonides lists the commandment in his *Sefer haMitzvot* as the "belief" in the existence of God. We are not obligated to pursue reason and create philosophical proofs for the existence of God, although we certainly are permitted to, if we so choose. The *mitzvah* is simply "to believe."

The first book of the *Mishneh Torah* is called "The Book of Knowledge." The opening section is titled "Laws Concerning the Foundations of the Torah." Most appropriately, the opening statement is: "The foundation of foundations and the pillar of wisdom is to know that there is a First Being." Maimonides wishes to establish the most fundamental of all truths, namely, the existence of God. To his way of thinking, this principle is the nucleus from which all knowledge emanates. In *Sefer haMitzvot* his purpose is to define and to explicate the commandments; he is not concerned with theories of knowledge. In the *Mishneh Torah*, however, this is precisely his concern, for he speaks of "the pillar of wisdom." If man is to *know* anything, says Maimonides, he must begin by knowing that there is a God.

Knowing that God exists is the foundation of wisdom, but knowing God's Essence is beyond human comprehension. Indeed, it was even beyond the potential of Moses, the greatest of all prophets, for when he asked the Almighty, "O let me behold Your Presence," the response was, "Man shall not see Me and live" (Exodus 33:18,20). It is important to bear in mind that this response does not imply that he who sees God is sentenced to death, but rather that "seeing God," that is, comprehending God's Essence, is beyond the capabilities of mortal man.[3]

Man can know only what God has chosen to reveal to him, namely, the Divine attributes that are expressions that connote God's ways in the world. Hence, when Moses asked, "Now if I have truly gained Your favor, let me know Your ways, that I may know You and continue in Your favor" (Exodus 33:13), the Almighty responded positively and declared:

> The Lord! the Lord! a God compassionate and gracious, slow to anger, rich in steadfast kindness, extending kindness to the thousandth generation, forgiving iniquity, transgression and sin; yet remitting nothing [from those who do not repent], visiting the iniquity of fathers upon children and children's children to the third and fourth generation. (Exodus 34:6-7)

Although a full exposition of the Divine attributes is beyond the scope of this letter, clarification of the phrase "visiting the iniquity of fathers upon children," which has been responsible for much misunderstanding and resentment, is certainly in order. As you will undoubtedly remember, in our discussion of the Ten Commandments I gave you the Hirsch translation of this phrase. I also said that I would discuss the issue at greater length in a future letter, so let me do so here.

"The Rock, His deeds are perfect, yea, all His ways are just; a faithful God, never false, true and upright is He" (Deuteronomy 32:4). To posit that God punishes innocent children is incomprehensible and simply unacceptable. For the true meaning of this Divine attribute, we must turn again to the Ten Commandments, where the expression first appears. In both cases, the context is the key to its meaning.

> You shall not make for yourself a sculptured image, or any likeness of what is in the heavens above, or on the earth below, or in the waters under the earth. You shall not bow down to them or serve them. For I the Lord your God am an impassioned God, visiting the iniquity of fathers upon children, upon the third and upon the fourth generation of those who reject Me, but showing kindness to the thousandth generation of those who love Me and keep My commandments.[4]

God punishes the children of the wicked and sinful when they walk in the ways of their fathers, and are themselves wicked and sinful. Such children are likewise referred to as "those who reject Me." Since the same phrase is found in our context, the clarifier there applies here as well.

Nahmanides, in his commentary to Exodus 20:5, writes, "Now the Torah states that this attribute of punishment applies only to 'those who reject Me,' namely, the children who reject God. If the sinner begot a righteous son, he does not bear the iniquity of the father." The matter is also discussed by the prophet Ezekiel:

> The word of the Lord came to me. . . . Consider all lives are Mine; the life of the father and the life of the son are both Mine. The person who sins, only he shall die. Thus if a man is righteous and does what is just and right . . . such a man shall live, declares the Lord. Suppose now that he has begotten a son who is a ruffian, a shedder of blood . . . shall he live? He shall not live. . . . Now suppose that he in turn has begotten a son who has seen all the sins

that his father has committed but has taken heed and has not imitated them . . . he shall not die for the iniquity of his father, but shall live. . . . The person who sins, he alone shall die. A son shall not share the burden of his father's guilt, nor shall a father share the burden of his son's guilt; the righteousness of the righteous shall be accounted to him alone, and the wickedness of the wicked shall be accounted to him alone.[5]

Nahmanides also notes that when a child walks in the evil ways of his father, he is punished not only for his own sins but for the sins of his father as well. This severe measure applies only to the grave sin of idolatry, however, which is the context of the phrase as it appears in Exodus, chapter 20. It does not apply to any of the other commandments.[6] I hope that the matter is now sufficiently clear.

Although the Essence of God has always been a mystery to man, he has been concerned with metaphysics and the implication of God's existence throughout history. Not only sages but poets and scientists have probed the matter of God's existence and His ways, and have offered theories and interpretations based on their culture and their experiences.

As Jews, we have more than the theories and interpretations; we have Divinely revealed truth, the truth that is found in the Torah. No other nation has been so endowed. Alas! no other nation has suffered so much because of this endowment. If nothing else, the very survival of the Jewish people through centuries of persecution and discrimination is valid testimony to the existence of God and to His concern for His nation of Israel.

We know God through the Torah, the Prophets, and the Writings; we know Him through the Oral Law. We know Him through the history of our people, and we know Him through our own personal experiences. But what we know is limited to *human* experience and *human* knowledge. This means that although what has been revealed to us in the Torah about God is absolute truth, our perception of that truth is limited by the fact that we are finite and imperfect mortals.

Would it then be more logical to opt for silence? Though one might make a strong argument for silence—and many have—it is not the most viable posture, for it is virtually impossible to relate to a God of whom one knows nothing and can say nothing, and *relating* is the lifeblood of Judaism.

An argument frequently heard from the skeptic goes something like this:

> If there really were a God, people should have no doubts on the matter. A true God would have made Himself known to humanity in no uncertain terms rather than rely on so-called miracles to establish His existence, for miracles have not convinced those who did not experience them. Considering that this has not happened, how can we believe that there is a God?

Assuming that God exists, we must approach the argument with the following principle in mind: since God has not made Himself known to man beyond question or doubt, it is preferable for man to be in his present condition of ignorance where he must ultimately rely on *faith* to establish in his mind that God exists. Why should that be?

If God were to make Himself known beyond question or doubt, it would deprive man of his uniqueness, namely, his freedom of choice. Faced with absolute proof of God's existence, what rational person would be an atheist? Moreover, the whole system of reward and punishment would crumble. Knowing that God exists—and assuming that it was likewise beyond question or doubt that He revealed the Torah—would make obedience axiomatic. Let us pursue this idea a bit further. If doubt were impossible, what would happen to charity, sympathy, and mercy, the things that bring people together and are fundamental to friendship? They would be endangered, for many people would tend to leave things to God. Finally, a life without faith in God would be bereft of the mystery that comes with the unknown and the unknowable, and the merit that such faith earns for man in the eyes of the Almighty.

Another point must be made regarding proofs: since the time of Immanuel Kant, the eighteenth-century German philosopher, the matter of proofs for the existence of God has been considered moot by most scholars. Kant has argued quite sensibly that God's existence cannot be proved by speculative reasoning. Finite man can deduce nothing concerning an "infinite" Being, he argued. It is rather the human heart and intuition, the encounters and experiences of man throughout history, that are the best sources of knowledge of God.

For these reasons, it is proposed that the "proofs" we are about to offer be taken as logical arguments rather than as definitive evidence, keeping in mind that when they are taken as a unit and put into perspective, they are impressive or at least "food for thought."

The Cosmological Argument

The world has come into existence through the process of cause and effect, for our observation of nature has established that all things have a cause. For example: we stand at the river's edge and witness the impressions made on the sand. How did they get there? The river, of course. But the river waters were driven by the current, the current was created by the ocean that feeds it, and the ebb and flow of the ocean was caused by the winds that themselves are caused. The same is true of objects. We see a table, and we know that it was created by a carpenter. The carpenter got the plans from a designer who modeled his table after a design he saw in a gallery, and so on. It can thus be demonstrated that in nature, everything has a cause. All things are dependent on other things. But a dependent thing cannot be a "final" or "first" cause. Indeed, the very term *dependent* contradicts the term *first.* Yet, there had to be a first cause to start the whole process of cause and effect that we see operating in the world. This First Cause we call "God."

Refutation and Weakness

The last statements are the problematic ones. If we postulate that God is the First or Final Cause who is Himself not caused, we contradict our original premise that all things are caused. For if we allow the possibility that one thing (God) is not caused, why can there not be other things that are not themselves caused? As such the whole argument of cause and effect is weakened. In any event, even if we were to accept the argument as being sound, it leads only to a First Cause. It says nothing of the nature of that First Cause, whether it is at all concerned with man, and whether it is the God spoken of by religion.

The Ontological Argument

The term *God* means "the Being greater than which nothing can be conceived." From this definition it follows that God must exist, for if God does not exist, one can conceive of something greater than God, namely, a God who exists.

Refutation and Weakness

The argument assumes that the term *exists* adds something to the subject, namely, that existence is a quality not already included in the term *God.* The truth is, however, that the term *exists* adds nothing to the subject. When I say, "The house has an oak door," I am qualifying the house and adding information that is not contained in the term *house.* But when I say, "The house exists," I am merely saying that the house is a house. I am not adding any quality to the term. The statement "God exists" adds nothing to the term *God*. This defeats the argument. It should also be noted that conception has no necessary bearing on truth or existence. I can conceive of a blue horse, yet no such animal exists. Interestingly, the ontological argument is the only one of the three to be discussed that is not found in Jewish sources.

The Teleological Argument

This is perhaps the most widely known and the most highly respected of all the arguments for the existence of God.[7] It is also called "the Argument from Design." There is evidence of design in nature, that things have been put together by a purposive mind, an "Intelligent Designer," so to speak. For example: the human body functions in a way that indicates that its parts are coordinated. The same can be said of animal and plant life. This principle also manifests itself in the universe as a whole. Our solar system with its circling planets that operate continuously in orbit, the rising and setting sun, the tides and the seasons, all imply an order or design, and a design implies a "Designer." Just as one who sees a beautifully constructed city knows that it didn't construct itself, but came into being through the skill, intelligence, and effort of architects and craftsmen, so must one who observes the heavens and the earth and all that is within them recognize that they have not come into being by chance but are rather the creations of a Supreme Being, a "Designer" whom we call God. Indeed, the Artist can be discovered from His work.

Refutation and Weakness

There are those who argue that from a scientific point of view there is evidence that the so-called design of the universe is somewhat faulty. They claim that earthquakes, tidal waves, meteors, and volcanos that wreak havoc on the world would all suggest this, and thus imply that there is really no design to the universe. Conversely, one might contend that these powerful destructive forces are themselves part of the design. But then again, the fact that they often leave many innocent and maimed people in their wake puts the whole matter of Divine beneficence into question. One could contend that the tragedies themselves are by Divine design. The fact that this is incomprehensible to man serves only to reinforce the position that man's intelligence is finite. Since all of these conflicting positions are logical, the argument is somewhat neutralized.

The Argument from Morality

Man has an inherent feeling that some forms of behavior are right while others are wrong. This feeling, often referred to as "conscience," though it differs in terms of standards and definitions from one culture to another and from one generation to another, is found in people of all societies. The terms *right* and *wrong*, however, are not synonymous with *pleasant* and *unpleasant*. Most of us would say that a given act might be unpleasant yet right; another, quite pleasant but unquestionably wrong. For example: to visit a hospitalized patient who is suffering from a terminal disease would not be a pleasant task, yet we would consider it the right thing to do. On the other hand, taking revenge on someone who, for personal gain, has caused us much pain and suffering could be a very pleasant task, but most of us would agree that revenge is immoral. Why is this so? From where do we get this sense of morality? It could come only from a source outside ourselves—from God, who has implanted it within our souls.

The Argument from Religious Experience

It is possible for people to experience God directly and indirectly. From the prophets of old, to the mystics, to the sages of talmudic times, people have claimed to have communed with God. Some of us today can testify to personal experiences that would make sense only if God exists. Now it could be argued that though the experience is authentic—far be it from us to question the credibility of the pious—to attribute it to God would simply be self-delusion. While we must recognize the strength of this argument, we must also recognize that many of the people of whom we are speaking were the most respected people of their community. Indeed, they were intelligent and sensible people of unquestionable integrity. Not only does history testify to this, but the literature these people have left for posterity does as well. If we entertain the notion that even the experiences of such individuals were merely delusions, the whole nature of reality is brought into question, human intelligence becomes farcical, and the thought processes of man become exercises in futility. One doubts whether civilized man would care to go so far, for to do so would challenge thousands of years of human progress. Finally, the fact that many of those who had such religious experiences spoke of similar things and came to similar conclusions, though they lived in different times and stemmed from different backgrounds, lends credence to the experience and, consequently, gives greater power to the argument.

The Argument from Tradition

For more than thirty centuries, the Jewish people have handed down a tradition—father to son and teacher to student—that attributes the Torah revealed at Sinai to the Almighty Himself. They have preserved this tradition through the centuries despite being exiled from their homeland and despite persecution in many lands of the Diaspora. Frequent attempts by the nations of the world to annihilate them because of this tradition and its implications have failed to deter them or to weaken their resolve. Now here again, we must recognize that a tradition could be in error or merely an illusion, but it is extremely unlikely that if such were the case it would have gone unchallenged by the prophets, the sages, the philosophers, and the great rabbinic scholars through the ages.

Let us now consider the atheist and the humanist. Atheism is not a philosophical position; it is a personal prejudice. Perhaps the best attack against the atheist is logic. If there is no God, and all that exists is the physical world, then the arguments offered by the atheist have no basis in reality; they result from his physical makeup alone, namely, the chemical reactions that take place in his brain. Were a different set of chemicals combined, a different kind of thinking would result. As such the atheist must admit that there can never be an objective assessment of reality, and though this line of reasoning must lead to the conclusion that it is impossible to prove the existence of God, it is likewise impossible to prove his nonexistence. If one refuses to accept the preponderance of evidence and testimony that has accumulated through the ages that implies the existence of a Supreme Being, the only logical position would be that of the agnostic, who admits ignorance and therefore takes no position. Of course, we must keep in mind that taking no position really means not acting on the position that God exists, which for all practical purposes is taking the position that God does not exist.

Humanism, by contrast, does not deal with proofs for the existence of God because it is simply not concerned with God. The humanist would say: "I don't need God to make me ethical. I am ethical and moral because I have chosen to be so out of personal conviction. It is possible to have an ethical society without God, so why complicate matters with a concept that none of us can agree upon anyway?" There is an appropriate answer to the humanist in a work called The Disputation.[8]

The reason for the close connection of religion and morality taught by Judaism is not far to seek. One of the essential elements in the religious consciousness is the sense of responsibility to God. Such a sense must at all times provide the most effective restraint upon bad action and the most powerful incentive to virtue. The fact that there are to be found agnostics and atheists of high moral life does not invalidate the claim of religion. One might just as well argue that work is not essential to the production of wealth because there are people who have wealth without ever having done any work. We live, after all, in a world that has been fructified for thousands of years by religious ideas, and in such a world, the fruits of religion are sufficiently rich and attractive to be shared by people who have neither worked nor done anything to contribute directly to their growth. Whether morality could exist independent of all religious influences has yet to be discovered. The religious impetus of hundreds of generations may carry people along the paths of moral life for some time, even as the train glides along after the steam is shut off; but without the driving force of religion, stoppage is inevitable, and with that stoppage, end the moral and spiritual values of life . . . wherever we turn, we find that the moral decline is proportionate to the extent of the religious decline; and where disbelief is complete, as in Nazi Germany, the moral decline is complete.[9]

One further comment on humanism: the humanist claims that he is motivated to achieve ethical and moral excellence by his concern for his fellowman. Perhaps this is so. But as virtuous as altruism and brotherly love are, they must be taken with a grain of salt these days. With few exceptions, even the humanist has his price. He is not impervious to the corruption around him. Quite the contrary. Because he believes that he is not being watched from above by the Almighty, he may more easily succumb to temptation, be it monetary or otherwise. In many cases, his humanism is merely a facade put on to impress others, and when he thinks that he will not be exposed, he will compromise his ethics for personal gain. The believer, on the other hand, cannot escape what to him is the scrutinizing eye of the Almighty and the threat of punishment. And though this may not be the ideal motivation for proper conduct and ethical behavior, it does frequently succeed in keeping people on the right path, and it is the end result here that is of ultimate importance.

I have presented to you some of the best arguments for the existence of God. They have been expounded ever so many times by philosophers and theologians through the ages. Almost all of them are found in Jewish sources, but as I have already indicated, none of them has won universal acceptance as a definitive statement on the matter. Together, however, they are certainly impressive. The first three are the product of reason; if anything, they prove the reasonableness of God's existence. The others are the result of man's contemplation of reality and are based on God's concern for the world. Reason provides indirect knowledge of God; it derives from independent thinking and analysis of the environment. Revelation is direct knowledge derived from the encounter with God. Reason is man's effort to find God; revelation is God's effort, as it were, to enable man to find Him.[10]

Study this letter carefully. It can be the basis for many discussions you will have with your professors as well as your friends, and it can serve as a good foundation for any further studies you may wish to pursue on this topic.

The Prophecy Phenomenon

My dearest daughter,

I concluded my last letter to you by pointing out that both revelation and reason have their place in Judaism. Reason provides indirect knowledge of God while revelation, namely, the encounter with God, provides direct knowledge. What it may take reason many generations to discover, revelation provides instantly. Of course, revelation is not something man can bring about on his own; he cannot summon it at will. Man must wait until revelation *comes upon* him from the Almighty Himself. In your last letter, you ask quite innocently how we know that revelation is authentic, that prophecy is a true encounter with the Divine and not deliberate chicanery or mere hallucination. I have, therefore, decided to devote this letter to a delineation of the principles of revelation and prophecy, as found in traditional Jewish sources.

One of the major concerns of philosophy is the meaning of the term *God* and the proofs or disproofs of His existence. Judaism takes God's existence as a given and concerns itself with the relationship between God and man, the community between Creator and Creation. It posits that even more than man is in search of God, God is in search of man, a desire that God has manifested through the medium of prophecy and revelation. Truthfully speaking, had God not been concerned with man and had He not manifested that concern in a clear and comprehensible way, His existence would be irrelevant to man, for it would have no impact on man's life. Let me once more emphasize that revelation is not to be taken as an awareness or understanding that man attains through his own thinking processes. Revelation is communication to man that derives from an outside source, namely, from the Supreme Being Himself. In the encounter, man plays a passive role; he is the recipient of God's word.

Revelation is God's *channel* to man just as prayer is man's *channel* to God. Through revelation, God establishes a relationship: He manifests His concern for man and communicates His message. The initial apprehension of God by the prophet is a frightening and overwhelming experience: "And Moses hid his face for he was afraid to look at God" (Exodus 3:6). It is a humbling experience: "I heard You with my ears, but now I see You with my eyes; therefore I abhor myself and repent, being but dust and ashes" (Job 42:5-6). Above all, it is a spiritually uplifting experience that confirms not only God's existence but man's importance and value to God. Thus revelation offers much more than an intellectual dimension; it is a Divine gesture that offers man security and reassurance, for it shows that God is concerned with the world and with man in particular.

All that we have said thus far is not meant to imply that revelation contradicts or in any way demeans the conquests man attains through reason. Indeed, the relationship of revelation to reason is a wholesome one. This relationship is delineated quite succinctly by the noted theologian of our time, the late Rabbi Isidore Epstein, who writes:

> The relation of reason to revelation can thus be said to be analogous to the relation of the body to the soul, and revelation is richer in content than reason, even as the soul is richer in energies than the body. Yet, both are closely interlinked; and even as the soul which escapes the body can have no existence in the context of earthly life, so can revelation which overthrows reason have no

existence in the context of the social and historical world in which revelation fulfills itself. In brief, while revelation need not necessarily be confined within the limited framework of reason, it can do no violence to reason. This is the test to which the teachings of Judaism, as revealed, may be readily submitted.[1]

As the channel through which the Almighty communicates His message to man, revelation, more particularly the revelation of the Torah, is the foundation upon which Judaism is built—the fact of revelation and its content. And it stands to reason that if God so cared for man that He revealed the Torah to him notwithstanding the fact that by doing so He aroused the envy of the heavenly angels, man should do his utmost to live in accordance with the lifestyle therein.

Now to your question. What about credibility? How can we be sure that the encounters between God and man actually took place? Could not the prophets have been deluded? And what of the Torah itself, could it not have been the work of Moses' hand?

In the argument from religious experience I pointed out to you that the prophets were the most intelligent and the most trustworthy individuals of the nation. To question either their integrity or their sanity would be illogical and would constitute an example of prejudiced thinking rather than reason. With regard to the revelation of the Torah by the Almighty at Sinai, we must keep in mind that it has been handed down by tradition that the entire nation stood at the foot of the mount and heard the words, "I am the Lord your God who brought you out of the land of Egypt, the house of bondage: you shall have no other gods beside Me" (Exodus 20:2). While the possibility exists that an individual may be deluded and by sheer charisma succeed in deluding others, that such an individual would succeed in deluding an entire nation into believing that they had heard a voice from God is simply unreasonable. But even if that had happened, it is hardly believable that such a charade would have endured through the centuries without being discovered.

The truth is that the facts imply the contrary. The history of the Jewish people is a strong argument (if not proof positive) for God's beneficence and the truth of revelation. Their inexplicable survival despite countless attempts by the nations of the world to annihilate them—a bleak reality even in our own day—makes it quite evident to the objective thinker that the Almighty has a personal hand in their destiny, and that He will not allow their future to be determined by the whims of man. Indeed, the enigma that has confounded historians the world over can only be resolved by recognizing that the Almighty did in fact reveal the Torah to Israel, who thus became the *covenantal community*, that this nation has been chosen to fulfill a Divinely ordained mission in the world, and that it will be shielded by the embracing arm of the Almighty so long as it remains committed to that mission.

And now to prophecy. Given that God exists, that He is concerned with man and that He has manifested that concern through revelation, it is quite in order that we investigate the subject of prophecy more fully. Among the medieval Jewish philosophers, Maimonides speaks at greatest length on this matter, and we shall turn to his works first.

Maimonides poses three theories on prophecy:

1. Among those who believe in prophecy, and even among our coreligionists, there are some ignorant people who think as follows: God selects any person he pleases, inspires him with the spirit of prophecy, and entrusts him with a mission. It makes no difference whether that person be wise or stupid, old or young, provided he be, to some extent, morally good. For those people have not yet gone so far as to maintain that God might also inspire a wicked person with His spirit. They admit that this is impossible, unless God has previously caused him to improve his ways.

2. The philosophers hold that prophecy is a certain faculty of man in a state of perfection, which can only be obtained by study. Although the faculty is common to the whole race, yet it is not

fully developed in each individual, either on account of the individual's defective constitution, or on account of some other external cause. . . . Accordingly, it is impossible that an ignorant person should be a prophet or that a person who was not a prophet in the evening should unexpectedly, on the following morning, find himself a prophet, as if prophecy were a thing that could be found unintentionally. But if a person perfect in his intellectual and moral faculties and also perfect as far as possible in his imaginative faculty, prepares himself . . . he must become a prophet; for prophecy is a natural faculty of man. It is impossible that a man who has the capacity for prophecy should prepare himself for it without attaining it. . . .

3. The third view is that which is taught in the Bible and which forms one of the principles of our religion. It coincides with the opinion of the philosophers in all points except one. For we believe that even if one has the capacity for prophecy and has duly prepared himself, it may yet happen that he does not prophesy. It is in that case the Will of God.[2]

The last point of the third theory, that which differentiates it from the theory of the philosophers, is of the utmost importance. As I have already pointed out to you, prophecy comes upon man, but it is an encounter initiated by the Almighty. In the final analysis it is *His* Will that determines who will prophesy. Though it is the law of nature that all those who have the proper constitution, intellect, moral fiber, and training attain prophecy, God may prevent a person so qualified from prophesying, if He chooses to do so. "According to my opinion," says Maimonides, "this fact is as exceptional as any other miracle, and acts in the same way. For the law of nature demands that everyone be a prophet who has the proper physical constitution, and has been duly prepared as regards education."[3]

Maimonides posits that the prerequisites for prophecy are alluded to in the statement of the sages: "Prophecy rests only on one who is wise, strong and rich" (*Shabbat* 92a). The term *wise* includes all intellectual faculties; *strong* implies moral fiber, as the Mishnah teaches, "Who is truly strong, he who subdues his inclination" (*Ethics of the Fathers* 4:1). The term *rich* alludes to contentment, as the sages indicated in the same statement, " . . . and who is truly rich, he who is content with his lot."[4]

What is prophecy? We must begin by clarifying a point in Arabic Aristotelian philosophy, which Maimonides accepted and employed in the development of his theories. There are ten intelligences or powers through which God controls the universe. Each of these intelligences has its own sphere of operation. The lowest of them is known as *Sekhel haPoel* ("the Active Intellect"); its sphere of operation is the material world. Man's soul is derived from the Active Intellect. At first, the soul is totally dependent upon the body. Through the pursuit of man's intelligence, however, the soul develops, converting potentiality into actuality, progressing from one level to the next. It is possible for a person to perfect his soul to the extent that it is able to gradually free itself from the body and reunite with the Active Intellect, says Maimonides. When this happens the person attains prophecy. Maimonides writes:

> Prophecy, in truth and reality, is an emanation set forth by the Divine Being through the medium of the Active Intellect, in the first instance to man's rational faculty, and then to his imaginative faculty; it is the highest degree and highest perfection man can attain; it consists in the most perfect development of the imaginative faculty. Prophecy is a faculty that cannot in any way be found in a person or acquired by man through the cultivation of his mental and moral faculties; for even if these were as good and perfect as possible, they would be of no avail, unless they were combined with the highest natural excellence of the imaginative faculty.[5]

Prophecy is the result of the influence of the Active Intellect upon both the rational and the imaginative faculties of man after he has developed them to near perfection. What is the imaginative faculty? According to Maimonides, it is the faculty of man's mind that receives and retains impressions by the senses, combines them, and forms images. Yet, the highest function of this faculty is performed in sleep, when the senses are at rest, for then it receives, to some extent, impulses from the Active Intellect. This is the nature of dreams that prove to be true and also of prophecy.[6] Indeed, the sages tell us, "A dream is a one-sixtieth part of prophecy."[7]

The difference between dreams and prophecy, says Maimonides, is that dreams reflect events of the day; they are the result of man's imaginative faculty acting upon his intellect while prophecy is the result of man's imaginative faculty reacting to the influence of the Divine Active Intellect. Consequently, the Almighty may choose to withhold impulses from the Active Intellect to a particular person and thus withhold prophecy as well.

As I have explained, in the experience of prophecy, two faculties of man interact with the Divine Active Intellect: his imaginative faculty and his rational faculty. But what happens when the Active Intellect acts only upon one of these faculties of man?

Those whose rational faculty is highly developed and receives influence from the Active Intellect, but whose imaginative faculty is defective either constitutionally or from lack of training so that it cannot receive such influence, are the wise men or philosophers, says Maimonides. Those whose rational faculty is defective but whose imaginative faculty is in good condition so that it receives impulses from the Active Intellect are the statesmen, lawgivers, diviners, and magicians. They believe that they have been given the gift of prophecy but they are in error.[8]

The prophets, wise men, and philosophers can be further subdivided: those upon whom the influence of the Active Intellect is sufficient only for their own perfection, and those upon whom the influence is so abundant that it impels them to influence others. We, therefore, have prophets who were also preachers, and wise men and philosophers who were also teachers.[9]

It is of crucial importance that we recognize that the prophets, despite their high level of perfection, physically, intellectually, and morally, were not angels. They were mortal: human beings with human frailties and human imperfections. Faculties of the body are weak and sometimes corrupted; the imaginative faculty is no exception. At such times, the prophet may be deprived of his ability to prophesy. Our sages tell us that for the entire period during which Jacob, the third patriarch, mourned for his son Joseph, he was unable to prophesy.[10]

In further analysis of the prerequisites of prophecy, Maimonides focuses his attention on the attributes of courage and intuition. Every human being possesses and exhibits at least a minimum amount of courage, says Maimonides, otherwise he would not act to prevent injury to himself. Nevertheless, people differ in their level of courage. In some, courage is limited to instances of self-preservation; in others, it is virtually unbounded. This is likewise true of intuition: all persons possess it to some degree. Most of us are able to perceive basic truths about the people we meet, including aspects of their character, even after the initial meeting. In some persons, their intuitive faculty is so highly developed that their perceptions usually prove to be true. It is as if their intuition is based on sensuous perception. In point of fact, the intuitive faculty in some people enables them to predict events in the future with uncanny accuracy.[11] In the prophets, the faculties of courage and intuition must have been developed to the highest levels possible, and when influenced by the Active Intellect, to near perfection. They were able to transcend the limits of reason and to conceive ideas and predict events that were beyond even the imagination of the most perceptive individuals of their day.[12]

The term *prophecy* is generic, for it encompasses many different levels of encounter between God and man, says Maimonides. These levels are as follows:[13]

The lowest forms of prophecy might more accurately be re-

ferred to as "conditions that have the potential for prophecy." The
first level is that of Divinely inspired courage. It is an outside force
that comes upon a person, inspiring him to do something extraordinary for his fellowman: to save a group of good people from
the hands of the wicked or to bring joy to the masses. In the
writings of the prophets, this influence from the Almighty is called
Ruah Hashem ("the spirit of the Lord"); it is one of action alone.
The recipient is not motivated to preach or write.

All the judges and kings of Israel possessed this influence.
Maimonides writes:

> This faculty was always possessed by Moses, from the time he had
> attained the age of manhood; it moved him to slay the Egyptian,
> and to prevent evil from the two men who quarrelled. It was so
> strong that after he had fled Egypt out of fear, and arrived in Midian,
> a trembling stranger, he could not restrain himself from interfer-
> ing. When he witnessed wrong being done [to the shepherdesses]
> he could not bear it.[14]

The second level is the experience of a compelling force that
motivates one to speak, to write hymns, to chastise one's fellowman when he does wrong, or to discuss theological problems and
the like, all of which are carried out when one is in full command
of his senses. It is called *Ruah haKodesh* ("Divine Inspiration").
All of the *Ketuvim* ("Writings") of the Bible were written through
Divine Inspiration. These two levels of Divine influence are considered prophecy only in the sense that what inspires the recipient is a force that comes from outside his own psyche.

The third level is the first degree of actual prophecy. The prophets introduce their prophecies with the words "And the word of
the Lord came upon me." The Divine influence manifests itself
in a dream experienced at night in which the prophet perceives
an allegory and its interpretation. No speech is heard. Most of
the prophecies of Zechariah were of this nature.

The fourth level, second of dreams, is where the prophet actually hears something clear and distinct but does not see a speaker. This was the case with Samuel in his first prophetic encounter.

The fifth level, third of dreams, is where the prophet sees a person addressing him. Some of the prophecies of Ezekiel were of this nature.

The sixth level, fourth of dreams, is where the prophet sees an angel speaking to him. It applies to most of the prophets.

The seventh level, fifth of dreams, is where the prophet senses that the Almighty Himself is speaking to him, but he sees no image. Some of the prophecies of Isaiah and Micah were of this nature.

The eighth level is the first of visions. A vision is an encounter with the Divine that occurs by day. Here again, the prophet sees allegorical figures and perceives their interpretation. The "covenant between the pieces" perceived by Abraham was of that nature.

The ninth level, second of visions, is where the prophet hears words but cannot identify the source, as with Abraham, when the Almighty told him, "This one [Ishmael] shall not be your heir" (Genesis 15:4).

The tenth level, third of visions, is where the prophet sees a man addressing him. Joshua experienced this at Jericho.

The eleventh level, fourth of visions, is the highest level attained by any prophet with the exception of Moses our teacher. It is where the prophet sees an angel who speaks to him. The vision Abraham saw at the "Binding of Isaac" was of that nature.

With regard to the perception of a speaker in a vision, whom the prophet identifies with the Almighty, Maimonides writes:

> It appears to me improbable that a man should be able to perceive in a prophetic vision God speaking to him; the action of the imaginative faculty does not go so far, and therefore we do not notice this in the case of ordinary prophets. Scripture says expressly, "In a vision I will make Myself known, in a dream I will speak to him"

(Numbers 12:6). The speaking is here connected with a dream, the influence of the action of the intellect is connected with a vision.[15]

Maimonides states emphatically that only Moses was capable of perceiving a voice from God Himself. While he was awake and in complete control of his senses, Moses heard the voice from God. No prophet before or after him was capable of an encounter with the Almighty on that level. This is the meaning of the words, "The Lord would speak to Moses face-to-face, as one man speaks to another" (Exodus 33:11).[16]

As we have seen, Maimonides contends that prophecy was a natural development in man, the result of natural endowments, training, and study. But this was by no means a unanimously held position. Rabbi Judah Halevi, the eleventh-century Spanish philosopher and poet, differs from Maimonides on this matter. He contends that the qualifications are moral, not intellectual. The candidate has to lead a contemplative life. He must have a deep yearning for spirituality and an enduring total absorption in God. Prophecy is a product of the land of Israel bestowed upon the people of Israel as citizens of the land, says Rabbi Judah Halevi. Already experienced by Adam and Noah, prophecy was bestowed upon Abraham, Isaac, and Jacob, and from them was vouchsafed to all the people of Israel.[17] The positions of Maimonides and Halevi are the extremes; the other medieval Jewish philosophers formulated their positions accordingly.

It is important for you to note that for all intents and purposes, the prophetic era ended with the Babylonian exile. This certainly lends credence to the position of Halevi, who held that the land of Israel is crucial to the prophetic experience. With this in mind, one might venture a response to the perennial question, "Why is there no prophecy today?"

The Talmud teaches that a prophet lost his ability to prophesy when he was in a depressed state. This principle was accepted unanimously by the sages. Coupled with the fact that the nation of Israel may never have suffered a greater calamity than being exiled from its homeland, could one not contend with at least a modicum of validity that the Babylonian exile marked the onset of a "national depression" in consequence of which Israel as a nation became totally disengaged from the prophetic experience? When the sages predicted that prophecy would be reinstated only with the return of the exiles to the land of Israel, the restoration of the kingdom, and the rebuilding of the Temple in Jerusalem, perhaps they meant to imply that only a monumental event such as the onset of the Messianic Era could relieve the national depression and thus bring about the return of prophecy.

I believe that we have delineated the matter of revelation and prophecy sufficiently. I urge you to study the material well and assimilate it. As soon as you accomplish this, let me hear from you so that we can continue our studies.

ELEVENTH LETTER

The Meaning of Miracles

My dearest daughter,

I am most pleased to hear that you find my letters both spiritually and intellectually rewarding, and that you look forward to them with the same anticipation as I do to yours. Regarding your request for my permission to show these letters to a friend whom you say is Jewish merely by accident of birth and is searching for a lifestyle that gives meaning to day-to-day living and offers a rational approach to God, a sincere young man who is willing to listen to the message of Torah; my answer is an unqualified "yes."

And now to your query on miracles. "Is the belief in miracles a fundamental principle in Judaism?" you ask. "For if God is the Creator of the world and the law of nature that governs it, why would He have His prophets perform acts that contravene this law? If God really does perform miracles, why have there been no miracles since biblical times and why are there no miracles today?" I see from your questions that you are obsessed with the idea of miracles and their significance in the Divine scheme of things, and that you have some doubts on their validity. Let me, therefore, devote this letter to the topic of miracles and try to resolve your dilemma.

The Talmud states in the name of Rabbi Yosi: "Why is Esther likened to the dawn? To tell you that just as the dawn is the end

167

of the whole night so is the story of Esther the end of all miracles."[1] For all intents and purposes, the historical period of Mordecai and Esther marked the end of the prophetic era and the onset of the nonprophetic era, and with this turn of events, the end of miracles as well.[2] Prophecy and miracles are inextricably bound up with one another: both are manifestations of Divine providence, and both bear a message conveyed through the prophet to the masses of the people. In prophecy, this message is conveyed to them through speeches and exhortations; in miracles, it is demonstrated visually. Rabbi Saadya Gaon, the ninth-century halakhist and philosopher, writes: "God's motive in the performance of a miracle is to have men lend credence to His prophet. Where such a motive does not exist, however, there is no reason for changing any substance."[3] It is, therefore, quite appropriate for our examination of the nature of miracles to follow our discussion on prophecy.

As with prophecy, the term *miracle* is generic. It may refer to an awesome event performed for a multitude of people for one or many different reasons, such as the splitting of the Reed Sea, or to a private act performed for a single person for a very special reason, such as the birth of Moses to Yocheved when she was 130 years old.[4] However, all miracles make the same statement: nature is under the jurisdiction of the Almighty; He uses it as a means for working out His plan for the universe. And although one must perceive everything that occurs in nature as miraculous—in the sense that nature is not a force that operates independently—only the unusual, the inexplicable event, draws one's attention, and upon reflection leads one to recognize in that event the *hand of God*. "I must turn aside to look at this marvelous event," said Moses, "why is the bush not burnt?" (Exodus 3:3).

This brings us to the matter of the essential meaning of miracles. Must we define a miracle as "a suspension of the laws of nature?" Might not an extraordinary act of Divine loving-kindness such as granting a child to a woman who had not conceived in many years and who, after extensive medical treatment, had been told that the chances of her having a child were infinitesimally small, be considered a miracle even though the conception and the birth occurred in a natural way? There is a difference of opinion among the sages on this matter.

Maimonides' position is somewhat ambiguous. On the one hand, he rejects Aristotle's theory of the eternity of the universe, for that would imply the impossibility of miracles. On the other hand, he posits that with Creation the laws of nature were fixed by the Almighty. True, miracles are a suspension of the laws of nature, says Maimonides, but they are of a temporary duration. At all other times, nature conforms with its fixed laws.[5] But there is another approach to miracles brought by Maimonides, which he introduces with "Our sages have said some very strange words. . . . " Let us look at his statement:

> They say that when God created the universe with its present physical properties, He made it part of these properties that they produce certain miracles at certain times, and the sign of a prophet consisted in the fact that God told him to declare when a certain thing would take place but the thing itself was effected according to the fixed laws of nature. If this is really the meaning of the words of the passage referred to, it testifies to the greatness of the author and shows that he held it to be impossible that there should be a change in any laws of nature, or a change in the Will of God after they have once been established.[6]

This position recognizes miracles as events structured within nature, as if nature were programmed by the Almighty, so to speak, to react in unique ways at certain predetermined times. Now it should be pointed out that despite his praise of this position, Maimonides rejected it and maintained that miracles are a temporary suspension of the laws of nature.[7]

As I have already pointed out to you, Saadya Gaon posits that miracles are performed to authenticate the words of the prophet.

For this reason, the miracle had to be a supernatural event such as the combining of natural elements and their transformation into a living organism, for such feats could be wrought only by God.[8] As such Saadya Gaon writes:

> Hence any messenger whom the Creator would choose to carry out His mission, would, as a matter of course, have to be provided by Him with one of these signs. This sign might consist in the subjugation of elements of nature such as preventing fire from burning or keeping water from running, or arresting a heavenly sphere in its course and the like. It might also take the form of the transformation of substances, such as the conversion of an animal into an inanimate object . . . or the transformation of water into blood. . . . When, therefore, one of these signs is presented to the prophet, it becomes the obligation of those men that see it to regard him as holy and to lend credence to what he tells them, for the All Wise would not have presented His sign to him unless he had been found trustworthy by Him.[9]

To emphasize the Divine origin of the miracle, says Saadya Gaon, the prophets were not granted the ability to perform miracles at will, for this might lead the uneducated masses to believe that this ability was natural to them, and that the miracles did not necessarily derive from God.[10]

Among the more contemporary Jewish thinkers, Rabbi Samson Raphael Hirsch also postulates that a miracle is a suspension of the laws of nature; it testifies to the fact that nature, rather than being an independent force, is totally dependent upon the Will of the Almighty. He writes:

> A miracle predicted and accomplished by God proves the Divine character of life's natural order. It becomes evident that the natural order of things not only derives its origin from God, but is rooted in its very existence in God. It exists, not because it once came into being through God, but because and so long as God

desires its continued existence, to teach the Divine character of life's natural order. This is the purpose of the miracle.[11]

A penetrating analysis into the significance of miracles, and the feasibility of their being a suspension of the laws of nature, is offered by the late Rabbi Eliezer Berkovits.[12] The miracle, writes Berkovits, may be one of God's ways to safeguard the world. Because man is free to choose good or evil, it is not at all inconceivable that as a result of human behavior, a situation arises where Divine intervention is necessary in a way clearly understood to be supernatural. For example: Should God's planned outcome of history be in jeopardy because of man's irresponsible actions, His intervention in the process of history might very well be in consonance with His own responsibility. Berkovits explains:

> As the human deed is a manifestation of human responsibility met in freedom, similarly—on an incomparably higher level—the miracle is an expression of Divine freedom made use of in the service of Divine responsibility. At times, when the deed fails, the miracle may be the only corrective. This, of course, means that miracles are not the ideal way of influencing men. Only the deed is according to plan; the miracle is a stopgap on history. The need for the miracle stems from the measure of freedom which is inherent in creation. When freedom misused threatens to break through the limits of the calculated risk that God took with His creation, the freedom of the Almighty might have to bring its trespassings to a halt.[13]

This approach of Berkovits relegates the miracle to a last resort action on the part of the Almighty; Divine interference with what should be exclusively human affairs. The miracle is used as a protective measure rather than a demonstrative impression-making device. It is Judaism's proclamation that the Almighty is the Supreme Lord over nature. He created it. He is its Master, and at times, He may choose to suspend or contravene its laws. There are instances where Divine intervention is initiated because of man's irresponsibility, says Berkovits, but there are other instances where man's behavior is totally irrelevant, and Divine intervention may be necessary for an entirely different reason.

God is the Perfect Being; nothing outside God can be perfect. By creating the universe as an entity outside Himself, as an act of self-denial or self-limitation, says Berkovits, God rendered it imperfect. Were the universe perfect, it would "roll back into God," so to speak. As an imperfect creation, one can conceive of potentially dangerous circumstances that might necessitate the intervention of the Almighty so that His imperfect creation does not run amok. Summarizing, Berkovits writes:

> It is, indeed, not impossible to interpret the laws of nature as nature's God granted independence from the Creator. Through the laws, God might have put His creation on its feet, as it were, enabling it to go its own way to some extent. . . . As human freedom may often result in man-caused suffering, so may—perhaps—nature's freedom, too, at times, lead to nature-caused suffering of the innocent and pure. And as in history, so in nature, too, the Creator's ultimate responsibility may occasionally require Divine intervention.[14]

As to whether the miracle must be a suspension of the laws of nature, Berkovits follows his predecessors and responds in the affirmative, adding:

> If the question means to imply that miracles are impossible because they are contrary to the laws of nature, we must regard it as completely devoid of meaning. . . . A miracle is, indeed, in its essence—even though not always in appearance—unnatural. . . . What is contrary to nature is, of course, naturally impossible. No one who is prepared to give credence to the possibility of miracles ever denied it. . . . That nothing within nature may disrupt the chain of cause and effect does not prove that the Lord of nature may not do it.[15]

The consensus of opinion I have presented to you thus far has been that miracles are Divinely induced events that suspend, albeit temporarily, the laws of nature. But in point of fact we must recognize that nature itself is a miracle. The rising and setting of the sun and the changing seasons, the ebb and flow of the tides, the growth of plant and animal from a single seed and the phenomenon of birth—are these not all manifestations of the Divine hand in the universe to no less a degree than the burning bush or the splitting of the Reed Sea? Even more: nothing in the universe operates independently; everything is continuously in God's hands. We affirm this truth in our prayers daily when we say, "In His goodness, He renews the creation every day constantly." What then makes a miracle so different? In a rather interesting essay on miracles, the noted scholar Dr. Isaac Breuer proposes the following rationale:[16]

The uniqueness of the miracle lies not in the fact that it was produced by the Almighty. He is the creator and master of all that exists in the universe. Nor is the character of the miracle to be recognized in its association with the moral education of man. "In the case of the Nile changing into blood because of the refusal of the Egyptian king to release the Israelites from servitude, the very fact that an upset in the laws of nature appears as a consequence of moral misconduct must not be regarded as out of the ordinary."[17] There is no difference between the law of nature and the law of morality; both derive from the Almighty. "All that nature grants becomes reward or challenge; all that it denies is punishment or trial."[18]

It is obvious to most of us that there is order and regularity in nature, says Breuer. Our experience and the experience of previous generations testify to this truth. Nevertheless, there are occasions when our set theories are challenged by some previously unobserved phenomenon, and we are forced to rethink the laws of nature and make revisions. What this means is that we can never be sure that what we are observing is a genuine suspension of the laws of nature. It may merely be the manifestations of a facet of nature never yet observed by man. Consequently, the theory that posits miracles to be Divinely induced events that suspend the laws of nature is highly questionable.[19]

What makes an event into a miracle is not the quality of the event, argues Breuer, but the fact that it is announced in the name of God. "The most astounding and wonderful event is far from being a miracle as long as it remains a part of the general system of nature." The simplest and minutest event, on the other hand, can be a miracle where it is announced that God is its active sponsor. In this light, the great drama of Purim is not an actual miracle, but the oil that lasted for eight days on Hanukkah is, indeed, recognized as a miracle. The experience of a miracle transforms man into a prophet. For a brief moment, he obtains an unobstructed view of the Almighty working through His design in the universe.[20]

Every miracle is a revelation, and as such it cannot be recognized by man through his normal channels of perception. Balaam's ass sees the angel of the Lord, but Balaam, the great prophet, cannot. Only after God grants him special faculties of perception does Balaam see the angel and react. Moses sees the burning bush as a great sight that beckons his investigation. Only when God calls out to him does he perceive the event as a miracle and hide his face. The Divinely induced special perception is what defines the uniqueness of the event.[21]

We shall conclude our discussion of miracles with an interesting rationale for the lack of public miracles today suggested by the contemporary halakhist and talmudic scholar Rabbi Chaim Zimmerman.[22]

Man's true uniqueness, that which differentiates him categorically from all other creations, is his freedom of will, says Rabbi Zimmerman. It is an attribute man shares with the Almighty alone, for even the angels are not free agents. Freedom is the prerequisite of responsibility. Indeed, without human freedom *mitzvot* would be futile; reward and punishment would be unjust. As such it can be stated unequivocally that freedom is man's most precious possession. In ancient times, when idolatry and magic prevailed in the world, people were readily deceived by witchcraft and the like. True miracles in no way endangered man's freedom of choice because the masses believed that even magicians could perform supernatural feats. A heretofore unobserved phenomenon would not *ipso facto* establish God's existence and His concern for mankind, for many people would take it as an act of magic performed by man. The more man learned about the world, the more sophisticated he became in his understanding of nature, and the more readily he relinquished his superstitions and his belief in magic. Were God to suspend the laws of nature today, the event would undoubtedly be meticulously investigated and subjected to all of the sophisticated knowledge and technology of science and, in the final analysis, says Rabbi Zimmerman, most likely be declared of Divine origin. Such an event might very well establish the existence of God and Divine providence beyond the shadow of a doubt. But God wants His existence and His providence to be left to man's free choice and his faith. This is precisely why there can be no miracles today, says Rabbi Zimmerman. The greater man's mastery of nature through science and technology, the more remote the likelihood of miracles. Only in the Messianic Era, when the existence of God and the commitment to His rule will be universally accepted, will public miracles return, for then man's freedom will no longer be an issue.[23]

The Theodicy—
The Problem of Evil

My dearest daughter,

We have discussed many issues in these letters, and I have felt comfortable with all of them, knowing that I had only to confront your intellect, to present the position of Judaism objectively, and you would "see the light." It was as simple as that, and I was right. The matter you now bring to my attention, that of the theodicy, namely, the vindication of Divine justice in allowing the existence of evil, is not at all like the others. It is perhaps the oldest and the most difficult problem that has confounded humanity throughout history. I know that an appeal to your intellect alone will simply not be enough to win your approval. Faith must play a major role in accepting most of the positions that our greatest Jewish thinkers have taken on this profound philosophical dilemma. But I believe that you have gained enough trust in the integrity of our sages and in the authenticity of the traditions that they have handed down to us, so that you can now make that gesture of faith. Let me begin.

In all honesty, I must tell you that my intent here is not to offer a definitive solution to the theodicy. Considering all that has been written on this subject by prophets, wise men, philosophers, and theologians through the centuries, even to attempt such a formidable task would be rather presumptuous. My purpose in this adventure into the perplexing unknown is to offer you some food for thought from the writings of our sages, both the ancient and the modern, and thus meet this latest challenge in your relentless pursuit of the fundamentals of Torah-true Judaism. My plan is to present and expound upon several ideas, and leave it to your discretion to accept, modify, or to totally reject what has been written and opt to pursue the matter on your own.

I

Why do the righteous suffer while the wicked prosper? Why do the innocent die while many of those stricken with terminal diseases—who suffer excruciating pain and mental agony and who avidly seek the release of death—go on living? Why are some children born physically handicapped or developmentally disabled while others—often unwanted and undeserved—are granted the blessing of good health, only to become a menace to society as adults? Last, the most horrendous tragedy of our time: why did the Almighty remain silent witness to the Holocaust of European Jewry?

The prophet Jeremiah wrote: "Who has commanded and it came to pass, unless the Lord ordained it? Is it not by command of the Most High that good and evil come?" (Lamentations 3:37-38). Indeed, the theodicy is a problem that has defied reason since man began to probe the meaning of his own existence. But it has been a relevant issue only for the believer. The atheist has no need to seek vindication of God. In consequence of his own thinking, he must postulate that whatever is . . . is.

Life is a complicated network of experiences: causes and effects, actions and reactions. It brings happiness to some, suffering to others, and in the end . . . death to us all. At times, it seems to us that things happen without rhyme or reason, that the wicked are free to pursue evil and to mock justice as being merely an illusion. How foolish it is for man to presume to know God's ways. King David wrote:

> How long shall the wicked, O Lord, how long shall the wicked exult? They bluster, they speak arrogantly; all the evildoers act boastfully. They crush Your people O Lord, and afflict Your heritage. The widow and the stranger they slay, and the fatherless they murder. And they think that the Lord does not see; the God of Jacob does not observe. Consider, you most stupid of people; you fools, when will you understand? He who sets the ear, will He not hear? He who forms the eye, will He not see? He who punishes the wicked, will He not punish you?[1]

King David addressed himself to the believer, reassuring him that although the wicked prosper and boast that God is unconcerned with man, their punishment will eventually come. To entertain the notion that the omnipotent Supreme Being of the universe is ignorant of the ways of the wicked or powerless to act upon them is sheer foolishness.

Much like the prophet who writes: "For My thoughts are not your thoughts, neither are My ways your ways, says the Lord" (Isaiah 55:8), it seems that King David would contend that man has neither the knowledge nor the intellectual capacity to probe God's ways, and he must accept that God is just on faith alone. Ultimately, we, too, may be forced to accept defeat and render the matter incomprehensible. I'm sure you can recall the words of Alexander Pope, "Know thyself, presume not God to scan; the proper study of mankind is man."[2] They ring true and on target. But unless and until that position becomes inevitable, we will proceed.

II

The sages spoke of three kinds of evil: evil in nature, namely, earthquakes, volcanos, and the like that leave a wake of innocent victims behind them (disease and death are in this category); evil of mankind, namely, the inhumanity of man against man; and finally the evil man inflicts upon himself through self-abuse. While the evil in nature can be attributed only to God, the others are clearly in man's domain, assuming, of course, that man has free will.[3] Consequently, the frequently voiced complaint "Where was God?" is misdirected. Under the circumstances, "Where was man?" would be more appropriate.

Let me now turn to our sages for some approaches to our problem. There are three statements in the Talmud that are of crucial importance on this matter.

1. "Whatever the All Merciful God does is for the good" (*Berakhot* 60b).

2. "No man bruises his finger [here on earth] unless it was so decreed against him in heaven" (*Hullin* 7b).

3. "There is no reward in this world for following the precepts" (*Kiddushin* 39b).

Although these statements are not necessarily interrelated, they do point in a certain direction and to my way of thinking suggest the following:

God is Good! Whatever God does is good by virtue of the fact that it emanates from His Will. When, from man's perspective, things appear to be unjust, it is due to his limited intellect and scope. Whatever happens to man—or for that matter, any of God's creations—whether it is perceived as good or evil, whether it results from some natural occurrence or from man's inhumanity to man, is in conformity with God's Will. This means that even so trivial a matter as man's bruising his finger, though it may not have been specifically decreed by God as punishment, is nevertheless in conformity with God's Will, namely, His law of nature that has rendered man susceptible to bruising. Whatever happens to man in this world is rooted in God's Will, but it is not necessarily a manifestation of reward or punishment. True retribution is reserved for the World to Come.

While this theory may help us understand *how* things happen to man, it does not explain *why* they happen. While it posits that all things are in conformity with God's inscrutable Will, it does not vindicate God for allowing evil to persist in the world. Nevertheless, it does make an important statement. It posits that ultimately there is justice, for in the end, whether in this world or the next, the "ledger will be balanced."

III

Among the medieval Jewish philosophers, Maimonides assumed the position of the neoplatonists who identify God with the Good. Since God is Good, evil of any kind cannot be derived from Him. If so, we must ask, "What is evil and from where does it come?" Maimonides writes:

> You know that he who removes the obstacle to motion is to some extent the cause of that motion. For example: if one removes the pillar that supports a beam, he causes that beam to move. In this sense, we say of him who removed a certain property that he produced its absence, although absence of a certain property is nothing positive. . . . All evils are negations. Thus for a man, death is evil; death is his nonexistence. Illness, poverty and ignorance are evils for man; all these are privations of properties. . . . It cannot be said of God that He has the direct intention to produce evil; this is impossible. . . . He creates evil only insofar as He produces the corporeal element such as it actually is; it is always connected with negatives, and on that account the source of all destruction and evil.[4]

All manifestations of man's inhumanity to man, says Maimonides, are also due to negation, namely, ignorance or the absence of knowledge and understanding.[5] In proportion to his ignorance, each person brings evil upon himself and upon his fellowman. If people possessed wisdom, they would harm neither themselves nor others, for wisdom prevents hatred and knowledge prevents injury.

There is another point made by Maimonides that we must consider in our quest to comprehend the rationale for the existence of evil in the world. Some of us imagine that there is more evil in the world than good, says Maimonides. When a person compares the happiness he has enjoyed in life to the evil that has befallen him, it may seem to him that the evil is of a far greater quantity. Even if this were true, is the life of one or even several individuals statistically significant? Can we draw conclusions on this matter concerning all of mankind from so small a number? Besides, says Maimonides, man is only a single species in the vast universe. He is of great importance, to be sure, but by what logic must the universe be anthropocentric? Perhaps there are other considerations with which the Almighty must reckon; at times, they may take preference over man's happiness. "It is of great advantage that man should know his station," says Maimonides, "and not imagine erroneously that the whole universe exists only for him."[6] The point is well taken and I will expound upon it presently when I discuss the Book of Job.

Maimonides' position on the theodicy is a common one in Jewish thinking, but I must point out to you that it does not address the suffering of the righteous or the death of innocent children. These are matters of crucial importance in any rationale for the existence of evil in the world. We will have to look further for these answers.

IV

The Book of Job, one of the earliest expositions of the perplexing lot of the righteous, has much to contribute to our understanding of the theodicy, the vindication of God in allowing evil to exist in the world. Let me summarize the narrative for you. In the opening scene of the first chapter, Job, the main character, is depicted as a righteous man. Indeed, the Almighty Himself testifies to Job's righteousness. For this, Job is rewarded with a full family: seven sons and three daughters, and much material wealth. He lives undisturbed, happy and content with his lot, for the first seventy years of his life.

The scene changes. The author transports us to heaven where we are privy to an interesting dialogue between God and Satan. Satan disparages Job for what he calls righteous self-interest, but God defends His trusted servant Job, whom He calls a sincere and pious man. Stubbornly, Satan disagrees: "But put forth Your hand now and touch all that he has," says Satan, "surely he will blaspheme You to Your face" (Job 1:11).

The stage is now set for the testing of Job. Satan is given permission by God to afflict him. First he takes his wealth, then his children, and finally he afflicts Job's body. Job becomes depressed, but he remains staunch in his faith. He cannot comprehend his lot, but he refuses to complain.

Sitting among the ashes mourning for his children, Job sees his three good friends approaching from afar. They have come a long distance to comfort him. For seven days and seven nights they sit with him in silence. Finally, Job ventures to speak. He curses the day on which he was born, wishfully thinking it out of existence. Why? For, were it to disappear from the world, he would not have been born on that day and would never have been destined to such unbearable suffering. Job condemns his lot in life and seeks a rationale for his misery. His friends offer arguments to justify his fate and to vindicate God, but their words fall on deaf ears. Job seeks a direct confrontation with God so that he can plead his case. Finally it comes.

The Lord speaks to Job out of the whirlwind, and His words topple Job from his "throne" of self-righteousness. In utter humility, Job repents, and the Lord forgives him. Job is then rewarded with double his previous wealth, and a new family identical in number. He lives for 140 more years, double the years of his life before the trial. As God had predicted, Job triumphs and Satan is defeated. Man has justified his existence.

One opinion in the Talmud asserts that Moses is the author of the Book of Job.[7] Yet, it is not at all clear from the discussions in the Talmud when Job lived. Opinions are offered that place him anywhere from the time of Abraham to that of Ahasuerus of Persia, a span of about thirteen centuries. Needless to say, if Job lived in the time of Ahasuerus, the book could not possibly have been written by Moses unless it was revealed to him by Divine inspiration. One sage contends that the book is an allegory, that there never was a Job, that he is merely an archetypal figure.[8] Indeed, the great Maimonides subscribes to this opinion.[9] Is this disagreement simply a matter of legitimate differences of opinion, or do the sages have something else in mind? I would suggest the following:

Every generation has its Job, for the character symbolizes man's confrontation with the inexplicable in life, a phenomenon with which he has wrestled since the beginning of time. Indeed, in every generation there are sages and philosophers who display compassion and foresight in an attempt to rationalize suffering and thus bring some understanding to those who are desperately searching for answers to this dilemma of life. And in every generation there is a "Job" who is perplexed by life, who believes that he is suffering unjustly, and who simply refuses to mouth the principle that God rewards the righteous and punishes the wicked, seeing that his own life's experiences testify to the contrary. Perhaps there is a little bit of Job in all of us, a facet of our psyche that is thoroughly perplexed with what is happening in the world, that loves God and disdains evil, and that is truly pained by the inequities of life and terribly disappointed by God's seemingly interminable silence. Conversely, there are those who contend that Job never existed, that no human being could ever be privy to the Divine rationale for life's inequities because no human being is capable of fathoming the Divine Will. Indeed, the thinking of the Infinite One is beyond the comprehension of finite man. And unlike Job in the book, no man can expect to have an encounter with the Almighty that resolves all the perplexities of life. Faith must take over to span the gap between that which is known to us and that which is still unknown . . . the knowable and that which can never be known.

The Book of Job presents four theories on the suffering of the righteous:

Eliphaz, the first of the friends to speak, posits that the righteous are always rewarded for their righteousness just as the wicked are always punished for their wickedness. Although the righteous do sometimes suffer, the purpose of such suffering is to cleanse them of the few sins that they have committed so that when they are taken to their final rest in the next world, it will be in perfect righteousness. Man has been endowed with freedom of will, but it is of a limited nature. Consequently, retribution is based only on what is in man's control.[10] In the words of Eliphaz: "Think now, what innocent man ever perished? Where have the upright been destroyed? As I have seen, those who plow iniquity and sow mischief reap the same" (Job 4:7-8). Sin is man's invention. God cannot be faulted when people sin and are made to suffer for it. Suffering also inspires introspection when it is inflicted upon the righteous, and as such serves to inhibit them from wrongdoing.

The position of Eliphaz on the suffering of the righteous is also found elsewhere in the Bible.[11] Regrettably, the approach does not resolve the problem of the theodicy to the satisfaction of many, nor is the argument for the suffering of the righteous very convincing. Of course, the matter of the suffering of innocent children is not addressed at all.

Bildad, the second speaker, also posits that God is just and man is free. His point of departure from Eliphaz concerns the suffering of the righteous. It may very well be that the righteous are

free of sin, says Bildad. In that case, God brings suffering upon
them in order to reward them twofold in the World to Come: once
for their suffering and once for their righteousness. In this way,
the ledger is balanced.[12]

Bildad's position is certainly not strange to Jewish thinking.
Indeed, the Talmud teaches:

> Rava, and some say Rav Hisda, says: If a man sees that painful suf-
> fering visits him, let him examine his conduct. . . . If he examines
> and finds nothing objectionable, let him attribute it to the neglect
> of the study of Torah. . . . If he did attribute it thus, and still did
> not find this to be the cause, let him be sure that it is chastisement
> of love.[13]

What is chastisement of love? *Rashi* explains: "The Holy One
blessed be He causes him suffering in this world in order to reward
him in the next world over and above his merits." Like the rationale offered by Eliphaz, Bildad's justification for the suffering of
the righteous is not very convincing. He does not offer a definitive answer to the problem of the theodicy or address the matter
of the suffering of innocent children.

Zophar, the third speaker, offers a rather unique approach to
the problem of the theodicy, as interpreted by Rabbi Meir Leibush
Malbim, the renowned Bible commentator of the late nineteenth
century. Man attempts to discover truth, says Zophar, but he is
severely handicapped in this endeavor by his limited intellectual
potential. In all realms, man's knowledge of reality is subjective;
he is intellectually incapable of objectifying truth. Consequently,
what he perceives as truth is continually being revised. (Any repu-
table scientist will admit that what is acceptable as scientific fact
today may very well be relegated to the wastebasket of discarded
notions tomorrow. How much more is this the case in the nebu-
lous realm of interpersonal relations.) Man's judgment of both
himself and his fellowman is highly tainted by subjectivity.[14] He
cannot know himself objectively. How then can he presume to

know others? Consequently, man can never ascertain true righteousness, neither in himself nor in others. Besides, man judges
himself by what he *is* and his fellowman by what he *believes* him
to be; the Almighty judges people by what they *are* in contrast to
what they *could be* by virtue of their potential. They are then rewarded or punished accordingly.[15] In Zophar's words: "But would
that God might speak and open His lips against you; and that He
would tell you the secrets of wisdom, that sound wisdom is mani-
fold, and know that God has overlooked for you some of your
iniquity" (Job 11:5-6). Indeed, there are two kinds of knowledge,
says Zophar, subjective knowledge that man acquires through investigation and experience, and objective knowledge, namely,
absolute truth that exists in God alone and can be acquired by
man only through revelation. The former, as I have already explained, is fallible and continually subject to revision and modification; the latter is infallible and eternally true and relevant. In
consequence of all this, says Zophar, we can speak about things
only with relative certainty. Recognizing our limitations, and in
fairness to both ourselves and others, we have no right to say more
than "it appears to me that such and such is true," knowing full
well that our judgment of reality is at best peripheral.

Zophar's theory is intriguing and certainly offers food for
thought, but here, too, objections can be raised. If it is true that
an individual whom one judges to be righteous and deserving of
reward may in reality be a sinner, what does this say about human
intelligence and perception? Indeed, how would such a theory
square with the Divinely revealed principle that man was created
in the image of God, an ingredient that most Bible commentators interpret as "intelligence superior to that of any other living
creature"? If man is prone to such colossal error and misjudg-
ment, would it not be better for him to disregard his propensity
for exploration and discovery and simply abandon his quest for
truth? Yet, man has been charged by the Almighty to subdue the
earth, and master all there is to know about it. Are we to believe

that the Almighty would charge man to pursue the impossible, to spend his time as an exercise in futility?

Elihu, the fourth speaker in the Book of Job,[16] posits, not unlike the others, that man is free and is essentially master of his own destiny. But he takes the argument much further. The righteous and the wicked have an effect upon *man*, says Elihu, not upon God. Having been endowed with freedom, man has been given the responsibility to preserve both his species and his environment. Righteousness creates a good society while wickedness creates a bad one. In every generation, it is man's responsibility to purge society of its wickedness. He has the ability to do so, for good people are always in the majority. In the words of Elihu: "If you sin, what do you do to Him? If your transgressions are many, how do you affect Him? If you are righteous, what do you give Him; what does He receive from your hand? Your wickedness affects men like yourself; your righteousness, mortals" (Job 35:6-7). The Almighty has equipped every living creature with the wherewithal to protect itself. Why should man alone need to turn to God in helplessness? When wickedness wreaks havoc with the world, therefore, the proper question is not "Where was God?" but rather "Where was man?"

The argument is as powerful as it is disquieting. The matter of the suffering of the truly innocent who are ravaged in crime and war must be recognized as man's doing, not God's. We have no argument with this. But we must also recognize that there are evils that are clearly outside man's domain, such as disease and cataclysmic occurrences in nature. These evils are not addressed by Elihu; they remain unresolved in our minds. Fortunately, we are not left in limbo on these matters. They are addressed in the final speech of the book, the one made by the Almighty Himself.

There are two aspects to God's reply to Job: the fact of the reply and its content. The fact that God replies to man's request for a hearing and his demand for a rationale for his suffering clearly establishes in the mind of the reader that God is concerned with the fate of man. The content of the reply is a powerful attack on anthropocentric thinking, for in truth, whether or not the book is historical, Job is an archetypal character. What is addressed to him applies throughout history to all people who identify with his lot.

In the reply, God is depicted as the "Lord of Wonders" whose deeds are not only beyond man's capability but beyond man's comprehension as well. Our attention is drawn to the beasts of the wild that are remote from man: the lion, the mountain goat, the wild horse, and the ostrich, creatures that not only are free from man's control but were never intended for man's use. Only one conclusion can be drawn from this excursion into the animal kingdom: The universe must not be seen nor its Creator judged from man's vantage point alone. The Almighty has other interests and other considerations with which to reckon, matters concerning which man may be totally irrelevant.

The argument is reinforced in God's second speech, where we are given a description of the hippopotamus and the crocodile. While in the first speech the animals depicted were at least colorful and thus aesthetically pleasing to man—though he cannot benefit from them, he can appreciate their beauty—the animals described in the second speech are repulsive to him. Again, the message is clear. Man must rise above his anthropocentric thinking. He must face reality and recognize that as important as he may be in God's eyes, he is not God's only consideration in the determination of the destiny of the universe. Indeed, just as some of God's creations are irrelevant to man, so are some of His decisions.

I have spoken to you at length concerning the Book of Job and you may be somewhat confused, so let me summarize the positions taken on the theodicy by the characters of this book. Eliphaz espouses the theory found in Scripture that the righteous receive their due reward. If they suffer in this world, it is to cleanse them of the few sins that they have committed, thus enabling them to enter the World to Come in perfect righteousness. Bildad disagrees with Eliphaz regarding the suffering of the righteous and posits that the righteous suffer only "chastisement of love," or punishment without guilt, in order to enhance their reward in the World to Come over and above that which they have earned. Zophar questions man's right and his capacity to judge both himself and others. Positing that man's knowledge is highly subjective—as compared to God's knowledge, which is objective and absolute—Zophar contends that man is capable of knowing only what *is*, not what *could be*. Consequently, man has no way of determining either true righteousness or true wickedness. Elihu considers man's complaint against God to be misdirected. The evil and suffering that prevails in the world is due to man alone; it is his responsibility, therefore, to uproot evil and thus end suffering in the world. Last, comes the response of the Almighty. In these speeches, man is told to leave the matter of managing the world in God's hands, and it is hinted to man, ever so gently, that when he contemplates his existence and God's rule, he should consider the possibility that he is not the center of the universe. A most sobering thought indeed!

V

Let me now turn again to Rabbi Dr. Eliezer Berkovits in his monumental work on the subject, *Faith after the Holocaust*. As the title suggests, Berkovits addresses the question of faith in a generation that has witnessed God's silence to the Holocaust of European Jewry. He introduces his work with the following words:

> There are two principle approaches to the Holocaust of European Jewry: the attitude of pious submission to it as a manifestation of Divine Will, and the more frequently met attitude of questioning and doubt, a position that may ultimately lead to outright rebellion against the very idea of beneficent providence.[17]

The point is well taken. Let me note, however, that these approaches apply not only to the Holocaust but to the whole matter of the theodicy. For as Berkovits himself says, the murder of six million human beings is no more challenging to the principle of beneficent providence than the murder of six. When we consider the problem of evil in the world, we have a tendency to focus on specific events. Why did God allow Pharaoh to build the pyramids with the bodies of Jewish children? Why did God allow the sages of Israel to be tortured and killed by the Romans? This is improper, says Berkovits. Events must be viewed in the context of history, both past and present. Only then is it possible to discern the principle that is in operation, and through this principle comprehend the meaning of evil and its roots. Concerning the Holocaust, Berkovits insists:

> Not for a single moment shall we entertain the idea that what happened to European Jewry was Divine punishment for any sins committed by them. It was injustice absolute. It was injustice countenanced by God. Such absolute injustice cannot be a mishap in the Divine scheme of things. Somehow there must be room for it in the scheme, in which case the ultimate responsibility for this ultimate in evil must be God's.[18]

God is involved in the process of history just as surely as man is, says Berkovits. According to the Bible, God's involvement is to punish the wicked and to reward the righteous. The trouble is that despite the promise, human experience seems to prove otherwise. God's hand is just not seen clearly enough in history. Quite the contrary. From man's vantage point, it seems that God has withdrawn from the historical arena. But to entertain the notion that His withdrawal was motivated by our sinful behavior, says Berkovits, is an oversimplification. Yet, what is the alternative? Must we posit that God allows the innocent to suffer while He remains silent?

The Torah speaks of *hester panim*, that is, "God's hiding of His face." This expression has two facets, says Berkovits. In one context, it means that God turns His face away from the wicked, so to speak, and lets them be punished; in another, that He is indifferent to the suffering of the innocent. While the first is clearly justifiable and quite in keeping with our understanding of the Divine attributes, the second is most perplexing. Why would God abandon the innocent to the machinations of the wicked? Some of the sages contend that *hester panim* is not always a manifestation of punishment, and that this reality must somehow be accommodated into our weltanschauung. But this is easier said than done, says Berkovits. How does one accommodate God's refusal to intervene in the plight of the innocent?

The prophet proclaims: "You are indeed a God who hides Himself, O God of Israel the Savior" (Isaiah 45:15). It is clear that Isaiah sees God as both hiding and saving. Accordingly, His hiddenness is not merely a reaction to man's behavior; it is an attribute of Divine nature. (One might contend here as we did in the Book of Job that it is because He has other considerations.) Were it not for the fact that God is capable of and at times willing to assume the posture of nonintervention into the affairs of man, says Berkovits, man as we know him to be—a creature of moral freedom and responsibility—could never have been created.

We believe that man's character is not predetermined. It is a basic tenet of Judaism that although there are some things about every individual that have been unalterably predetermined by God, over which man has absolutely no control, God does not determine in advance whether a person will be righteous or wicked. For unless the possibility exists for man to be either righteous or wicked, he can be neither righteous nor wicked in God's eyes. We must recognize, argues Berkovits, that what is good is so, because of the possibility of evil and vice versa. With remarkable insight he writes:

If God did not respect man's freedom to choose his course in personal responsibility, not only would the moral good and evil be abolished from the earth, but man himself would go with them. For freedom and responsibility are the essence of man. Without them, man is not human. If there is to be man, he must be allowed to make his choice in freedom. If he has such freedom, he will use it. Using it, he will often use it wrongly; he will decide for the wrong alternative. As he does so, there will be suffering for the innocent.[19]

These words summarize precisely the approach Berkovits takes to the theodicy. To ask why God has allowed evil to exist is to ask why God created man. Since man has been endowed with the wherewithal to create the ideal society where justice and righteousness reign supreme, he has been given the responsibility to do so. Man can create a "Heaven" or a "Hell" on earth. If it becomes a Heaven, he must preserve it; if it becomes a Hell, he must change it. Again, the ultimate question regarding evil in the world must be "Where was man?" We must recognize with whom the burden of responsibility lies, and if putting blame somehow becomes a positive factor that will lead to the establishment of the "good society," we must put the blame on man, where it belongs.

Berkovits makes another important point. Man is both ready and eager to accept God's mercy. Indeed, one of the thirteen Divine attributes revealed to us in the Torah is "long-suffering." God is patient; He tempers justice with mercy. When man sins, God waits. Rather than punish him immediately, God gives man the opportunity to repent; He takes a chance, as it were, with man. But what happens to humanity while God waits for the sinner? Berkovits explains:

While God tolerates the sinner, He must abandon the victim; while He shows forbearance with the wicked, He must turn a deaf ear to the anguished cries of the violated. This is the ultimate tragedy of existence: God's very mercy and forbearance, His very love for man, necessitates the abandonment of some men to a fate that they may well experience as Divine indifference to justice and human suffering. It is the tragic paradox of faith that God's direct concern for the wrongdoer should be directly responsible for so much pain and sorrow on earth. We conclude then: He who demands justice of God must give up on man; he who asks for God's love and mercy beyond justice must accept suffering.[20]

The Berkovits approach is painfully logical and most thought provoking. Like all good theories, it is alluded to in the Talmud.[21] God's greatness does not manifest itself in the display of power, but rather in its restraint. His plan was to appeal to man's conscience, his sense of responsibility to preserve the world. Yes, the Almighty is silent; He sits patiently and waits for man to see the light. He intervenes only when He sees that His ultimate plan for the world is being threatened. Perhaps the best example of such intervention is the history of the Jewish people. The survival of the Jewish people throughout the ages despite the concerted efforts of so many nations to annihilate them is an enigma of history, to be sure.

In all fairness, I must treat the Berkovits approach to the theodicy with the same scrutiny as I did the others and point out to you that he does not address the evil in nature that afflicts the innocent, namely, catastrophic events and disease. In no way can these things be attributed to man. In an earlier work, however, Berkovits does deal with this problem, and he offers the following rationale.[22]

Since God created the world, shouldn't it be perfect? Not at all, argues Berkovits. Quite the contrary. Creation is certainly filled with awe-inspiring beauty, but it also contains elements of sordidness and misery. God is Perfect, but that does not mean that the world must be perfect. Quite the contrary. "It is the worst form of anthropomorphism," says Berkovits, "to suggest that an omnipotent and omniscient God would only be responsible for an immaculate universe."[23] We know from experience that there are imperfections in the universe. It follows, therefore, that imperfection in the universe is in accordance with God's Will. "A perfect universe would have extinguished itself by tumbling back into God," says Berkovits, "a faultless universe, devoid of evil, would not be distinguishable from the Creator."[24] The universe is material; all its components are finite. All life is subject to disease, decomposition, and destruction. Evil in nature is the result of imperfection in nature, a condition that does not differentiate between the young and the old, the guilty and the innocent.[25] Only God is Perfect!

I have offered several approaches to the resolution of the problem of the theodicy, all of which have a common denominator: the only way that God can be vindicated in allowing evil to exist in the world is by accusing man, and by doing so, putting the responsibility where it belongs. Of course, we have had to postulate that man has freedom of will, for without such freedom, man cannot be accused of anything. Human freedom, however, offers a formidable challenge to the doctrine of omniscience, and I will devote the remainder of this letter to an exposition of that issue and several approaches to handling it.

VI

Unless man is free to choose good or evil, he cannot be charged with *mitzvot*. Unless he is free to choose that which will bring him life or death, he cannot be charged to choose life. Maimonides explains the principle of human freedom as follows:[26]

> Every man was endowed with a free will: if he desires to incline toward the path of good and be just, it is within his power to do so. And if he desires to incline toward the path of evil and be wicked, it is within his power to do so. This is known from the

verse, "Behold, the man has become as one of us, to know good and evil" (Genesis 3:22). In other words, man is unique in the world . . . he . . . of his own accord comprehends good and evil and does whatever he desires.[27]

More is implied in this statement than meets the eye. It teaches us not only that man is free but, perhaps even more importantly, that he has been endowed by the Almighty with the ability to distinguish between good and evil, a faculty that makes him responsible for his actions, to be sure, but that also enables him to mend his ways when he has sinned. Indeed, as a free agent he has been given that unparalleled of Divine gifts, the power of repentance. But would not the principle of human freedom preclude Divine omniscience? In the words of Maimonides:

> If you were to ask: "Does the Holy One blessed be He know what will be before it happens? Did He know whether a certain person will be just or wicked or did He not know it? If He knew that a person would be just then it would be impossible for him not to be just. If you say that God knew that a person would be just but that it would be possible for him to be wicked, God did not know the matter clearly."[28]

If man's destiny is not predetermined by God, meaning that he is free to determine his own destiny, does that not make it impossible for God to know what man's choice will be until the moment it is made? Conversely, if God knows what man's choice will be in a given situation, would that knowledge not compel man to make that choice, thereby neutralizing his freedom of will? How can Divine omniscience be reconciled with human freedom? Maimonides takes an epistemological approach to the problem. He writes:

> The Holy One blessed be He does not know things with a knowledge that exists outside Himself, like, for instance, man does. For man and his knowledge are two separate entities; but God and His

knowledge are one, and it is not within the power of the knowledge of man to attain this matter clearly, just as it is not within the power of man to attain and find the truth of the Creator, as it is said, "For man shall not see Me and live" (Exodus 33:20). . . . This is as the prophet said: "For My thoughts are not your thoughts, neither are your ways My ways, says the Lord" (Isaiah 55:8). This being so, it is not within our intellectual power to know in what manner the Holy One blessed be He knows all the creatures and their actions, but we do know without a doubt that man's behavior is in the hands of man and that the Holy One blessed be He neither forces him nor issues edicts against him to do as he does.[29]

Unlike some of the other Jewish philosophers who tried to resolve this problem by compromising either man's freedom or God's omniscience, Maimonides accepted these principles as a given. But for him, it is not a paradox. Man's knowledge and what is termed "God's knowledge" are not merely quantitatively different from one another; they are qualitatively different. Man's knowledge is sequential . . . not so with God. God knows the past, present, and future as one. Time, as man knows it, does not exist in God. From the standpoint of eternity, every moment is absolutely "now."[30] As such God's omniscience in no way precludes man's freedom.

While Maimonides and others attempted to resolve the dilemma by focusing on Divine omniscience, Rabbi Simon Duran, the fifteenth-century Bible commentator and philosopher, focused on human freedom, defining its parameters and limiting its role.[31] The Talmud teaches: "Bat Sheva, the daughter of Eliam, was predestined for David from the six days of Creation but she came to him with sorrow."[32] The Divine plan was for Bat Sheva to marry David, the second king of Israel. Had he waited until the appropriate time, the marriage would have been consummated legitimately. But he was impatient, says Duran, and he took her before the death of her husband Uriah the Hittite. For this reason, the Almighty considered King David's act a sin. While it was predestined for the king to marry Bat Sheva, it was his own decision to take her before the appropriate time because man has the final word in the determination of his destiny. Similarly, we find in the Talmud: "One who is born under Mars will be a shedder of blood: either a surgeon, a thief, or a circumcisor. Rabbah said: 'I was born under Mars.' Abaye retorted: 'You, too, inflict punishment and kill.'"[33] Rabbah had implied that the contention was invalid because he was none of those things mentioned. But being a judge in Israel, Rabbah had the power to sentence people to death. This is what Abaye meant. The meaning here is clear: one may have an inherent predisposition, but how he handles this predisposition is entirely in his own hands. Our sages tell us that the Almighty decrees upon a drop of semen whether the person developed therefrom will be rich or poor, strong or weak, wise or foolish. All of these tendencies are carried within the genetic code of that drop of semen. But the Almighty does not decree who will be righteous and who will be wicked, for "All is in the hands of Heaven except the fear of Heaven."[34]

For all intents and purposes, man has no control over his genetic makeup. In his formative years, he has little control over his environment. His genetic code predetermines his development in some things and predisposes him in others. But he has the power and as such he has been given the responsibility to discover himself and to work out his personality so that he becomes a good person and an asset to society. He must make a concerted effort to sublimate any predisposition toward evil.

Man's ability to overcome adversity by sheer willpower is phenomenal. In a fascinating study of human behavior in the concentration camps during the Holocaust, Dr. Viktor Frankl, a survivor and a psychiatrist of note, who was the father of "logotherapy," wrote the following:

> Human freedom is finite freedom. Man is not free from conditions, but he is free to take a stand in regard to them. The conditions do

not completely condition him. Within limits it is up to him to decide whether he succumbs and surrenders to the conditions. He may as well rise above them and by doing so open up and enter the human dimension. . . . In the concentration camps . . . the beast was unmasked but so was the saint. The hunger was the same but people were different. . . . Ultimately, man is not subject to the conditions that confront him; rather these conditions are subject to his decision. . . . All choices are caused but they are caused by the chooser.[35]

If man is capable of ethical heroism even under the most adverse conditions, as Frankl contends, if he has demonstrated that in the final analysis he is governed by his sovereign will even in life-threatening situations, all the more so is this the case under normal conditions. Despite heredity, environment, or any predispositions that may influence his decision-making process, man has the ability to turn away and do that which was totally unpredictable. This is the meaning of human freedom.

A thought-provoking essay on human freedom was written by the renowned Rabbi Eliyahu Dessler in his masterful work, *Mikhtav me'Eliyahu*.[36] He, too, insists that man has freedom of will, though he limits that freedom to specific realms and times, what he calls "points of conflict between man's good and evil inclinations." For example, the addicted smoker who experiences severe chest pains may resolve in his mind and promise himself never to smoke again. Considering the circumstances, it would certainly be a logical and sensible decision. Experience teaches us, however, that addicted smokers are notorious for breaking such promises. As many a smoker will tell you, "I can stop smoking whenever I want to; I've done it many times." On the morning after his decision to stop smoking, when he craves for a smoke, his evil inclination will begin to work on him, appealing to his sense of logic, reasoning with him that one cigarette will surely not harm him. Before long, the precarious barrier that he had set up to thwart his desire will be broken. He will smoke one cigarette, then another, and continue to smoke until the next chest pain. Such a cycle of self-deception can go on for years. What it proves, says Dessler, is that man is free to choose either of two alternatives: the rational or the irrational. Despite the fact that he knows that the irrational choice will bring him harm or even death, man frequently makes that choice, and he does so of his own free will.[37]

The will is the most powerful facet of the human psyche; it can turn saint into sinner, but it can also turn sinner into saint. Freedom of will is the true "image of God" in which man was created, say many of the sages. Indeed, from among all of God's creations, man alone shares this attribute with his Creator.

There is a great deal of material that I have brought to bear on this most difficult topic. Study it. Think hard on it. Discuss it with your friends, and let me know how you feel about it. I will conclude this letter with some inspiring words written by the revered halakhist and philosopher of our times, the late Rabbi Dr. Joseph B. Soloveitchik:

> Indeed, man's entire spiritual existence is enhanced by his unique privilege to create himself and make himself into a free man. The voluntaristic motif finds its full expression here, for in the final analysis it is the will which is the source of freedom. . . . More power and strength to the will! . . . God created the world for the sake of His Will. Therefore, when God apportioned some of His Glory to mortal man and bestowed upon him the power of creation, He grounded this creative power in man's will. The will outwits the structured lawfulness of the species; it creates a new, free mode of being in man, one which is not enslaved by the rule of the structured lawfulness of the universal but which ascends to the very heavens and cleaves to the Divine overflow. The will is the source of repentance, prophecy and the freedom of the spirit.[38]

THIRTEENTH LETTER

The Messianic Era and Resurrection

My dearest daughter,

Your delay in answering my last letter was to be expected. It takes time to digest philosophical material, and when the topic is one where faith is called for, and it plays a major role, it takes a while after the material has been assimilated before one finds the approach with which he or she can live. You say that you are confused about what Judaism has to say on such important topics as the Messianic Era and the doctrine of the Resurrection of the Dead, and you cannot understand why very little was taught to you in *yeshivah* on these topics. The truth of the matter is that there is so much to be taught and so little time in which to do it, that only the major issues are covered. Assigning priorities in the high school curriculum is a very difficult task. Of course, you must also keep in mind that Judaism is a "this world" religion; it emphasizes the *mitzvot*, our guide to life in *this* world. Eschatology, namely, matters of the next world, are left to the students to pursue on their own. Although the topics with which you are concerned are certainly discussed in the Talmud and Jewish philosophical literature—in point of fact, the belief in the Messiah and resurrection are fundamental tenets of our religion—greater emphasis is put on how to bring on the Messianic Era than on what will take place during that period in history. Be that as it may, I will devote this letter to an exposition of the doctrine of the Messianic Era as well as the belief in the Resurrection of the Dead. I mention the latter separately because, according to Maimonides, resurrection will not necessarily take place during the Messianic Era.

Judaism teaches that the ultimate goal of history is the perfection of society. In the most general sense, the Messianic Era can be understood to be a Divine promise that the ethical and moral values promulgated in the Torah will eventually triumph in the minds of humankind. Zion will become the *spiritual* center of the world and universal world peace will be established. Indeed, the Talmud states: "There is no difference between this world and the Messianic Era except that [in the latter] there will be no subjugation [of the Jewish people] to foreign powers" (*Berakhot* 34b). The doctrine of the Messianic Era is a religious doctrine by virtue of the fact that it is linked to God and to the Bible. Yet, it is also linked to man, for man has the power to initiate the Messianic Era through his commitment and through his behavior. In terms of its realization, therefore, the doctrine has a strong human component, at least potentially. Whether hastened by man or brought in its own time, the Divine promise *will* be realized.

Jewish literature is replete with references to the Messianic Era, yet there is confusion among laymen and differences of opinion among scholars as to what will transpire during this period. Are the pertinent verses in the Prophets and the statements in the Talmud and Midrash to be taken literally or symbolically? Will the Messianic Era be one of miracles? How can the apparent contradiction between one talmudic or midrashic text and another be reconciled? I will attempt to clarify these matters by referring to the writings of medieval and contemporary sages, and we will witness this doctrine emerge, at least to some extent, from beneath the veil of mystery and confusion.

Although there are allusions to the Messianic Era in the Torah, the doctrine as such was not spelled out until the period of the Prophets. This must not be misconstrued to indicate that the doctrine is a product of the mind of man, for the Bible contains only those ideas that were communicated to the prophets directly by the Almighty. Some historians contend that this teaching was born out of social and political conditions, namely, the faltering Jewish state, which in the hands of clever and insightful men was used to create a doctrine that would placate the people. Let me make clear at the outset that this is not only sacrilegious but presumptuous and totally demeaning of the prophets of Israel, whose character and integrity are beyond suspicion.

Although the prophets Amos and Hosea speak of the Messianic Era, it is not until Isaiah that the doctrine is spelled out in detail. In the second chapter of the book, Isaiah begins to speak of the Messianic Era, and in the eleventh chapter, he speaks of *Melekh haMashiah*, the Messianic King himself. Contrary to the belief of some, the Messiah will be mortal, a normal human being of the Davidic dynasty, upon whom will rest "the spirit of wisdom and understanding, the spirit of counsel and courage, the spirit of knowledge and the fear of the Lord" (Isaiah 11:2). His mission will be to establish justice and to gather the dispersed of Israel to their homeland, where they will live in peace and in security. Israel will set the example for the rest of the nations of the world, who will themselves come to the Messiah for guidance and inspiration. In the words of Isaiah:

> He shall sense the truth by his reverence for the Lord:
> He shall judge not by what his eyes behold,
> Nor decide by what his ears perceive.
> Thus he shall judge the poor with equity,
> And decide with justice for the lowly of the land.
> He shall strike down a land with the rod of his mouth,
> And slay the wicked with the breath of his lips.
> Justice shall be the girdle of his loins,

And faithfulness the girdle of his waist.
The wolf shall dwell with the lamb,
The leopard lie down with the kid;
The calf, the beast of prey and the fatling together,
With a little boy to herd them.
The cow and the bear shall graze,
Their young shall lie down together,
And the lion like the ox shall eat straw.
A babe shall play over a viper's hole,
And an infant pass his hand over an adder's den.
In all of My sacred mount nothing evil or vile shall be done;
For the land shall be filled with devotion to the Lord,
As the waters that cover the sea.[1]

The vision of the Messianic Era presented by Isaiah is as spiritually uplifting as it is beautiful. It is reassuring to all those who yearn and work for the triumph of justice, the reward of the righteous, and the recognition of ethics and morality as the noblest of human pursuits. But are the words of Isaiah to be taken literally? Of what import is it to man that the wolf shall dwell with the lamb or that the leopard lie down with the kid? Maimonides enlightens us on this matter:

Let no one think that in the days of the Messiah any of the laws of nature will be set aside, or any innovation will be introduced into creation. The world will follow its normal course. The words of Isaiah, "And the wolf shall dwell with the lamb . . . " are to be understood figuratively, meaning that Israel will live securely among the wicked of the heathens who are likened to wolves and leopards. . . . They will accept the true religion, and will neither plunder nor destroy, and together with Israel earn a comfortable living in a legitimate way, as it is written, "And the lion like the ox shall eat straw." All similar expressions used in connection with the Messianic Era are metaphorical. In the days of King Messiah, the full meaning of these metaphors and their allusions will become clear to all.[2]

The prophet Micah, who lived late in the eighth century B.C.E., almost a contemporary of Isaiah, also prophesied about the Messiah and the Messianic Era. Like Isaiah, Micah prophesied that the Messiah will be of the Davidic dynasty, and that he will gather the dispersed of Israel to their homeland. The nations of the world will look to Israel for spiritual guidance, and war will become a relic of the past. In his own words:

> In the days to come,
> The mount of the Lord's house shall stand
> Firm above the mountains;
> And it shall tower above the hills.
> The people shall gaze upon it with joy,
> And many nations shall go and say:
> "Come, let us go up to the mount of the Lord,
> To the house of the God of Jacob;
> That He may instruct us in His ways,
> And that we may walk in His paths."
> For instruction shall go forth from Zion,
> The word of the Lord from Jerusalem.
> Thus He will judge among the many peoples,
> And arbitrate for the multitude of nations,
> However distant;
> And they shall beat their swords into plowshares
> And their spears into pruning hooks.
> Nation shall not take up sword against nation;
> They shall never again know war.[3]

Micah also introduces new ideas in his prophecies. The Almighty will unite the gathered exiles into a great nation, and He will reign over them in Mount Zion through His appointed King Messiah. The nations of the world will fear the now mighty nation of Israel, for God will give them "horns of iron" and "hooves of bronze,"[4] and they will "crush many people."[5] Those very nations that had taunted Israel and had mocked the name of God will "now be covered with shame"[6] and fear God. They will come to the house of God to seek instruction on how they may walk in His ways. The punishment exacted upon Israel for their sins will endure until the birth of the Messiah and the return of the dispersed of Israel to the land of Israel.[7]

According to the prophets, the reconstitution of the State will bring about the reunification of the kingdom of Judea with the kingdom of Israel. The new State will be blessed with political stability and spiritual perfection. All Jews will accept upon themselves the commitment to God and to the Torah, and they will exert a profound ethical influence upon the rest of the world. For Zion will become the spiritual center of the world, in which capacity it will remain for the duration of the Messianic Era.[8] It should be understood, however, that spiritual supremacy means just that; it does not imply political control over the world. The national aspiration prophesied by the prophets meant that the Jewish people would be sovereign; they would be forever free from foreign rule or intrusion. It is also important to note that the doctrine of the Messianic Era as prophesied and preached is a universal one, for the perfection of Israel would affect the rest of the world and would inspire universal commitment to God. According to the prophet Zechariah, there will even be a yearly pilgrimage of the nations to Zion. He writes: "And it shall come to pass that everyone that is left of all the nations which came against Jerusalem shall go up from year to year to worship the King, the Lord of Hosts, and to keep the feast of Sukkot" (Zechariah 14:16).

In terms of the fate meted out to the wicked in the Messianic Era, there will be no differentiation made between the wicked of Israel and those of the other nations. All the wicked of the world will be punished for their sins; it will be meted out to them measure for measure.

I must bring to your attention the unequivocal posture of Jewish Messianism. Unlike its counterpart in Christianity, even the Messianic Era is a *this world* concept. It does not profess that the solution to the vexing problems of this world is escape into another, a world that is unconnected with the struggles and the hopes of the present. On the contrary, it is totally congruent with the most fundamental principle of Jewish thought that posits that man is essentially good and he is capable of bringing about his own salvation. Indeed, optimism is the hallmark of Jewish Messianism. In contradistinction from Christianity, one might say that Jewish Messianism is an escape from *fantasy into reality*. Rabbi Isidore Epstein expressed the idea of a "this world" Messianic Era quite succinctly when he wrote: "The kingdom of God as Judaism sees it, as Judaism originally created it, is full of life, of earthly life. It is a kingdom which is to be built here on earth, under Divine guidance, by the hands of man and realized as the result of human struggles and Divine discipline."[9]

Let me develop this idea more fully. An important distinction must be made between the Messianic Era as depicted by the prophets and that which is depicted by the apocalyptists, whose writings span a four-hundred-year period from the second century B.C.E. to the second century C.E. The apocalyptic literature deals with eschatology, the period referred to as "the end of days." Parenthetically, let me point out that the apocalyptic books—whatever value they may have historically—were never accepted by the sages into the canon as part of the Bible, that is, as holy writings. The prophets and the apocalyptists differed on matters such as the designated time of the Messiah, whether man has the power to bring the Messianic Era sooner than its designated time, and how the Messiah will come. While the prophets optimistically concentrated on the human element of Messianism, namely, man's perfectibility, the apocalyptic writers—disillusioned with man—concentrated on the Divine element. Epstein delineates the fine distinction:

> The prophets laid emphasis on the present life. They saw in the present, Divine forces at work for the training of humanity in righteousness, and conceived the future not as something unconnected

with the present but as an organic result thereof. . . . The apocalyptic writers, on the other hand, despaired of this world and of human nature. They saw around them only misery and human suffering and could not believe in the establishment of a Divine order in any world organically connected with the present. They consequently directed their hopes to a future on the celestial stage, in essential opposition to the present—a future in which a new world would be brought into existence, catastrophically, by Divine intervention, to take the place of the old. To this eschatological future, man can do nothing to contribute.[10]

How ironic that the condition of life in today's society is such that the position of the apocalyptic writers is almost plausible. International greed, widespread dishonesty among people of all backgrounds and nationalities, rampant crime, and the threat of a nuclear catastrophe—the ultimate insult to man's intelligence—has cast man into the depths of despair. Indeed, man is overwhelmed by his situation, a condition he believes to be getting progressively worse, day by day, and many have abandoned all hope for man to redeem himself in the near future.

The apocalyptic writers spoke subjectively of man not much differently than people speak of man today, but they missed the point. They saw the human condition as it manifested itself in their day quite clearly, but they were unable to envision the human potential for good, let alone predict its actualization. The prophets, on the other hand, were well aware of the evils of the society in which they lived, but they did not allow it to blind them to the potential with which man has been endowed by the Almighty. Their prophecies were not mere wishful thinking, as some would contend. Quite the contrary. Their words resulted from a proper understanding of the Torah, one that was confirmed by revelation.

Truthfully speaking, even a superficial understanding of Judaism will lead to the conclusion that the apocalyptic writers could never have been given official recognition in Judaism, for such pessimism is contrary to the Jewish spirit. And although some elements of that literature did gain a foothold, they never changed or in any way affected the core of Jewish thinking or preaching about the Messianic Era.

Let me clarify here that the term *Meshiah Hashem*, as generally found in the Bible, refers to one anointed with sacred oil, which is a ritual of inauguration into the priesthood. The Book of Samuel refers to the king of Israel, who was also inaugurated with the sacred oil. Later in history, the term *Meshiah Hashem* was applied to any person chosen by the Almighty to fulfill a special mission. (In Isaiah 45:1, Koresh, the king of Persia, was spoken of as a *Meshiah Hashem*.) But the first appearance of this term referring to the awaited redeemer of Israel is in the apocalyptic literature. (It should be noted, however, that the term was undoubtedly a familiar one to the masses of the people much earlier in history.) From then on, we read of *Melekh haMashiah*, the Messiah King, and *Yemot haMashiah*, the Messianic Era.

No discussion of the Messianic Era would be complete without mention of the role of the prophet Elijah, a major event-moving character, and *Meshiah ben Yosef*, a minor one. Elijah is first mentioned in his role by the prophet Malachi: "Behold, I shall send you Elijah, the prophet, before the coming of the great and awesome day of the Lord" (3:23). Elijah will arrive before the "Day of Judgment" to announce the coming of the Messiah. According to the Talmud, the announcement must come at least one day before the Messiah arrives.[11] Elijah will also have another role: to settle unresolved halakhic issues.[12] The Talmud appended the term *Teku* to such issues, which is an acronym for *Tishbi yitaretz kushyot ve'abayot*, meaning "[Elijah] the Tishbite will resolve the [halakhic] difficulties and questions."

Meshiah ben Yosef is alluded to in the *Tirgumim*[13] and the Midrash.[14] Rabbi Saadya Gaon delineates his role as follows:

It has been transmitted by the traditions of the prophets that God will cause misfortunes and disasters to befall us that would compel us to resolve upon repentance so that we would be deserving of redemption. This is the sense of the remark of our sages: if Israel will repent, they will be redeemed; if not, the Holy One blessed be He will raise up a king whose decrees will be ever more severe than those of Haman, whereupon they will repent and thus be redeemed (*Sanhedrin* 97b). Our sages also tell us that the cause of this visitation will be the appearance in upper Galilee of a man from among the descendants of Joseph, around whom there will gather individuals from among the Jewish nation. This man will go to Jerusalem after its seizure by the Romans and stay in it for a length of time. Then they will be surprised by a man named Armilus who will wage war against them and conquer the city and subject its inhabitants to massacre, captivity and disgrace. Included among those who will be slain will be the man from among the descendants of Joseph.[15]

Strangely enough, the prophets make no mention of *Meshiah ben Yosef* in their writings. We find mention of him in the apocalyptic books, however, to the effect that he will restore Israel to their homeland and rebuild the Temple in Jerusalem. There, too, we find mention of the fact that he will subsequently be killed by Armilus. But the apocalyptic writers posit that he will be revived by the prophet Elijah in order for him to live in the Messianic Era with *Meshiah ben David* as his viceroy. The battle in which it is said that *Meshiah ben Yosef* will be killed is identified by *Rashi* as the battle of *Gog u'Magog*, which is the last battle before the onset of the Messianic Era.[16]

Putting the events that I have thus far explained into sequential order, the following pattern emerges:

Sin brings punishment in its wake. The sinfulness of the nation of Israel will bring national punishment on the awesome "Day of the Lord." At that time there will be cataclysmic catastrophes: wars, exile, and destruction. This period is known as *Hevle haMoshiah,* which is the difficult prelude to the Messianic Era. (It may very well be upon us today.) Some of the prophets see this period simply as one of judgment, while others feel that it will bring about moral improvement as well. Following these events, there will be a period of national repentance through which Israel will return to their position of favor in God's eyes as they were in the days of old. This will lead to the awaited redemption announced by Elijah the prophet, and will be marked by the ingathering of the exiles and the reunification of the kingdom of Israel. All the world will then recognize and accept the existence of God as well as the merit of Israel, and will accord Zion spiritual supremacy in the world. This will lead to universal peace and security among the nations. The prophet Ezekiel adds that the great wars of *Gog u'Magog* will take place during this period.[17] Some of the sages place these wars before the redemption while others place them after it. This is also true of the Resurrection of the Dead, of which I shall speak later. Regarding the duration of the Messianic Era, there is a wide variety of opinion in the Talmud, with estimates that range from forty to two thousand years.

It is interesting that the medieval sages ventured calculated guesses on when the Messianic Era will arrive, despite the talmudic admonition: "Withered be the bones of those who calculate the end, for they would say, 'Since the predetermined time has arrived, and yet he has not come, he will never come,' but wait for him."[18] Saadya Gaon calculated the Messianic Era to begin in 965 c.e., while *Rashi* figured the year 1352 and Nahmanides, 1358. Perhaps the interminable years of exile produced such a feverish longing for redemption that, to avoid national breakdown, the leaders of the generation felt the necessity to venture guesses. It is of vital importance that you understand, however, that these calculations resulted from compassion and sensitivity to the feelings and yearnings of the people; they were not at all grandiose gestures of egoism, as some have suggested.

With the birth of the State of Israel in our own time, the question of the advent of the Messiah has become a more practical one. Are we presently in the throes of the Messianic Era? Are we in the stage referred to by our sages as *at'halta de'Geulah* (the beginning of the redemption)? While some contemporary rabbinic authorities would regard an affirmative answer to these questions as heresy, others, of equal repute, would tend to agree with it. The matter is discussed at length by Rabbi Chaim Zimmerman, a renowned contemporary talmudic scholar. In a series of questions and answers, he defines the concept of *at'halta de'Geulah* and its parameters, making the following points:[19]

Those of the *Neture Karta*, a religious political group in the State of Israel, argue that the existence of the State of Israel is totally irrelevant to the coming of the Messiah. The period referred to by our sages as *at'halta de'Geulah*, they say, must commence through miracles. In point of fact, the Talmud asserts that this period will be marked by even greater miracles than in the time of the redemption of the Israelites from Egypt.[20] Since this is not happening in the State of Israel today, we could not possibly be living in the stage of *at'halta de'Geulah*.

The belief that the period of *at'halta de'Geulah* must be initiated by miracles is a mistaken one, says Rabbi Zimmerman. Maimonides, for one, adopted the position put forth in the Talmud that, other than the fact that the Jewish people will no longer be subjugated by foreign powers, life in the Messianic Era will be very much like life in the world today. Rabbi Akiva believed the Jewish general Bar Kokhba to have been the Messiah, and he did not expect that great leader to perform miracles.

Some posit that the redemption can be initiated only through the repentance of the masses of Israel. Since this has not taken place—in point of fact, most of the citizens of Israel are not observant of *mitzvot* and the laws of the State of Israel are not made in accordance with the Halakhah—we could not possibly be living in the period of *at'halta de'Geulah*.

The contention that repentance is a prerequisite for redemption is contrary to statements in the Talmud, says Rabbi Zimmerman. In *Megillah* 17b it is explained that the daily *Amidah* alludes to the exile of Israel from their land and the process of redemption. Each benediction symbolizes a particular period, and the benedictions are sequential. The tenth benediction, "Sound the great shofar," speaks of the gathering of the exiles in the Messianic Era. The Talmud states: "When the exiles are assembled, judgment will be visited upon the wicked, as it is said: 'And I will turn My hand upon you and purge your dross away as with lye'" (Isaiah 1:25). It is clear from this statement that the wicked will be among the gathered exiles; they will not have repented. Now, since the benedictions are sequential, and the stage of *at'halta de'Geulah* is alluded to in the seventh benediction,[21] "Look upon our affliction," it will evidently take place before the gathering of the exiles, says Rabbi Zimmerman. It follows likewise that we may very well be in the period of *At'halta de'Geulah* today, despite the fact that the repentance of the entire nation of Israel has not yet taken place.

There are those who claim that the Messianic Era cannot be initiated by nonobservant Zionists, for they do not think and act according to the Torah and the Halakhah.

This, too, is an erroneous argument, says Rabbi Zimmerman. Everything that happens in this world is in accordance with God's ultimate plan. Maimonides explains that there are times when reality is not at all as it appears to us. We observe the wicked fool living in wealth and security, and in his employ is a venerable sage who virtually serves him. Is this justice? The truth is that the wealth that the fool thinks he has amassed for himself is in reality being prepared for a sage who will in the future inherit him. The point is made in the Book of Job: "Should he [the wicked] pile up silver like dust, lay up clothing like dirt—he may lay it up but the righteous will wear it and the innocent will share the silver" (27:16-17).[22] The Talmud teaches that in the Messianic Era, the nations of the world will appear before the Almighty and claim that their accomplishments in technology and economy and their acquisitions of gold and silver—indeed, all that bears the stamp

of human endeavor—was done by them to enable Israel to study
the Torah.

But the Almighty will challenge their claim and reveal that their
motivation was nothing more than self-interest and self-aggrandizement. The meaning of this, says Rabbi Zimmerman, is explained
by the great halakhist of the early twentieth century, Rabbi Hayyim
Soloveitchik of Brisk. The nations of the world will actually be
speaking the truth, he says, for in the Messianic Era even they will
realize that the world was created for the Torah, for Israel to study
the Torah, and for life in the Messianic Era. They will acknowledge the supremacy of Israel in the realm of Torah study and
practice, and they will finally understand that it was the Will of
God that all their accomplishments in this world be for the benefit of Israel. But rather than confess their sins and bear their
punishment, they will add insult to injury and claim that their
intentions had been honorable all along, that the welfare of Israel
had been uppermost in their minds. But the Almighty will chastise
them severely for their deceit, and will spell out their sins with
little compassion. This teaches us an important lesson, says Rabbi
Zimmerman. "Preparation and means for Torah . . . can be affected
by a wicked person or by an entire generation of wicked people,
for a future generation of righteous people."[23] It is a principle stated
in the Talmud and affirmed by Maimonides, that the Almighty
works through the nonobservant to prepare the way for the righteous. As such, argues Rabbi Zimmerman, the nonobservant Zionists will surely take part in the *at'halta de'Geulah*, but their role
may not at all be what they envision it to be.

There are those who argue that the Messianic Era cannot be
brought about by natural historical events, for if that were so, what
would be the purpose of the Messiah? They point out that
Maimonides explains that the Messiah will be a charismatic personality who will gather the exiles of Israel and influence them
to repent and commit themselves to the Torah. He will rebuild
the Temple in Jerusalem and bring all the nations to recognize

the Almighty as the Supreme King of the universe. But there is no one today who has done even one of these things, they say. How then can it be claimed that we are presently in the period of *at'halta de'Geulah*?

We must recognize that the redemption will come in one of two ways, says Rabbi Zimmerman: in its designated time, or "hastened," that is, whenever the Jewish nation proves itself worthy. This tradition is alluded to by the prophet Isaiah. He speaks of the glory of Jerusalem in the Messianic Era, concluding, "The smallest shall become a thousand and the least, a mighty nation; I, the Lord will hasten it in its time" (Isaiah 60:22). A first reading detects a contradiction here. An event that occurs in its time is not hastened. This led the sages to deduce that if Israel is worthy, God will hasten the Messianic Era; if they are not, it will come in its designated time.[24] The former is referred to by the prophet as *ahishenah*; the latter as *b'ito*.

Different rules apply to these conditions, says Rabbi Zimmerman. If the entire nation repents and commits itself one and all to the observance of the *mitzvot*, they will be redeemed immediately through the Messiah, the son of David, and miracles even greater than those that had occurred during the redemption from Egypt will be performed. This is the condition of *ahishenah*. But if the nation does not repent and society follows its normal way, the Messianic Era will come about in its predestined time through the normal historical process, in stages determined by the Almighty. In the latter case, the redemption will be a slow process, according to the Jerusalem Talmud, but once it begins, nothing will stop it from reaching fruition. The people of Israel will return to their homeland and set up their own government. They will no longer be subjugated to foreign powers, and they will repent and accept the *mitzvot*. This will initiate the coming of the Messiah. When the redemption is *b'ito*, there are no miracles. In point of fact, says Rabbi Zimmerman, we are presently in this period of redemption through the normal historical process.

We now come to the last topic of this letter, the doctrine of the Resurrection of the Dead. It is of the utmost importance that it be stated unequivocally at the beginning of this exposition that Resurrection of the Dead, as preached by the prophets and as spoken of by the writers of the Apocrypha and the Apocalypse, as put forth in the Talmud and as expounded by the medieval as well as the modern traditional Jewish philosophers, is *physical resurrection*, namely, the return of the soul to the body, and the revival of life as it once existed in this world. Though there are differences of opinion regarding who will be resurrected and when the resurrection will take place, there has never been any doubt in the minds of the sages of Israel throughout the generations as to what resurrection means. In my letter to you on the theodicy, I spoke of the importance of confidence in the integrity of our sages and the relationship of faith to reason. With regard to resurrection as well, we must rely on the integrity of our sages, and we must let faith take over where reason ceases to function.

The earliest documented expression of the doctrine of the Resurrection of the Dead is found in Isaiah 26:1-19. The prophet sings a song of thanksgiving for the protection of Jerusalem and the fall of the enemy cities. He looks to the future optimistically, prophesying the reinstatement of the kingdom of Israel in the city of strength whose bulwarks are salvation and whose gates are open to accept the righteous. Indeed, says Isaiah, the righteous dead will rise to share the blessedness of the new kingdom. In his own words:

> The dead live not, the spirits rise not; to that end you have punished and destroyed them and made all their memory to perish.[25]

> Your dead shall live, My dead bodies shall arise. Awake and sing, you that dwell in the dust! For your dew is like the dew of light and the earth shall bring to life the spirits.[26]

The resurrection as seen by Isaiah is a limited one; it is a gift promised to the righteous alone. Only those who dedicated themselves to the Torah way of life are worthy to be resurrected; they alone from among God's creations are termed by the prophet "Your dead," that is "the dead who belong to the Almighty."[27]

The second biblical source for the doctrine of resurrection is the Book of Daniel. Written in the middle of the second century B.C.E., Daniel is the first book to speak of a resurrection of both the righteous and the wicked:

> And many of those that sleep in the dust of the earth shall awake, some to everlasting life, and some to disgrace and everlasting abhorrence. And the intelligent shall shine brightly, like the brilliance of the expanse; and they that bring many to righteousness shall be like the stars forever and ever.[28]

Even in the Book of Daniel, the resurrection is not a general one, for he speaks of the "many" who will be resurrected. Of those, the righteous will rise to everlasting life and the wicked to everlasting punishment. Indeed, the wicked will be forced to endure the righteous.[29] But among the righteous another class is distinguished: the wise. They will shine with celestial brilliance, for not only did they observe the *mitzvot* meticulously, but they influenced others to do so as well. Through their instruction and discipline, they set right the masses.[30]

Some contend that a further enlightenment will take place at that time. A select few from every generation will arise and proclaim the true faith to those who are living, and on that day the Lord shall be One and His name One.[31]

These references in Isaiah and Daniel are the only sources in biblical literature for the doctrine of resurrection. The prophecy of the "dry bones," namely, Ezekiel 37, has been accepted by most commentators as an allegory symbolizing the revival of the nation of Israel. There are, of course, sources in the Apocrypha and the Apocalyptic literature that make reference to this doctrine, namely, the books of Hanokh, Barukh, and Maccabim, but since these books were not accepted by the sages as authoritative, I will not discuss them here.

The first of the medieval Jewish philosophers to discuss the doctrine of the Resurrection of the Dead in detail is Rabbenu Saadya Gaon, in his book *Beliefs and Opinions*.[32] He opens his treatise with a declaration that resurrection is a unanimously accepted doctrine in Judaism, its purpose being the execution of retribution. Man, the goal of Creation, has been singled out by the Almighty to serve Him, says Saadya Gaon. In reward for his having freely chosen to do so, he is given eternal life in the world of recompense. Being the philosopher par excellence, Saadya Gaon poses the question of validity: Is the doctrine of the Resurrection of the Dead in conformity with nature and reason, Torah and Jewish tradition? He then systematically refutes the arguments that might be advanced against this doctrine in the aforementioned areas and says the following:

To deny resurrection because it conflicts with the law of nature is inconsistent to the monotheist who believes in the omnipotence of the Creator. Nature is the pattern for existing things created by God; He can abrogate that pattern if he so chooses. To deny this would be to reject the miracles described in the Torah. (You recall this point from our discussion of miracles.) Moreover, says Saadya Gaon, such a position carried to its logical conclusion would negate the doctrine of *creatio ex nihilo* and contradict the definition of the Divine attributes taught by the Bible. This being untenable, Saadya Gaon concludes: "It is therefore clear that whoever admits that the Creator produced everything that exists out of nothing and supported His prophets with marvelous miracles, cannot reject the resurrection or adhere to arguments from nature."[33]

Perhaps the doctrine is a logical inconsistency, continues Saadya Gaon, and as such unreasonable. With the decomposition of the body after death, each cell returns to the earth and is assimilated into those elements from which it was created, that is, earth, fire, air, and water. When a second body is created, portions of the elements are again combined, which, after a given time, again decompose and return to their source. This process is continuous. How then can each body be resurrected in its original form when elements of the first body form part of the second? The argument is based on a false premise, says Saadya Gaon. There is no reason to assume that one body is composed of elements that existed in another. Nature's raw material is so plentiful that the Creator can use new material for each creation. The elements of the decomposed body are never used again; they remain in their basic form until the resurrection. In his words:

> The Creator can therefore afford to disregard the disintegrated portions of the first and second and third and all succeeding bodies in and by themselves, not using them in all subsequent combinations. Thus they would be ready for Him to reunite out of them the parts of every body and to restore the latter whenever it might please Him.[34]

The question of validity is still not fully resolved. What textual proof is there for resurrection? Here Saadya Gaon contends that there are biblical references to it, and he brings the material in Isaiah and Daniel. Although these texts are interpreted figuratively by some, he says, there is no basis for rejecting the literal meaning. And here, Saadya Gaon makes an important qualification. Unless we are forced to interpret biblical passages figuratively for any of four reasons,[35] they should be taken literally.[36]

On the other hand, there are verses in the Bible such as "So He [God] remembers that they were but flesh: a wind that passes away and comes not again" (Psalms 78:39) and "As a cloud is consumed and vanishes away, so he that goes down to the grave shall come up no more" (Job 7:9), and the like, which could be misconstrued to contradict resurrection. If these passages are studied carefully, says Saadya Gaon, it will readily be seen that they are characterizations of *man's* inability to transcend death, a condition of impotence to which he must ultimately yield. The power of God is neither mentioned nor implied in these texts.

On the contrary, man's inability to escape his destiny heightens the power of God, for only God can perform the miracle of resurrection.[37] As you will see later, Maimonides takes the identical approach to this matter.

The last source to be examined by Saadya Gaon is rabbinic tradition. Needless to say, the doctrine of the Resurrection of the Dead is confirmed and strengthened by all that is found in rabbinic literature. Several of the examples he brings to confirm his contention will suffice.

With regard to redemption, we read in the Bible, "Then shall we raise against him [the nation of Ashur] seven shepherds, and eight princes among men" (Micah 5:4). When the sages were asked who these shepherds were, they replied, "We have it on the basis of tradition that they are David, who will be in the center, Seth and Methusaleh, who will be on his right, and Abraham, Isaac, Jacob, and Moses, who will be on his left." Asked who the princes were, they replied, "We have it on the basis of tradition that they are: Ishai, Samuel, Saul, Amos, Zefaniah, Hizkiah, Elijah, and the Messiah."[38] Thus we have an explicit statement in the Talmud that these men will be resurrected in the time of the redemption.[39]

The sages have said that whoever rejects the resurrection of the dead will himself have no share in it. This is a retaliatory measure that is illustrated in the Bible. In chapter 7 of the Book of 2 Kings, the prophet Elisha brought good tidings to the nation of Israel, telling of the period of plenty that would follow the famine in the land. Yehoram son of Ahav disbelieved these good tidings and Elisha said to him, "You shall see it with your own eyes, but you shall not eat of it" (2 Kings 7:2). So, too, will it be with those who deny the resurrection, says the Talmud.[40]

Saadya Gaon concludes his treatise on the Resurrection of the Dead with ten questions and answers in which he indicates the following:

Every righteous and penitent Jew will be resurrected in the Messianic Era. They will rise with whatever blemishes they had when they died so that their families will recognize them; then they will be healed. They will partake of food, marry, and live no differently than they had lived before. Eventually, they will be taken to the World to Come where, much like Moses on Mount Sinai, they will live a purely spiritual existence. Regarding the people who will be alive at the onset of the Messianic Era, there is no established dogma, says Saadya Gaon. Some contend that they will never die; others, that they will die a normal death but return to life again so that they would be no different from those who had been resurrected. Still others contend that they will live long lives (400-500 years), then die, but come to life again in the World to Come. It is clear that Saadya Gaon favored the last position, but good arguments can be brought to substantiate all three positions.[41]

Let me now delineate the position of Maimonides, for no discussion of Jewish philosophy would be considered adequate without consulting his writings. Motivated by a letter from the Jews of Yemen, Maimonides wrote a treatise entitled "The Treatise on the Resurrection of the Dead."[42] The Jews of Yemen had requested that he enlighten them on the matter, for they were confused by the fact that he had postulated that the greatest reward for man is in the World to Come, where existence is purely spiritual. Some had misinterpreted this as a denial of resurrection. Despite his answer to their query, notes Maimonides, the community remained confused, so he decided to write an entire treatise on the subject. His treatise made the following points:

Resurrection is a cardinal principle of the Jewish faith, and whoever rejects it will have no share in the World to Come. As taught by the prophets, this doctrine postulates that at a time that pleases the Creator, the departed will return to life. This means that their souls will return to their bodies and they will live again, says Maimonides. Like Saadya Gaon, Maimonides posits that these individuals will live normal physical lives, and after a long life they will die. As to when the resurrection will take place, there is no established time, says Maimonides. It may come about before, during, or after the Messianic Era.[43] It should not be assumed that all biblical passages that seem to refer to physical resurrection of the individual were unanimously accepted by the sages at face value, says Maimonides. Although some of these passages must be taken literally, others should be taken figuratively; still others were subject to differing opinions. Some of the Bible commentators contended that the vision of the "dry bones" (Ezekiel 37) speaks of the resurrection of the individual while others contended that it refers to the restored kingdom of Israel. In such instances, says Maimonides, one may adopt either opinion.

If resurrection is a doctrine that is so fundamental to our religion, one may wonder why is it not mentioned explicitly in the Torah. In point of fact, says Maimonides, there are many biblical passages that appear to deny resurrection, such as "When a man dies, will he live again" (Job 14:4) and "For the nether world will not praise You, death will not extol You; they that go down in the pit will not hope for Your truth; the living, only the living can give thanks to You, as I do this day . . . " (Isaiah 38:18-19). The resolution of this problem is put forth by Maimonides in a detailed analysis of the vein in which the prophets wrote, and he concludes his analysis with the following:

With regard to the problematic texts in Job and in Isaiah, we must recognize that the prophets spoke on these subjects in terms of the natural potential of things. When Job asked whether man will live again he meant to imply that it is not within the laws of nature that man should rise up and live again after death. By natural law death is permanent. But the law of nature is irrelevant in this regard, for resurrection is a *supernatural* act, namely, a manifestation of God's intervention in the process of nature. There is no difference between Job's query and that of Moses, who asked, "Shall we bring forth water for you out of this rock?" (Numbers 20:10). Both questions were asked in accordance with the law of nature, and as such, both would certainly be answered in the negative. Of course, what is true regarding the verse in Job is likewise true regarding the verse in Isaiah and would be true of any other biblical text.[44]

Regarding the lack of a specific text in the Torah that teaches resurrection, Maimonides' approach is unique. We must recognize the nature of prophecy and the level of understanding of the masses of Israel at the time of the enslavement in Egypt, says Maimonides. The encounter with Divinity that took place at this juncture in Jewish history was not only beyond the experience of both the Hebrews and the Egyptians; it was beyond their comprehension as well. Neither the Hebrews nor the Egyptians believed in miracles. When Moses appeared before Pharaoh and turned his rod into a serpent, he was thought to be merely a magician, and Pharaoh commanded his magicians to do the same.[45] The new nation of Israel had to be reoriented. The people had to learn to accept prophecy as communication with the Divine, and the miracle as an act of God performed through his prophet. But the process had to be a gradual one, says Maimonides, the learning had to be experiential. In the beginning, everything said to the people had to be on their level of understanding. The prophet could not expose them to ideas that were beyond them. Reward and punishment would be given to them in this world, which in their idiom meant that their crops would either be successful or they would fail. Miracle after miracle were performed for them until at last, when they witnessed the greatest miracle of all, namely, the revelation of the Torah at Mount Sinai, they were convinced of the Divine origin of these acts, and they exclaimed, "Behold, the Lord our God has caused us to see His glory and His greatness, and His voice have we heard out of the midst of the fire: this day we have seen that God speaks with man, who nevertheless may live" (Deuteronomy 5:21).

Only after many generations, when prophecy and miracles became firmly rooted in the culture of Israel and there no longer existed any doubt as to the authenticity of the prophet and the validity of his word as the word of God, was the doctrine of the Resurrection of the Dead presented to the people. For such a doctrine had to be accepted on the prophet's word alone; it could not be subjected to either logical or empirical verification. Had it been presented to the people of Israel prematurely, at a time when the authority of the prophets had not yet been firmly established, says Maimonides, it might have been totally rejected by them.[46]

From Maimonides, we move to Joseph Albo, the fifteenth-century Spanish philosopher of whom I have already spoken in my letter to you on prayer. Albo was quite familiar with the works of both Saadya Gaon and Maimonides. Much of his philosophy is based on their ideas. Not so with regard to his explanation of the doctrine of resurrection, however. Here his thinking is unique. Resurrection is a doctrine that is not only conceivable, says Albo, it is one that is confirmed by events that occurred in the Bible. The revival of the son of the widow of Zerafat by Elijah and the revival of the son of the Shunammite woman by Elisha are two such events. This being the case, says Albo, it is not at all unreasonable that we be expected to accept resurrection as a fundamental principle of our religion.[47] In point of fact, says Albo, resurrection is less miraculous and more logical than the origin of life. In his words:

> The body of the righteous man, by reason of the impression remaining in it of the Divine spirit which it lodged, is more prepared without doubt to receive the same Divine spirit a second time than it was at first, as the sages say: "If those who never had been, came to life, surely those who once had been would come to life again."[48]

According to the sages, says Albo, the resurrection will be initiated by a heavenly dew that will cover the earth and cause the bodies to be revived. This process has been likened, figuratively of course, to the process of human fertilization.[49]

One of the fundamental questions that presents itself regarding resurrection is "Who will be resurrected and to what end?"

Here Albo develops an interesting approach. If we posit that resurrection will include all mankind or all the people of Israel—the
purpose being to reward the righteous and to punish the wicked—
then Daniel 12:2 must be given an allegorical interpretation, as
referring to "the exaltation of the lowly nation in the days of the
Hasmoneans or in the Messianic Era," rather than the resurrection.[50] But this assumption raises another problem. Since the body
of man is continuously regenerating, technically, he has many
bodies in his lifetime. Which body will be resurrected? Do they
not all deserve retribution of some kind or another? This problem can readily be resolved, says Albo, if we postulate that reward
and punishment is meted out only to man's soul. The purpose of
resurrection then would be either to afford the individual the
opportunity to further perfect himself in this world or if not, simply to make known to the world the great power of the Almighty.
Consequently, the verse in Daniel that speaks of the *many* who
will be resurrected would refer to the righteous alone. They will
be revived for either or both of the aforementioned purposes. The
wicked will be revived for no other purpose than to witness the
success of Israel. Moreover, argues Albo, from the last verse of
Daniel, chapter 12, we can place the resurrection sometime before
or during the Messianic Era, and he explains the verse as follows:

> But you go on to the end; you shall rest and arise in your destiny
> at the end of days (Daniel 12:12).

> The word "end" when used without qualification applies to the
> redemption from exile. "You shall rest and arise" alludes to the
> resurrection which will take place in the Messianic Era. . . . [51]

To summarize: The doctrine of the Resurrection of the Dead
as prophesied by Isaiah and Daniel and as postulated by the sages
of Israel is to be taken literally and understood to be physical
regeneration, namely, the return of the soul to the body and the
resumption of normal living. Although this doctrine first appears

in the books of the prophets, it undoubtedly existed as a tradition much earlier, for there are allusions to it in the Torah. Perhaps the reason it does not appear in biblical literature earlier than Isaiah is because the people were not yet ready to assimilate a doctrine that would have to be accepted on the word of the prophet alone. With the exception of Joseph Albo, all of the sages postulate that the purpose of resurrection is to execute judgment, that is, reward or punishment, to the body and soul of man as a unit. The rationale for this position is delineated in the Talmud as follows:

> Antoninus said to Rabbi: "The body and the soul can both free themselves from judgment. Thus the body can plead: the soul has sinned, [the proof being] that from the day it left me I lie like a dumb stone in the grave [powerless to do anything]. While the soul can say: the body has sinned, [the proof being] that from the day I departed from it I fly about in the air like a bird [and commit no sin]." He replied: "I will tell you a parable. To what may this be compared? To a human king who owned a beautiful orchard. . . . Now he appointed two watchmen therein, one lame and the other blind. [One day] the lame man said to the blind, 'I see beautiful figs in the orchard. Come, take me upon your shoulder, that we may procure and eat them.' So the lame bestrode the blind, procured and ate them. Some time later, the owner came and inquired of them, 'Where are those beautiful figs?' The lame man replied, 'Have I then feet to walk with?' The blind man replied, 'Have I then eyes to see with?' He placed the lame upon the blind and judged them together. So will the Holy One blessed be He bring the soul, place it in the body, and judge them together."[52]

Since it is the joined body and soul that has lived in the world, it must be the joined body and soul that is judged, and subsequently rewarded or punished. The verses in the Bible that seem to deny resurrection actually refer to man's potential according to natural law. They assert and emphasize strongly that man cannot escape death, which is the destiny of all living things, nor can he return to life. God and His power are not the object of these passages, nor are they in any way taken into consideration. God, the creator of nature, can superimpose His Will over nature and act as He chooses. Most of the sages contend that resurrection will take place in the Messianic Era, as prophesied by Isaiah and Daniel. Maimonides disagrees. He refuses to pinpoint the time for this event because of his strict adherence to the talmudic dictum: "There is no difference between this world and the Messianic Era except that [in the latter] there will be no subjugation [of Israel] to foreign powers."[53] Isaiah prophesied the resurrection of the righteous of Israel alone while Daniel prophesied the resurrection of both the righteous and the wicked: the former to receive their reward and the latter to be punished. Joseph Albo and Saadya Gaon align themselves with Isaiah while Maimonides makes no statement at all on this matter.

In conclusion: The doctrine of the Messiah and the Messianic Era is a fundamental principle in our religion. It was preached by the prophets and delineated by the sages as well as the Jewish philosophers throughout the ages. It is the hope of humanity for a better, more equitable world. Both the doctrine of the Messianic Era and the doctrine of the Resurrection of the Dead are listed by Maimonides as basic tenets of the Jewish Faith. They have been recited as such by Jews throughout the world in what is known as the "Thirteen Principles of Faith," according to the following formulation:

I firmly believe in the coming of the Messiah: and although he may tarry, I daily await his coming.

I firmly believe that there will be a resurrection of the dead at a time which will please the Creator, blessed and exalted be His name forever and ever.

Postscript

He has told you O man what is good and what the Lord
requires of you: only to do justice and to love righteousness
and to walk humbly with your God.

Micah 6:8

First and foremost, the Torah is a book of law. It is a compendium of 613 commandments revealed by the Almighty to the
ancient Israelites at Sinai with the intent that they should study
it intensively and assimilate it into their personalities so that it
becomes the very fiber of their being, indeed, their *raison d'être*.
They were to become the nation of Israel, a people unique in their
way of life, and they were charged to transmit this way of life to
their children after them throughout the generations.

Given this goal, why does the Torah not commence with the
first commandment given to the Jewish people as a nation, namely,
"This month shall mark for you the beginning of the months; it
shall be the first of the months of the year for you" (Exodus 12:2),
rather than with the story of Creation?

Many of the sages have discussed this question at length, and
they have come up with a variety of answers, all of which point
in the following direction. Creation is a cornerstone of the Jewish faith; it is the foundation of the Torah and fundamental to
the belief in God and in providence. In the words of Nahmanides,
"It is the root of faith, and he who does not believe in this and
thinks that the world is eternal denies the essential principle of
the [Jewish] religion and has no Torah at all.[1] Creation establishes
Divine freedom, but it teaches that man, who was created in the

image of God, has freedom as well, and that on the basis of that freedom he is rewarded or punished. Were the Torah not to have begun with the story of Creation, establishing these truths, there would be no basis for the law.

Interestingly enough, there is a also a great deal that we can learn from what has been omitted in the Creation story.

What is the significance of the phrase "And God saw that it was good"? It appears in the text at the close of each day of Creation and serves as a lesson to us that everything that the Almighty created on that day conformed precisely with His design. This phrase is conspicuously missing, however, on the second day. Why? What is created is not evaluated until it is completed, said the sages. What was created on the second day, namely, the firmament that separated the upper and lower waters, was not completed until the third day. It was then that the waters were concentrated into lakes, seas, and oceans, allowing for the appearance of dry land. Thus the third day's activity is aptly followed by the proclamation "And God saw that it was good."

Of far greater significance, however, is the omission of this phrase entirely after the creation of man. Are we to infer from this omission that man does not conform with the design intended for him by the Almighty? Heaven forbid! Let me rather offer a more logical explanation, one that is both complimentary to man and in harmony with his having been created in the image of God.

"A rose is a rose is a rose." Each and every object of Creation, the inanimate as well as the animate, can be evaluated at the moment it is created. Not only is its potential predetermined, but the degree to which that potential will be actualized in every member of every species is predetermined as well. Inanimate and animate life is subject only to the necessary vicissitudes and imperfections of nature. Not so with man! Though he was created of "dust from the earth," man was also created "in the image of God," the Torah tells us. This teaches us that man is a composite of the earthly and the heavenly, the physical and the spiritual . . .

body and soul, and he operates on both levels. While man's physiology is essentially the same as that of the animal, the similarity ends there. In terms of his essence and his potential for greatness, man is far more than an animal. Most importantly, as I have already pointed out to you, he has been endowed with freedom of will, namely, the ability to superimpose his intellect over his desires and attain a measure of control over his destiny. For better or for worse, man is continually "becoming"; he is perpetually in a state of flux. It has been said that man does not step into the same river twice. But what applies to the river applies to man as well. Let us rather say, "The same man does not step into the same river twice." Today he is good; tomorrow he could be better; the day after . . . better still. This is why man cannot possibly be evaluated and judged until he has completed his life. The words "And God saw that it was good" were omitted with the creation of man to teach us this important lesson.

The meaning of the term *good* vis-à-vis man is of vital concern to every human being. Needless to say, philosophers and theologians have been concerned with the "good life" since early times. For the Jew, of course, the question is more specifically focused. What is the prescription for the "good life" preached by the Torah?

> See I have set before you this day life and good, and death and evil, in that I command you this day to love the Lord your God, to walk in His ways, and to keep His commandments and His statutes and His social laws; then you shall live and multiply, and the Lord your God shall bless you in the land in which you go to possess it.[2]

Rashi explains the message as follows: "If you do good, behold there is life for you, and if you do evil, behold, there is death for you." The ambiguity of this verse led the renowned Rabbi Ephraim Solomon Luntschitz to pose the following question: "Why is the text not written 'good and life, evil and death,' for it is the good that earns man the reward of life, and the evil that incurs the punishment of death?" The answer, says Rabbi Luntschitz, is to teach us that it is improper to do good simply for the reward it promises or to shun evil simply because of the punishment it carries. One must live to do good rather than do good to live![3]

What is the "good life" that is prescribed in the Torah? First, it is to love God and to walk in His ways. And how does one come to love God? Maimonides writes:

> And what is the way that will lead to the love of Him [God] and the fear of Him? When a person contemplates His great and won-drous works and creatures, and from them obtains a glimpse of His wisdom which is incomparable and infinite, he will immedi-ately love Him, praise Him, glorify Him, and long with an exceed-ing longing to know His great name.[4]

The overwhelming experience of the greatness of the Creator as being unbounded and inestimable leads to the feeling of love, says Maimonides, the desire to praise Him, and the yearning to know Him. And how does one express his great love of God? Again, Maimonides writes:

> Whoever serves God out of love, occupies himself with the study of the law and the fulfillment of the commandments and walks in the path of wisdom, impelled by no external motive whatsoever, moved neither by fear of calamity nor by the desire to obtain material benefits; such a man does what is truly right because it is truly right, and ultimately, happiness comes to him as a result of his conduct.[5]

To walk in God's ways is a charge to man not only to follow the commandments in the Torah, but *imitatio Dei*, literally, to imi-tate the ways of God. Just as we perceive God to be merciful, so must we be merciful; just as He is truthful, so must we be truth-ful; just as he is slow to anger, so must we be slow to anger. Even more, says Rabbi Naphtali Zevi Judah Berlin in his Torah commentary. To keep God's commandments alludes to the Written Law; to keep His statutes and His social laws alludes to the Oral Law.[6]

The prophets also spoke of the "good life." To wit: "He has told you O man what is good and what the Lord requires of you: only to do justice and to love righteousness and to walk humbly with your God" (Micah 6:8). "Good" implies the laws between man and his fellowman; "what the Lord requires of you" implies the laws between man and God. The former are for the preservation of society; the latter for the perfection of the individual.[7] King David advised all those who seek the lifestyle ordained by God to "shun evil and do good, seek peace and pursue it" (Psalms 34:15). Our sages teach us that to shun evil means to follow the negative commandments of the Torah; to do good means to follow the positive ones.[8]

What is the "good life?" It is the life to which the Creator Himself testifies, "And God saw that it was good," for it has been lived in conformity with what He intended for it. It is a life that focuses not only on man's relationship with God, but on his relationship, indeed, his responsibility to his fellowman as well. It is the life in which the pursuit of Torah means not only study but practice, where scholarship leads not only to self-improvement but also to an involvement with the improvement of the status of one's fellowman as well. It is a life in which integrity is at least as important as erudition, where religiosity is synonymous with ethics and morality.

We are living in paradoxical times. On the one hand, exponents of the "good life," let alone its adherents, are becoming increasingly difficult to find, but on the other, there is significant movement, particularly among young adults, to seek out the "good life" as preached by the Torah, the life we identify as traditional Judaism. In these thirteen letters, I have addressed matters of God and matters of man. I have discussed many principles of the Jewish faith. In some of these letters my purpose was simply to impart knowledge, the heritage of our forefathers; in others, it was to offer an approach to a vexing problem, an explanation that might help to clear the air or ease the agony of confusion. I do not claim to have a monopoly on truth, nor do I purport to have fully tapped the sources on these issues. My purpose was only to whet the appetite and thus inspire further study. If I have succeeded in influencing but a single person, in touching one Jewish soul, one outstretched hand, I shall forever be thankful to the Almighty. For, "Whoever preserves a single soul in Israel, Scripture ascribes merit to him as though he had preserved a complete world" (*Sanhedrin* 37a).

Notes

First Letter

1.Purim Lecture, March 1973.

Second Letter

1. The material in this letter is based partially on a lecture given by Rabbi Dr. Joseph Soloveitchik at Yeshiva University in Spring 1957.

2. Samson Raphael Hirsch, Torah Commentary on Genesis 1:5 (London: Isaac Levy, 1959).

3. There are seven Noachide commandments: appointment of judges, sanctification of God, prohibition of idolatry, prohibition of murder, prohibition of illicit sexual relations, prohibition of theft, prohibition of eating a limb from a living animal.

4. Cf. *Rosh Hashanah* 33a; also *Eruvin* 96a.

5. David Abudraham, *Abudraham haShalem* (Jerusalem: Usha, 1960), p. 25.

6. This rationale is found in the *Anaf Yoseph* commentary in *Siddur Otzar haTefillot* (New York: Sepher, 1946), vol. 1.

7. Abudraham, p. 42.

8. Cf. *Siddur Rashi* (Jerusalem: *Kiryah Ne'emanah*, 1963), no. 267, and the *Biur Halakhah* to *Shulhan Arukh, Orah Hayyim: Hilkhot Berakhot* 47:14. *Tallit* and *Tefillin* are prohibited to women today because of other considerations.

9. Emanuel Rackman, "Arrogance or Humility in Prayer," *Tradition* 1 (1958): 17.

10. This material is part of a major address given by Rabbi Aaron Soloveitchik at the Midcontinental and National Leadership Conference of the Union of Orthodox Jewish Congregations of America, November 1969.

11. Ibid.

Third Letter

1. The material in this letter is based in part on my introduction to *The Cantor's Manual of Jewish Law* (Northvale, NJ: Jason Aronson, 1994).

2. *Sanhedrin* 22a.

3. Cf. *Pirke De'Rebbi Eliezer,* chap. 19.

4. Cf. David Hoffmann, Torah Commentary, Leviticus, intro. (Jerusalem: Mossad Harav Kook, 1953), pp. 64-65.

5. Cf. Rashi on Genesis 4:3, also Hoffmann, op. cit., p. 64.

6. Cf. Hoffmann, op. cit., p. 65.

7. *Yoma* 36a.

8. *Berakhot* 23a.

9. *Taanit* 27b.

10. *Berakhot* 26b.

11. See my article "The Maimonides Rationale for Sacrifice," *Hebrew Studies* 24 (1983): 33-39.

12. Moses Maimonides, *Guide of the Perplexed,* III, chap. 32.

13. Maimonides, *Mishneh Torah: Laws of Kings* 11:1.

14. Ibid., *Me'ilah* 8:8. Additionally, we read: "How much more should man be on guard not to rebel against a commandment decreed for us by the Holy One blessed be He, only because he does not understand its reason; or to heap words that are not right against the Lord, or to regard the commandments in the manner in which he regards ordinary affairs."

15. Maimonides, *Guide of the Perplexed,* III, chaps. 23 and 24.

16. The point is emphasized by I. Twersky, *Introduction to the Code of Maimonides* (New Haven and London, 1980), pp. 410-411: "The second pitfall warned against in the *Me'ilah* passage is that of 'regarding

the commandments in the manner in which he regards ordinary affairs,' i.e., dismissing as worthless the laws for which one understands no cause ... divinely revealed laws are by no definition rooted in reason and geared to advancing perfection; they are intrinsically true and valuable. Hence failure to find their underlying truths is a temporary setback not an irreversible censure."

17. *Babylonian Talmud: Introduction to Seder Kodoshim*, ed. I. Epstein (London: 1948), pp. xx-xxxii. See also *Redak* (Rabbi David Kimhi) Commentary on Jeremiah 7:21, *Mikraot Gedolot* (Lublin: *Mefitze Torah*, 1898) who likewise differentiates between obligatory and voluntary sacrifices.

18. Maimonides, op. cit., chap. 26, p. 125.

19. Epstein, op. cit., p. xxvi.

20. Hoffmann, op. cit., p. 63.

21. It is certainly a logical assumption from the writings of Maimonides. Cf. *Guide of the Perplexed*, III, p. 51, where he clearly postulates thought or contemplation of God to be the highest perfection of man. In his words: "Our sages have pointed out to us that it is a service of the heart, which explanation I understand to mean this: man concentrates all his thoughts on the First Intellect, and is absorbed in these thoughts as much as possible."

22. Cf. Aaron HaLevi, *Sefer haHinukh*, trans. C. Wengrov (Jerusalem, 1978), vol. 1, p. 363.

23. Maimonides, *Sefer haMitzvot: Mitzvat Aseh* 5.

24. Maimonides, *Guide of the Perplexed*, III, chap. 32, p. 152.

25. Ibid., chap. 17, p. 74.

26. Eliezer Berkovits, *Prayer* (New York, 1962), p. 28.

27. Ibid., p. 74.

28. *Yevamot* 64a.

29. Cf. *Berakhot* 10b.

30. Cf. *Berakhot* 34b.

31. Ibid.

32. Joseph B. Soloveitchik, *Halakhic Man* (Philadelphia: Jewish Publication Society, 1983), p. 43.

33. Berkovits, op. cit., p. 77.

34. Joseph Albo, *Sefer haIkkarim*, IV, chap. 18.

35. Ibid.; cf. also Berkovits, op. cit., pp. 78-80.

36. *Yevamot* 64a.

37. *Shulhan Arukh, Orah Hayyim* 119:1.
38. *Berakhot* 21a.
39. *Bereshit Rabbah* 14:11.
40. Cf. *Berakhot* 26b.
41. *Shulhan Arukh, Orah Hayyim* 90:9.
42. *Berakhot* 28b.
43. *Pirke Avot* 2:18.
44. *Berakhot* 31a.
45. Maimonides, *Mishneh Torah: Laws of Prayer* 4:16.
46. *Shulhan Arukh, Orah Hayyim* 98:1.
47. *Mishnah, Berakhot* 5:1.
48. *Berakhot* 7a.
49. Maimonides, op. cit., *Laws of the Foundations of the Torah* 1:1-3.
50. Louis Jacobs, *Hasidic Prayer* (New York, 1973), p. 23.
51. According to the Kabbalah there are ten *sefirot* (levels of emanation) through which God acts upon the world. The highest (or most removed from the world) is *Keter* ("Crown"); the lowest, which is the one that acts directly upon the world, is *Shekhinah* ("Presence"), also called *Malkhut* ("Kingship"). These emanations are the intermediary agents between the spiritual and the material worlds.
52. Cf. *Rashi* on Genesis 1:1.
53. *Yoma* 44a.
54. *Mishnah, Berakhot* 3:3.
55. Cf. *Berakhot* 20b and *Rabbenu Yona*, commentary 11b.
56. *Shulhan Arukh, Orah Hayyim* 70:1.
57. Cf. *Mishnah Berurah*, commentary on *Shulhan Arukh, Orah Hayyim* 70:1.
58. *Sanhedrin* 74a-74b.
59. *Berakhot* 21a.

Fourth Letter

1. *Kiddushin* 29a.
2. *Mishnah, Sotah* 3:4, cf. *Bemidbar* 5:11-31.
3. *Shabbat* 116a.

4. *Sotah* 21b.

5. Maimonides, *Mishneh Torah: Laws of Torah Study* 1:13.

6. *Rashi* on *Pesahim* 91a.

7. Cf. Moshe Meiselman, *Jewish Woman in Jewish Law* (New York: KTAV, 1978), pp. 34-35.

8. There seems to be evidence from the Jerusalem Talmud, *Mishnah, Sotah* 3:4, that would prove to the contrary.

9. *Shulhan Arukh, Yoreh De'ah* 246:6.

10. *Perishah* commentary to the *Tur Shulhan Arukh, Yoreh De'ah* 246.

11. Judah HaHasid, *Sefer haHasidim*, no. 313.

12. Joseph Saul Nathanson, Responsa *Shoel U'Meshiv*, vol. 4 (Jerusalem, 1972) 3:41. See also Z. Serotskin, *Moznayim Le'Mishpat* (Jerusalem, 1968), 1:42, who takes the matter still further.

13. Israel Meir HaKohen, *Likute Halakhot, Sotah* 20a, p. 11a.

14. This letter dated 23 *Shevat* 5693 was published in the magazine *Bet Yaakov* in *Elul* 5723.

Fifth Letter

1. *Shabbat* 31a.

2. Moses Nahmanides, Torah commentary: introduction.

3. Cf. Abraham Korman, *Mavo Le'Torah Shebikhtav v'Sheb'al Peh* (Tel Aviv, 1987), p. 17.

4. Cf. Eliezer Shulman, *The Sequence of Events in the Old Testament* (Tel Aviv: 1975), p. 42.

5. Cf. Nahmanides, op. cit. who presents two opinions on this matter; also *Bava Batra* 15a, where we read: "So Moses the servant of the Lord died there" (Deuteronomy 34:5). Now is it possible that Moses, being dead, could have written the words "Moses died there"? The truth is that up to this point Moses wrote; from this point on Joshua wrote. This is the opinion of Rabbi Judah. . . . Said Rabbi Simon to him: "Can we imagine the scroll of the law being short of one word? What we must say is that up to this point, the Holy One blessed be He dictated and Moses repeated and wrote, and from this point on, He dictated and Moses wrote with tears."

6. Cf. Moses Maimonides, *Mishneh Torah: Introduction*.

7. Cf. Korman, op. cit., p. 28. The division of verses was likewise clarified. An open paragraph, i.e., where the remaining space in the line is left blank, indicates a major break in the theme between paragraphs; a closed paragraph, i.e., where a space equivalent to nine letters is left between paragraphs, indicates a minor break in theme. There are a total of 669 such paragraphs or *parshiyot* in the Torah: 290 are open and 379 are closed.

8. Cf. *Rashi* on *Bava Batra* 14b, where he notes the following: The reason Ezekiel and Daniel did not write and publish their own books was that they lived outside the land of Israel and prophecy could not be written outside the land. When Ezra returned to the land of Israel, beginning the Second Jewish Commonwealth, the prophecies were edited and published. Since the custom was for prophets to record their prophecies in old age, Hizkiah and his court edited and published the prophecies of Isaiah because the latter was executed by Menasseh. Regarding the prophecies of the twelve minor prophets, considering that they were few in number and might easily be lost, Haggai, Zechariah, and Malachi edited their own works, to which they appended the smaller works totaling twelve or *Tre Asar*.

9. Cf. Maimonides, op. cit.

10. For a discussion on this, see Zevi Hirsch Chajes, *The Student's Guide Through the Talmud*, trans. J. Schachter (London: East and West Library, 1952), chap. 3.

11. Ibid.

12. *Gittin* 60b.

13. Cf. Maimonides, op. cit.

14. Ibid.

15. Ibid.

16. Ibid.

17. Ibid.

18. Ibid.

19. Ibid.

20. Ibid.

21. Exodus 12:40.

22. Cf. *Megillah* 9a.

23. Cf. *Bava Batra* 123b and *Rashi* on Genesis 46:26.

24. *Sukkah* 35b.

25. Cf. *Kiddushin* 15a.

26. Chajes, *The Student's Guide.*

27. Ibid., p. 13.

28. Korman, op. cit., p. 296 n. 1.

29. Ibid., p. 15.

30. Cf. Ibid., p. 17, and *Hullin* 28a.

31. Ibid.

32. Ibid., pp. 19-20.

33. Ibid., p. 29.

34. Cf. *Zevahim* 2a and *Berakhot* 4b.

35. Cf. Chajes, op. cit., p. 32. This is true despite the difference in rank.

36. Cf. 1 Samuel 14:34 for content. Since the term *ba'zeh* can also mean "with this," it is assumed that King Saul had given the people an examined knife with which to slaughter the animals.

37. Cf. Chajes, op. cit., p. 36, who brings this question in the name of Nahmanides.

38. Ibid., p. 35.

39. Ibid., p. 36, in the name of Maimonides.

40. Cf. Chajes, op. cit., pp. 38-45 and 80-87, for the sources of these *takkanot* and *gezerot.*

41. Cf. *Mishnah, Shevi'it* 4:1.

42. Cf. *Shabbat* 40a.

43. Cf. *Avodah Zarah* 21a.

44. *Mishnah, Terumot* 8:4,5.

45. *Mishnah, Hullin* 2:5.

46. Cf. *Sanhedrin* 87b and Maimonides, op. cit., *Laws of Rebels* 1:3.

47. Maimonides, ibid., 1:4.

48. Cf. Chajes, op. cit., pp. 120, 127.

49. Ibid., pp. 127, 129.

Sixth Letter

1. Cf. Maimonides, *Mishneh Torah: Introduction.*

2. Ibid.

3. Ibid.

4. *Midrash Temurah*, chap. 3.

5. *Bava Kamma* 85a.

6. Ibid., in the commentary of the Tosafists, *D. H. Shenitnah.*

7. Baruch HaLevi Epstein, *Torah Temimah* (New York: Hebrew Publishing, 1928), Exodus 21:19.

8. Cf. *Sanhedrin* 73a, on which Maimonides based his ruling.

9. Moses Maimonides, *Perush haMishnayot: Nedarim* 4:4.

10. *Shulhan Arukh, Yoreh De'ah: Hilkhot Rofeh* 336:1.

11. In the commentary of David Halevi (*Ture Zahav*) on *Shulhan Arukh, Yoreh De'ah: Hilkhot Rofe* 336:1.

12. Cf. Jacob Ibn Shelomo Haviv, *Eyn Yaakov Kiddushin* 82a.

13. Moses Nahmanides, *Torat HaAdam*, (Warsaw, 1840), p. 43.

14. Hayyim David Azulai, *Perush Birke Yosef: Shulhan Arukh, Yoreh De'ah* 336:1.

Seventh Letter

1. Exodus 19:3-6.

2. *Rashi* on Exodus 19:24.

3. Exodus 19:16-19.

4. Cf. Samson Raphael Hirsch, Torah Commentary on Exodus 24:12 (London: Isaac Levy, 1959).

5. *Rashi* on Exodus 24:12.

6. Cf. Exodus 32:16.

7. Cf. Exodus 32:8.

8. Exodus 31:18.

9. Deuteronomy 9:9.

10. Exodus 34:28.

11. *Shabbat* 86b.

12. Cf. *Bava Kamma* 54b.

13. Cf. Nahmanides, Torah Commentary on Exodus 20:8.

14. It is quite clear that, with the exception of the fourth commandment, the differences are minor.

15. *Zevahim* 115b.

16. *Bemidbar Rabbah* 18:17.

17. *Pesikta Rabbati* 21.

18. Ibid.
19. Cf. *Mekhilta: Yitro* 20:13.
20. Jerusalem Talmud, *Berakhot* 1:5.
21. *Pesikta Rabbati* 22.
22. Maimonides, *Guide of the Perplexed*, III, chap. 33.
23. Ibid., p. 166.
24. Ibid., p. 167.
25. Ibid.
26. Ibid.
27. Cf. Exodus 20:17.
28. *Berakhot* 11b-12a.
29. Cf. *Shemot Rabbah* 40:1.
30. *Mekhilta, Yitro* 20:1.
31. The interpretation of this midrash is taken from a lecture given by Rabbi Joseph B. Soloveitchik on June 22, 1972.
32. Cf. Maimonides, *Mishneh Torah: Laws Concerning the Foundations of the Torah* 1:1-6.
33. Cf. Hirsch, op. cit., 20:1.
34. *Bereshit Rabbah* 14:11.
35. *Mekhilta* 19:9.
36. Cf. *Rabbenu B'haye,* Torah Commentary on Exodus 20:1.
37. Cf. Second Letter, n. 3, for a listing of the Noachide laws.
38. Cf. Jacob Zevi Mecklenburg, *HaKetav ve'haKabbalah*, Exodus 20:1.
39. Cf. Hirsch, op. cit., Genesis 4:3 on this matter.
40. Cf. Maimonides, op. cit., *Laws of Idolatry,* chap. 1.
41. Cf. Nahmanides, Torah Commentary on Exodus 20:3.
42. Cf. Maimonides, op. cit., *Laws of the Foundations of the Torah* 1:2.
43. Ibid., *Laws of Idolatry* 3:9.
44. Cf. Hirsch, op. cit., Exodus 20:4.
45. *Avodah Zarah* 43b.
46. *Sanhedrin* 61b. See also Baruch HaLevi Epstein, *Torah Temimah* (New York: Hebrew Publishing, 1928) on Exodus 20:5, n. 29.
47. Hirsch, op. cit., Exodus 20:5.
48. Cf. *Berakhot* 7a.
49. Cf. Malbim, Torah Commentary on Exodus 20:5 for further discussion on this matter.
50. Cf. Hirsch, op. cit., on Genesis 21:23.
51. Ibid., Exodus 20:7.

52. Cf. *Shevuot* 39a and commentary of *Maharsha* (ad loc.), also Maimonides, op. cit., *Laws of Repentance* 1:4.

53. Cf. Epstein, *Torah Temimah,* Exodus 20:7, n. 23.

54. *Rabbenu B'haye,* Torah Commentary on Exodus 20:7 in the name of Nahmanides.

55. Nahmanides, op. cit., 20:8.

56. Ibid.

57. Malbim, op. cit., 20:8.

58. Ibid., cf. also N. Berlin, *Haamek Davar* (Jerusalem: *Vaad haYeshivot,* 1967), Exodus 20:8.

59. Aaron HaLevi, *Sefer haHinukh,* trans. C. Wengrov (Jerusalem: Feldheim, 1978), *Mitzvah* 31.

60. *Shabbat* 119a.

61. *Mekhilta* 20:8.

62. *Betzah* 16a. cf. Nahmanides, op. cit., Exodus 20:8.

63. Cf. *Rabbenu B'haye,* op. cit., 20:8, and Gersonides, Bible Commentary on 2 Kings 4:23.

64. Hirsch, op. cit., Exodus 20:8.

65. Cf. *Da'at Zekenim* Torah Commentary on Exodus 20:8.

66. Hirsch, op. cit.

Eighth Letter

1. Nahmanides, Torah Commentary on Exodus 20:12.

2. Malbim, Torah Commentary on Exodus 20:12.

3. Cf. *Kiddushin* 30b.

4. Cf. Maimonides, *Mishneh Torah: Laws Concerning Rebels* 6:2.

5. *Kiddushin* 32a.

6. Jerusalem Talmud, *Pe'ah* 5:5.

7. *Kiddushin* 31b.

8. Ibid., 32a.

9. Ibid.

10. Samson Raphael Hirsch, Torah Commentary on Exodus 20:12 (London: Isaac Levy, 1959).

11. Ibid.

12. *Sanhedrin* 37a.

13. *Bereshit Rabbah* 34:20.

14. Cf. Nahmanides, op. cit., 20:12.

15. *Sanhedrin* 74a.

16. Ibid.

17. Cf. *Shulhan Arukh, Hoshen Mishpat* 425:1 and Rema (ad loc.). This law is not exercised today.

18. Ibid., 425:2.

19. Cf. *Mishnah, Semahot* 1:1-4 and *Shulhan Arukh, Yoreh De'ah* 339:1.

20. Bahya ben Yosef, *Hovot haLevavot: Shaar haBitahon* (Jerusalem: Feldheim, 1970), chap. 4, p. 327.

21. Cf. *Niddah* 13b and Aaron HaLevi, *Sefer haHinukh,* trans. C. Wengrov (Jerusalem: Feldheim, 1978), *Mitzvah* 35.

22. HaLevi, op. cit.

23. *Sanhedrin* 86a.

24. Ovadiah Seforno, Torah Commentary on Exodus 20:13.

25. *Bereshit Rabbah* 9:9.

26. Cf. *Kiddushin* 30b and *Avot De'Rebbi Natan* 16.

27. Cf. *Makkot* 4b and Hirsch, op. cit., 20:13.

28. Ibid.

29. Cf. Hirsch, op. cit.

30. Jerusalem Talmud, *Nedarim* 3:2.

31. Cf. *Rabbenu B'haye,* op. cit., 20:13.

32. Cf. Seforno, op. cit.

33. Maimonides, op. cit., *Laws of Robbery* 1:9.

34. Cf. Hirsch, op. cit., 20:14.

35. Ibid.

36. Cf. Ibn Ezra, Torah Commentary on Exodus 20:14, also Rabbenu B'haye and Seforno (ad loc.).

37. *Bava Batra* 21a.

38. Cf. Rabbenu B'haye, op. cit.

39. *Pesikta De'Rav Kehana* 12.

Ninth Letter

1. Maimonides, *Mishneh Torah* 1:1.

2. Maimonides, *Guide of the Perplexed*, II, chaps. 1-4.

3. Nahmanides, Torah Commentary on Exodus 32:20.

4. Exodus 20:5.

5. Ezekiel 18:1–20.

6. Nahmanides, op. cit., 20:5, also Hirsch, Torah Commentary (ad loc.).

7. Cf. Isidore Epstein, *The Faith of Judaism* (London: Soncino Press, 1954), p. 111, n. 1, where he writes: "Notwithstanding the speculative difficulties against the argument from design which Kant raises, he confesses that 'this argument always deserves to be mentioned with respect. It is the oldest, the clearest and the most in conformity with human reason . . . and it would be utterly hopeless to rob this argument of the authority it has always enjoyed' (Critique of Pure Reason Dialect I, chap. iii, section 7, E.T., J.M.D. Meiklejohn, 1924), p. 383. Even Darwin was so impressed with the Argument of Design that he is led to write with regard to it: 'I am conscious that I am in an utter muddle [about it]' (Life and Letters, II, p. 353)."

8. *The Disputation* (London: 1972), p. 55.

9. Cf. Epstein, op. cit., p. 27.

10. Cf. Louis Jacobs, *Principles of the Jewish Faith* (Northvale, NJ: Jason Aronson, 1988), pp. 33–69, for further discussion and proofs.

Tenth Letter

1. Isidore Epstein, *The Faith of Judaism* (London: Soncino Press, 1954), p. 110.

2. Maimonides, *The Guide of the Perplexed*, II, chap. 32.

3. Maimonides, op. cit., chap. 32, p. 163.

4. Cf. Moses Maimonides, *Hakdamah le'Masekhet Avot*, chap. 7.

5. Cf. Maimonides, *Guide of the Perplexed*, II, chap. 36, p. 173.

6. Ibid., p. 174.

7. *Berakhot* 57b.

8. Maimonides, op. cit., chap. 37, p. 179.

9. Ibid., p. 180.

10. Cf. Maimonides, *Hakdamah le'Masekhet Avot*, op. cit.

11. Maimonides, *Guide of the Perplexed*, chap. 38, p. 182.

12. Ibid.

13. Ibid., chap. 45, pp. 206–214.

14. Ibid.

15. Ibid., p. 212.

16. Cf. Moses Maimonides, *Mishneh Torah: Laws Concerning the Foundations of the Torah* 7:6.

17. Cf. Judah HaLevi, *The Book of the Kuzari*, trans. H. Herschfeld (New York: Pardes, 1946), I, p. 56 n. 95.

Eleventh Letter

1. *Yoma* 29a.

2. The point was made by Rabbi Dr. Joseph B. Soloveitchik in a lecture he gave in March 1973 at Yeshiva University on the Book of Esther.

3. Saadya Gaon, *Book of Beliefs and Opinions*, trans. S. Rosenblatt (New Haven: Yale University Press, 1948), p. 148.

4. *Bava Batra* 119.

5. Maimonides, *Guide of the Perplexed*, II, chap. 29, p. 139.

6. Ibid., p. 139, based on *Bereshit Rabbah* 5:4.

7. Ibid., p. 140.

8. Saadya Gaon, op. cit., p. 147.

9. Ibid.

10. Ibid., p. 150.

11. Samson Raphael Hirsch, Torah Commentary on Exodus 3:20 (London: Isaac Levy, 1959).

12. Eliezer Berkovits, *God, Man and History* (New York: Jonathan David, 1959), chap. 14.

13. Ibid., p. 149-150.

14. Ibid., p. 192 n. 15.

15. Ibid., p. 150.

16. Isaac Breuer, *Fundamentals of Judaism* (New York: Feldheim 1949), pp. 252-263.

17. Ibid., p. 252.

18. Ibid.

19. Ibid., p. 254.

20. Ibid., pp. 258-261.

21. Ibid., p. 262.

22. Cf. Chaim Zimmerman, *Torah and Existence* (Jerusalem, 1986).

23. Ibid., pp. 420-422.

Twelfth Letter

1. Psalms 94:3-7.

2. Alexander Pope, "Essay on Man," *Eleven British Writers* (New York, 1940), Epistle I, line 294.

3. Maimonides, *Guide of the Perplexed*, III, p. 39.

4. Ibid., p. 33.

5. Ibid., p. 36.

6. Ibid., p. 38.

7. *Bava Batra* 14b.

8. Ibid., 15b.

9. Maimonides, op. cit., p. 93.

10. Cf. Meir Leibush Malbim, Bible Commentary on Job, (New York: Grossman Publishers, 1953) introduction to chap. 4.

11. Maimonides, op. cit., p. 107.

12. Ibid., p. 105.

13. *Berakhot* 5a.

14. Cf. Malbim, op. cit., 11:6.

15. Cf. Gersonides, Bible Commentary on Job, 11:6.

16. The book speaks of "three" friends who came to Job, which has led some to suggest that the argument of Elihu is an interpolation. Others disagree, and posit that the author portrays Elihu as a member of the audience who, after hearing all the speeches fall on deaf ears, was compelled to speak out himself.

17. Eliezer Berkovits, *Faith After the Holocaust* (New York: KTAV, 1973), p. 3.

18. Ibid., p. 89.

19. Ibid., p. 105.

20. Ibid., p. 106.

21. Cf. *Yoma* 69b.

22. Eliezer Berkovits, *God, Man and History* (New York: Jonathan David, 1959).

23. Ibid., p. 75.

24. Ibid., p. 76.

25. We recognize that disease and illness may at times be a manifestation of Divine retribution, but to assert that this is always the case is simply unwarranted and unjustifiable.

26. Although Maimonides did not list freedom of will as one of his

Thirteen Principles of Faith, the concept is implied in his Eleventh Principle, which states: "The Almighty rewards those who obey His commandments and punishes those who disobey them." This principle follows immediately after that of Divine omniscience.

27. Maimonides, *Mishneh Torah: Laws of Repentance* 5:1.

28. Ibid., 5:5.

29. Ibid.

30. Cf. Maimonides, *Guide of the Perplexed*, III, chap. 20; also Yom Tov Lippman Heller, commentary on Ethics of the Fathers 3:15 (New York: Hebrew Publishing).

31. Cf. Simon Duran, *Magen Avot* 3:15 (New York: Light, 1944).

32. *Sanhedrin* 107a.

33. *Shabbat* 156a.

34. *Berakhot* 33b.

35. Viktor Frankl, *The Unheard Cry for Meaning* (New York: Simon & Schuster, 1978), pp. 47-48.

36. Eliyahu Dessler, *Mikhtav me'Eliyahu* (New York: Committee for the Publication of the Writings of E. L. Dressler, 1965), pp. 111-120.

37. Ibid., p. 111.

38. Joseph B. Soloveitchik, *Halakhic Man* (Philadelphia: Jewish Publication Society, 1983), pp. 136-137.

Thirteenth Letter

1. Isaiah 11:3-9.

2. Maimonides, *Mishneh Torah: Laws of Kings* 12:1.

3. Micah 4:1-3.

4. Ibid., 4:13.

5. Ibid.

6. Ibid., 7:10.

7. Cf. *Rashi* and *Redak* on Micah 5:1-2.

8. It is important to take note of the fact that there are references to the Messianic Era in the writings of other prophets as well: Zephaniah, chap. 3; Habakkuk, chap. 2; Jeremiah, chap. 3; Ezekiel, chap. 20; and Obadiah, chap. 1; but to discuss them fully would be beyond the scope of this letter.

9. Isidore Epstein, *The Faith of Judaism* (London: Soncino Press, 1954), p. 315.

10. Ibid., pp. 316-317.

11. *Eruvin* 43b. The Talmud refers here to *Meshiah ben David.*

12. This is according to Rabbi Simon in *Mishnah, Eduyot* 8:7.

13. *Tirgum* to Song of Songs 4:5.

14. Cf. *Yalkut Shimoni* to Isaiah 60.

15. Saadya Gaon, *Book of Beliefs and Opinions: Redemption* (New Haven: Yale University Press, 1948), pp. 301-302.

16. Cf. *Sukkah* 52a.

17. Ezekiel 38.

18. *Sanhedrin* 97a.

19. Chaim Zimmerman, *Torah and Existence* (Jerusalem, 1986), pp. 25-78.

20. *Berakhot* 12b.

21. Cf. *Megillah* 17b.

22. Cf. *Avodah Zarah* 2b.

23. Zimmerman, op. cit., p. 36.

24. *Sanhedrin* 98a.

25. Isaiah 26:14.

26. Isaiah 26:19.

27. Cf. David Kimhi, Bible Commentary on Isaiah 26:19.

28. Daniel 12:2-3.

29. Cf. Malbim commentary *Yipah leKetz* and *Mezudot David* on Daniel 12:2.

30. Cf. *Rashi* and Ibn Ezra commentaries (ad loc.).

31. Malbim, op. cit.

32. Saadya Gaon, op. cit., treatise vii.

33. Ibid., p. 411.

34. Ibid., p. 413.

35. They contradict what is observed by the senses; they contradict reason; they conflict with another biblical passage; they conflict with what has been transmitted by rabbinic tradition.

36. Cf. Ibid., p. 424. To interpret the passage in Isaiah and in Daniel figuratively as allusions to the revival of the Jewish kingdom is unwarranted. "Furthermore," says Saadya Gaon, "if it were allowable to interpret all these passages that deal with the resurrection of the dead in this figurative manner . . . then by the same token, it might be necessary or permissible to interpret all revealed laws . . . and the miracles mentioned in Scripture, by means of other types of allegory, so that none of them

would retain their literal meaning, but be given totally different significance."

37. Ibid., p. 418.

38. *Sukkah* 52b.

39. Saadya Gaon, op. cit., p. 429.

40. *Sanhedrin* 90a.

41. Saadya Gaon, op. cit., p. 430.

42. Moses Maimonides, "The Treatise on the Resurrection of the
Dead," *Iggrot u'Teshuvot* (Jerusalem).

43. On this point, Maimonides differs from most Jewish philosophers,
who put the resurrection of the dead in the Messianic Era.

44. Maimonides, op. cit., pp. 18-19.

45. Cf. Ibid., pp. 20-21.

46. Ibid.

47. Joseph Albo, *Sefer haIkkarim*, IV (Warsaw, 1877), p. 339.

48. Ibid., pp. 342-343.

49. Cf. Isaiah 26:19 and *Hagigah* 12b.

50. Albo, op. cit., p. 349. As such, the only biblical source for resurrection would be Isaiah 26:19.

51. Ibid., pp. 354-356.

52. *Sanhedrin* 91a.

53. *Berakhot* 34b.

Postscript

1. Moses Nahmanides, Commentary on the Torah to Genesis 1:1.

2. Deuteronomy 30:15-17.

3. Ephraim Solomon Luntschitz, *Keli Yakar* on Deuteronomy 30:15,
Mikraot Gedolot (New York: Schulsinger, 1950).

4. Moses Maimonides, *Mishneh Torah: Foundations of the Torah* 2:1.

5. Maimonides, op. cit., *Laws of Repentance* 10:3.

6. Naftali Zevi Yehudah Berlin, *Haamek Davar* on Deuteronomy 30:16
(Jerusalem: *Vaad haYeshivot*, 1967).

7. Cf. Meir Leibush Malbim, Commentary on the Prophets, Micah
6:8 (New York: Grossman Publishing, 1963).

8. Moses Ibn Ezra, Commentary on Psalms 34:15 (Lublin: *Mefitze
Torah*, 1898).

Index

Aaron ben Asher, 65
Abduction, 132-134
Abortion, 130
Abraham, 3-4, 22
Abudraham, David, 13
Active Intellect, 160-161
Adultery, 55, 107-108, 130-132
Agnosticism, 151
Ahai Gaon, 84
Ahishena, 215
Albo, Joseph
  on efficacy of prayer, 35
  on resurrection, 224-225
Alfasi, Isaac, 85-86
Amidah, 34-35, 37, 47-48, 212-213
Angels, 30, 35, 164
Animal sacrifice. *See* Sacrifice
Anthropocentrism, 182, 189-190
Apocalyptic literature, 207-210, 216-217
Arukh HaShulhan, 89-90
Arvit, 22
Asher ben Yehiel, 86-87

Ashkenazic Jewry, 86, 88-89
At'halta de'Geulah, 212-215
Atheism, 145-146, 151, 178
Azulai, David, 96

Babylonian Talmud, 70
Baraitot, 70, 77
Belz, Rebbe of, 61
Ben Azzai, 55, 57
Berkovits, Eliezer
  on existence of evil, 190-195
  on miracles, 171-172
  on prayer, 32, 35
Berlin, Naphtali Zevi Judah, 232
Bet Yaakov, 60-61
Bet Yosef, 87-88
Bible, 64-67. *See also* Oral Law
  apocalyptic writings not
    included in, 207-209
  authority of, 64-65, 76, 93
  Hebrew text of, 65
  Pentateuch. *See* Written Law
  Prophets, 64-66, 76
  Writings, 64-65, 67, 76

Birkhot haShahar, 9-14
  for women, 13, 48
B'ito, 215
Breuer, Isaac, 173-174

Chajes, Zevi Hirsch, 73-74, 77
Chanting, 40-41
Chastisement of love, 185-186
Children of wicked, punishment
    of, 116-118, 142-143
Codes, 83-90
  Arukh HaShulhan, 89-90
  Bet Yosef, 87-88
  Halakhot Gedolot, 84-85
  Kitzur Shulhan Arukh, 89
  Mapat HaShulhan, 88-89
  Mishnah Berurah, 89-90
  Mishneh Torah, 87-89
  Riff (Alfasi), 85-86
  Rosh, 86-87
  Sefer haTurim, 87-88
  Sheiltot, 84
  Shulhan Arukh, 87-89
Compassion, Divine. *See* Mercy,
    Divine
Compassion, of women, 16
Concentration
  music and, 40-41
  in prayer, 39-41
  separation of sexes and, 40
Conquest, gift of, 15-16, 187-
    188
Contemplation, 28-29
Conversion, to Judaism, 10
Courage, 162-163
Covenant by God and Israel, 19-
    20, 99-103, 113-114, 144,
    158, 206-207

Coveting, 107-108, 135-136
Creation, 229-231. *See also*
    Nature
  by God, 112-113, 146-147,
    169-170, 172, 229-231
  goodness of, 7-8, 230
  havdalah in, 8
  heterogeneity of, 7-8, 131
  imperfection of, 148-149, 172,
    194-195
  man's place in, 31-32, 182,
    189-190, 230-231
  purpose of, 43-46
  symbolized in *Shabbat,* 121-
    123
  through Ten Sayings, 106
Cultivation, gift of, 15-16
Custom, local, 71, 89

Danzig, Abraham, 89
Davar halamed me'inyano, 132
Day of Judgment, 209-211
Deborah, 5
Dessler, Eliyahu, 199-200
Determinism. *See* Free will
Dietary laws, 58, 81
Din, 45-46, 110-111
Divine Emanations, 44
Divine Inspiration, 64, 163
Dreams, prophecy and, 161,
    163-164
Duran, Simon, 197-198

Eliezer, 56
Elijah, 209-210
E-lohim, 110-111
Epstein, Isidore
  on Messianic Era, 207-208

on reason and revelation, 156-
  157
on sacrifice, 25-26
Epstein, Yehiel Mikhel HaLevi,
  89-90
Eruv, 78
Eschatology, 201, 207-209
Esther, 5, 167-168
Euthanasia, 130
Evil, 177-200. *See also* God,
  inscrutability of; Goodness
children punished for fathers',
  116-118, 142-143
existence of under just God,
  148-149, 177-200
freely chosen, 33-34, 43-45,
  145-146, 174-175, 192-
  200, 229-232
God's mercy on, 34, 36, 43-
  47, 110, 193-194
in man, 12-13, 44-45, 133-
  134
in nature, 148-149, 179-180,
  188, 194-195
retribution for, 210-211
sources of, 133-134, 181-182,
  195
Evil inclination, 133-134
Evil speech, 46
Exodus from Egypt, 99-103
Ezekiel, 143, 211

Faith, 30, 112-113, 139-146
False swearing, 104, 107-108,
  118-120
False witness, 106-108, 134-135
Family, women's responsibility
  to, 6, 47, 56

Feminism, 2-3
Frankl, Viktor, 198-199
Free will. *See also* Evil; Goodness
Divine, 32-33, 121, 171-175,
  218, 229-230
human, 33-34, 43-45, 145-
  146, 174-175, 192-200,
  229-232
God's limits on, 43-44, 171-
  172, 194, 198-200

Gansfried, Solomon, 89
Geonim, 83-84
Gezerah shavah, 50
Gezerot, 70, 77-80
God, 139-153
covenant of, with Israel, 19-20,
  99-103, 113-114, 144,
  158, 206-207
as Creator, 113, 146-149, 169-
  170, 172, 218
equality of men before, 34-35
exclusive worship demanded
  by, 116-118
existence of
  faith in, 30, 112-113, 139-
    146
  philosophical proofs of,
    146-153, 158
freedom of, 32-33, 121, 171-
  175, 218, 229-230
goodness of, 43-47, 180-181
inscrutability of, 25-26, 32-33,
  111-112, 142, 179-181,
  189
Kingdom of. *See* Messianic Era
man's influence on, 31-35,
  121, 202, 207, 215

God (*continued*)
mercy of, 34, 36, 43-47, 110,
193-194
names of, 8, 110-111
omnipotence of, 113, 121,
167-175, 218, 222
omniscience of, 33, 178-179,
185, 187, 195-197
prayer of, 42-46
Ten Intelligences of, 160
voice of, 109, 165
Gog u'Magog, 210-211
Goodness. *See also* Evil
of Creation, 7-8
freely chosen, 33-34, 43-45,
145-146, 174-175, 192-
200, 229-232
God as source of, 43-47, 180-181
of man, 230-232
hastens Messianic Era, 202,
207, 215
Great Assembly, 64, 66-67

Hafetz Hayyim, 59-60
Hakhel, 11
HaKohen, Israel Meir
Mishnah Berurah of, 90
on Torah study by women,
59-60
Halakhah (law)
Ashkenazic practices in, 86,
88-89
corpus of. *See* Bible; Codes;
Oral Law
equality of men in, 34-35
human nature considered in,
79-81

local custom and, 71
majority opinion in rulings of,
80
natural law considered in, 81
Sefardic practices in, 86, 88
tradition considered in, 70-71,
75-76
Halakhah LeMosheh MiSinai, 75
Halakhic method, 67, 72-76, 80-
81
example of (practice of
medicine), 90-97
logic in, 75-76, 91
Halakhot (Alfasi), 85-86
Halakhot Gedolot, 84-85
Hanukkah, 11
Havdalah (principle)
definition of, 8
expression of, in contrasted
ideas, 9-10
minyan and, 48-51
in *mitzvot,* 9-14
in prohibition of adultery,
131
Havdalah (ritual), 9, 122
Healing, permissibility of, 90-94
Hermeneutical principles, 50, 67,
70, 73-74, 132
Hillel the Elder
on deriving Oral Law, 73
on *Shabbat,* 122
Hirsch, Samson Raphael
on false swearing, 118
on *havdalah,* 8
on honoring parents, 128
on miracles, 170-171
on *Shabbat,* 123

Historical process. *See also*
    Messianic Era
    God's intervention in, 43-44,
        113, 121-122, 171-172,
        194, 214-215
    human perfection goal of, 202
Hoffmann, David, 26-27
Holocaust, 190-195, 198-199
Home, women's responsibility in,
    6, 47, 56
Hukkim, 25
Humanism, 151-153
Humility, 12, 30-31, 34

Idolatry
    children punished for fathers',
        144
    First Commandment on, 107-
        108, 114-118
    as forbidden transgression,
        49
    origins of, 114-116
    sacrifice as replacement for,
        24-26, 29
    theft as, 132-133
Incense offering, 46
Inheritance by women, 4-5
Intuition, 162
Isaiah
    on Messianic Era, 203-205
    on resurrection, 216-217
Israel (modern), Messianic Era
    and, 211-215
Isserles, Moshe *(Rema),* 88-89

Jacob ben Asher, 87
Jerusalem Talmud, 70

Jewish lifestyle. *See* Torah way of
    life
Job, Book of, 182-190
Judah HaHasid, 58-59
Judah Halevi, 165
Judah HaNasi, 68, 70
Judgment, Day of, 209-211
Justice, Divine, 45-46, 177-200
    strict, 45-46, 110-111

Kaira, Simon, 84-85
Kant, Immanuel, 146
Karaites, 91
Karo, Joseph, 87-88
Kashrut (kosher) laws, 58, 81
Kavanah
    music and, 40-41
    in prayer, 39-40
    separation of sexes and, 40
Keriat Shema, 108
Ketoret, 46
Kiddush, 122
King David, 179
Kingdom of God. *See* Messianic
    Era
Kitve haKodesh, 64-67
Kitzur Shulhan Arukh, 89
Knowledge. *See also* Reason
    Divine, 33, 178-179, 185, 187,
        195-197
    human, 32-33, 181-182, 186-
        187, 196-197, 213-214

Law. *See* Halakhah
Law of pursuit, 129-130
Levi, Rabbi, 108
Levi (tribe of), 15, 101

Logic, rabbinic. *See* Halakhic
    method
Lord of Hosts, 8
Love
    of God for man, 34-36, 43-47,
        155-158, 185-186
    of man for God, 18, 30-32, 35-
        36, 232-233
Lubavitch, Rebbe of, 61
Lulav, 14, 74
Lunschitz, Ephraim Solomon,
    231-232
Luria, Isaac, 39

Maariv, 22
Maimonides, Moses
    on coveting, 135
    on evil, 181-182
    on existence of God, 140-142
    on faith, 140-142
    on free will, 195-197
    on God's omnipotence, 43
    on healing, 93-94
    on idolatry, 115
    on love of God, 232
    on Messianic Era, 23-29, 204,
        212
    on miracles, 169, 223-224
    Mishneh Torah of, 85-86
    on prayer, 23-29, 39
    on prophecy, 158-160, 160-
        165, 223-224
    on resurrection, 221-224, 227
    on sacrifice, 23-29
    on the Sages, 69-70
    on Ten Commandments, 109,
        112-113

Malbim, Leibush Meir, 186-187
Mapat HaShulhan, 88-89
Matriarchs, equal status of, 3-6
Medicine, permissibility of
    practicing, 90-94
Mehitzah, 40
Menstrual cycle, 14
Mercy, Divine, 34, 36, 43-47,
    110, 193-194
Meshiah ben Yosef, 209-210
Messiah, 203-206, 209, 214-215
Messianic Era, 201-215
    in apocalyptic literature, 207-
        210
    conditions for, 212-215
    events of, 203, 205-206, 209-
        211
    human character in, 16
    man's goodness can hasten,
        202, 207, 215
    miracles in, 175, 212, 215
    present day as, 211-215
    resurrection in, 201, 216-234
    role of repentance in, 212-213,
        215
    sacrifice in, 22-29
    timing of, 207, 211-212, 215
Messorites, 65
Mezuzah, 47
Micah, 203-206
Mikvah, 79
Minhah, 22
Minyan
    necessity of, 38
    origin of, 48-49
    women not counted in, 17,
        48-51

Miracles, 113, 167-175, 223-
224. *See also* Prophecy;
Resurrection; Revelation
cessation of, 168, 175
in Messianic Era, 175, 212,
215
nature and purpose of, 168-
174
Miriam, 5
Mishnah, 68-71. *See also* Oral
Law
Mishneh Berurah, 89-90
Mishneh Torah, 85-86
Mitzvot observance, 7-16. *See also*
Oral Law; Prayer; Written
Law
elucidated in Oral Law, 71-
74
elucidated in posttalmudic
Codes, 71-74, 83-90
forbidden transgressions of,
49, 75, 129
havdalah in, 8-14
negative, 13, 77-79, 120-121
positive, 13-14, 77-78, 120-
121
relative importance of various,
109-110, 126
time-oriented, 10-11, 13-15,
47-48, 120-121
Torah study as, 53-54
transforming power of, 10, 14-
18, 112, 133-134, 136-
137, 231-233
women exempted from, 10-16,
47-48, 57-58, 120-121
Monotheism, 114-116

Morality
derived from God, 149
humanism and, 151-153
Morning benedictions, 7, 9-14
special, for women, 13
Moses
Book of Job by, 184
God spoke directly to, 109,
165
Oral Law revealed to, 67
rabbinic enactments of, 78
Written Law revealed to, 64-
65, 99-103, 109, 157-
158
Murder
as forbidden transgression, 49,
75
in Halakhah, 129-130
Sixth Commandment on, 107-
108, 128-130
Music, 40-41

Nahmanides
on practicing medicine, 96
on punishing children of
wicked, 143-144
on *Shabbat,* 120
on timing of Messianic Era,
211
Nathanson, Joseph Saul, 59
Natural law, 80
Nature. *See also* Creation
evil in, 148-149, 179, 188,
194-195
goodness of, 7-8, 180
havdalah in, 8
heterogeneity of, 7-8, 131

Nature (*continued*)
  laws of
    fixed, 8, 113, 121, 169, 172,
      230
    God's power over, 113, 121,
      167-175, 218, 222
    God's will as, 8
    in Messianic Era, 204
    resurrection and, 222-223
Neture Karta, 212
Nonobservant Jews, and
    Messianic Era, 213-214
Nusah, 40-41

Oaths, false, 118-120
Oral Law, 64, 67-80
  authority of, 67, 76-77
  chain of transmission of, 67-
    70
  clarifies Written Law, 63-64,
    71-75, 110-136
  compiled in Mishnah, 68
    posttalmudic commentary
      on, 83-90, 140-142
    rabbinic enactments and,
      77-80
    talmudic commentary on,
      70-71
  derived from Written Law, 50,
    70, 73-76
  hermeneutical principles in,
    50, 67, 70, 73-74, 80,
    132
  mitzvot elucidated in, 71-74
  necessity of studying, 63-64,
    71-72
  oral teaching of, 67-70, 74

revealed to Moses, 67, 73-74
Ten Commandments
  interpreted by, 110-136
women's study of, 56-61

Parents, honoring, 107-108, 125-
  128
Passover, 11
Pentateuch. *See* Written Law
Polytheism, 114-116
Prayer, 17-51
  concentration in, 39-41
  daily services, 9-14, 22, 36-42
  efficacy of, 31-35
  equality of men in, 34-35
  by God, 42-46
  humility in, 12, 30-31, 34
  minyan and, 17, 38, 48-51
  as *mitzvot,* 29
  music in, 40-41
  nature and purpose of, 17-18,
    30-40
  obligatory, 36-42
  prophecy compared to, 18,
    156
  as replacement for sacrifice,
    21-30
  spontaneous, 36-38
  transforming power of, 35-36
  women exempted from, 10-14,
    47-48
Prophecy, 158-166, 223-224. *See
  also* Miracles; Revelation
  authenticity of, 155-158, 223-
    224
  cessation of, 165-166
  dreams and, 161, 163-164

forms of, 162-165
initiated by God, 155, 159,
  161
miracles and, 168-169
prayer compared to, 18, 156
prerequisites for, 158-162,
  165-166
workings of, 160-162
Prophets (books of Bible), 64-
  66, 163
authority of, in Halakhah, 76
Purim, 11

Rabbinic enactments, 77-80
Rabbinic logic. See Halakhic
  method
Rachel, 4
Rackman, Emanuel, 14
Rahamim, 16
Rashi
  on evil inclination, 133
  on origin of minyan, 48-49
  on role of Sarah, 3
  on Ten Commandments, 110-
    111
  on timing of Messianic Era,
    211
  on Torah way of life, 231
Rav Ashi, 70-71
Reason. See also Knowledge
  existence of God proved by,
    146-149, 153
  in halakhic method, 75-76
  inadequacy of, 25-26, 32-33,
    141-142, 146, 179-180
  relation to revelation, 25-26,
    156-157, 160-161

Redemption. See Messianic Era
Redemption from Egypt, 99-103,
  113-114
  Shabbat commemorates, 121-
    123, 127-128
Rema (Moshe Isserles), 88-89
Repentance, 21, 193-194, 196,
  212-215, 220-221
Responsa literature, 83
Resurrection, 216-227
Revelation, Divine, 31, 144,
  150, 153. See also
  Knowledge; Miracles;
  Prophecy
  initiated by God, 115, 155,
    159, 161
  nature and purpose of, 155-
    158
  of Oral Law, to Moses, 67, 73-
    74
  relation to reason, 25-26, 156-
    157, 160-161
  truth of, 155-158, 223-224
  of Written Law, to Moses, 99-
    103, 109, 119, 157-158
Riff (Alfasi), 85-86
Ritual. See Mitzvot observance;
  Prayer
Rosh, 86-87
Ruah haKodesh, 163
Ruah Hashem, 163

Saadya Gaon
  on Meshiah ben Yosef, 209-210
  on miracles, 168, 170
  on Resurrection, 218-221
  on timing of Messianic Era, 211

Sabbath. *See Shabbat*
Sacrifice, 19-30
  obligatory *versus* voluntary, 25-
    26
  purpose of, 19-21, 29-30
  replaced by prayer, 21-30
  restoration of, in Messianic
    Era, 22-30
Sages
  integrity of, 2, 64, 157
  Oral Law transmitted by, 67-
    71
  on resurrection, 220
Salvation. *See* Messianic Era
Sanhedrin, 68, 77
Sarah, 3-5
Sefardic Jewry, 86, 88
Sefer haTurim, 87-88
Sefirot, 44
Sekkel haPoel, 160-161
Semikhah, 20
Separation of sexes
  in socialization, 4
  in worship, 40
Sexual relations, illicit, 55, 107-
    108, 130-132
  as forbidden transgression, 49
Shabbat
  commemorates redemption
    from Egypt, 121-123,
    127-128
  Fourth Commandment on,
    107-108, 120-123
  havdalah after, 9
  observance by women, 11, 58,
    120-123
  rabbinic enactments
    concerning, 78-79

Shaharit, 22
Sheiltot, 84
Shekhinah, 44
Shema
  observance by women, 47-48
  Ten Commandments in, 108
Shofar, 14, 74
Shulhan Arukh, 87-89
  on prayer, 39, 47
  on Torah study for women, 57
Sifra, 70
Sifre, 70
Sin. *See* Evil
613 commandments. *See Mitzvot*
    observance; Written Law
Slaughter, ritual, 74, 76
Slavery, 132-134
Slaves, 9-11, 47
Soloveitchik, Aaron S.
  on spiritual superiority of
    women, 14-16
Soloveitchik, Hayyim, 214
Soloveitchik, Joseph B.
  on equality of man before
    God, 34-35
  on free will, 200
  on status of women, 5
  on Torah study by women, 61
Sotah, 55
Soul, 160-162, 225-227
Speech, 18, 46
Suffering of righteous, 185-195
Suicide, 130
Sukkah, 14, 74
Sukkot, 75
Supernatural, 113, 121, 167-175,
    218, 222
Synagogues, 40

Takkanot, 70, 77-80
Tallit, 11
Talmud. *See* Oral Law
Tamid sacrifice, 22
Tanakh. See Bible
Tefillat haTzibbur, 38
Tefillat Hovah, 36
Tefillin, 11, 47
Ten Commandments, 99-137
  correspondence between pairs
    of, 107
  as interpreted by Oral Law,
    125-137
    on man and God (First
      through Fourth), 110-
      123
    on man and man (Fifth
      through Tenth), 125-
      137
  intrinsic totality of, 111
  revelation of, 99-103, 109,
    119
  symbolize Ten Sayings, 106
  texts of, 103-106
  Written Law derived from,
    101, 106
Ten Intelligences, 160
Ten Sayings, 106
Tetragrammaton, 110-111
Theft, 107, 132-134
Theodicy, 148-149, 177-200
Thirteen Hermeneutical
    Principles. *See*
    Hermeneutical principles
Tiflut, 56-57
Time
  -oriented *mitzvot,* 13-15
  -oriented prayer, 10-14, 47-48

  sanctity of, 14
  women's awareness of, 14
Torah. *See* Written Law
Torah study, 17, 53-61, 136-137
  by women, 53-61
Torah way of life, 17-18, 136-
    137, 231-234. *See also*
    Mitzvot observance; Prayer
Tosafists, 93
Tosefta, 70
Tradition
  authority of, 150-151
  considered in Halakhah, 70-
    71, 75-76

Uniqueness. *See Havdalah*
    (principle)
Universe. *See* Creation

Visions, prophetic, 164-165

Will. *See* Free will
Wine, 122
Wisdom Literature, 65
Women
  exempted from *mitzvot*
    observance, 10-14, 47-48,
    57-58, 120-121
  inheritance rights of, 4-5
  not counted in *minyan,* 17, 48-
    51
  obligated to *mitzvot*
    observance, 10, 11, 13,
    47-48, 120-123
  prayer obligations of, 10-14,
    47-48
  role in the home, 6, 47, 56
  spiritual superiority of, 14-16

Women (*continued*)
  status of, 3-6, 10
  Torah scholars, 56-57
  Torah study by, 53-61
Worship. *See* Prayer
Writings (books of Bible), 64-65,
    67, 163
  authority of, in Halakhah, 76
Written Law, 64-67, 99-137. *See
    also Mitzvot* observance;
    Oral Law; Revelation
  authority of, 64, 76, 93
  books of, 66
  clarified by Oral Law, 50, 71-
    80, 110-136
  derived from Ten Command-
    ments, 101, 106
  elucidated in Codes, 83-90,
    141-142
  forbidden transgressions of,
    49, 129
  immutabilty of, 25-26
  Oral Law derived from, 50, 70,
    73-76

Prophets (Bible), relation to,
    64-65, 76
relative importance of
    commandments in, 109-
    110, 118-119, 126
revelation of, to Moses, 64-
    65, 99-103, 109, 157-
    158
supported by rabbinic
    enactments, 77-80
unquestionable statutes of, 25-
    26
women's study of, 56-61
Writings (Bible), relation to,
    64-65, 76

Yom Kippur, 12

Zimmerman, Chaim
  on beginning of Messianic Era,
    212-215
  on miracles, 174-175
Zundel, Hanokh, 95-96

About the Author

Rabbi Walter Orenstein studied at Yeshiva University, where he received his baccalaureate degree in Jewish education, his master of fine arts, and his doctorate in Hebrew literature. Subsequently appointed to the faculty as professor of Jewish studies and religious guidance counselor, Dr. Orenstein taught at both the Teachers Institute for Women and Stern College for a total of thirteen years. The author of *The Cantor's Manual of Jewish Law* (1994), *Etched in Stone* (1989), *Torah and Tradition* (1972), *Sheliah Tsibbur B'Halakhah* (1965), and *Torah as Our Guide* (1960), he has also published several scholarly articles on Judaism. Dr. Orenstein was a recipient of the Outstanding Educator Award from the organization Outstanding Educators of America in 1974 and the Senior Professor Award from Stern College in 1983. He and his wife live in Brooklyn, New York. They have two daughters.